Sophie now lives in the north west of England and works at a senior level for a national child protection charity. She is a volunteer for Samaritans and was recently appointed as a trustee for the organisation. She can be contacted via her website www.sophieandrews.co.uk

Scarred

Sophie Andrews

HODDER

First published in Great Britain in 2008 by Hodder & Stoughton
An Hachette UK company

First published in paperback in 2009

4

Copyright © Sophie Andrews 2008

A CIP catalogue record for this title
is available from the British Library

ISBN 978 0 340 93737 2

Typeset in Sabon by Hewer Text UK Ltd, Edinburgh

Printed and bound by Clays Ltd, St Ives plc

Broken Man written by Paul Young and Ian Kewley.
Reproduced here by kind permission of Bright Music Ltd

Hodder & Stoughton policy is to use papers that are natural,
renewable and recyclable products and made from wood grown in
sustainable forests. The logging and manufacturing processes are expected
to conform to the environmental regulations of the country of origin.

Hodder & Stoughton Ltd
338 Euston Road
London NW1 3BH

www.hodder.co.uk

*To Fran – forever in my thoughts
and heart*

Acknowledgements

I have often heard the statement that 'everyone has a book in them' and over the years I have come to believe that maybe this is true and that maybe I do have a story inside me to tell. Through my teenage years I wrote every day and found it a cathartic experience to release the words that were screaming out in my head onto a piece of paper. The first part of my book was therefore written many years ago and the challenge for me as an adult has been to release both the past and my present onto a page once again.

This hasn't been easy and has taken me back to places in my head where I would have preferred not to go. In going back to those places I have relived some of the pain but it has rekindled my writing and put me back in touch with being able to express my thoughts in words   a power that cannot be underestimated.

I can't mention everyone that has been there, but that doesn't mean I have forgotten the many people who have passed through my life and reached out a hand when I needed it most.

Here's an acknowledgement of just a few of those people: I'd like to work backwards, for without a publisher the book that was 'inside me' would not have been published. So, thanks to Helen Coyle and Rowena Webb at Hodder & Stoughton for giving me the opportunity to tell my story, believing in me and for handling me with sensitivity. Thanks to my agent, Judy Chilcote for her support and guidance and belief in me and thanks to Caro Handley for her special care of me and her expert help in filling in the gaps in my manuscript – in doing this she helped me to deal with the parts that had been too hard to write about before.

Thanks to Richard McCann for helping me believe that I should find an agent and for recommending Judy to me, and to Stuart Howarth for making me believe that however bad the experiences we go through, there is always space for the human spirit to shine through and survive.

I have been touched by the hands of some very special people and friends in my life; Jenny and Anna who have both been there for me in good times and bad, Kay who is special to me and has been there for many years and given me the support and boundaries that were needed when my life was out of control, Katrina who is a special friend and has made a difference to the way that I see the world and myself as well as being a great support to me in finishing the book and helping me to talk about the details that have been locked inside. Some people in life we are destined to meet. Thanks to them all for their love and support.

Thank you to those who were 'there' at the time – to my social worker, my English teacher, the staff in the hospital . . . all of whom I waited for a rejection from. I must have been a challenge but they were always there and did all they could to keep me alive.

Thanks to Katie, for being Katie . . . the closest person to a sister I will ever have. Her spirit kept me going on the darkest days.

Whilst the past can never be fully erased, the very darkest days are over so it's fitting that my final thanks go to the organisation and people that have had such a huge effect on my life. Thanks to the late Rev Dr Chad Varah, the founder of Samaritans who dedicated his life to the provision of emotional support and in 1953 had the inspiration and fore-sight to found Samaritans for the suicidal and despairing. Samaritans is a confidential organisation that is based on the simplest philosophy of them all – listening really does make a difference. Thanks to Pam for answering the phone at Samar-itans when I was at my lowest ebb and for still being there today, but now as a friend and colleague.

My final thanks to 'Fran' – the Samaritan who supported me through it all who is sadly not alive to see the end product of my writing. I truly believe her support and care through the simple act of listening is the reason that I am here today. I hope she would have been proud of the final product and hope the book helps someone else in some small way, which would be a fitting tribute to her support of me and the support of all Samaritan volunteers who spoke to me at that time.

I often tell people that I have been lucky, and to that they ask why – it doesn't make sense to them. But I have been lucky as I have been touched by people at every stage who have helped me to believe in myself a little more and have brought me to a place where I can accept my past.

So . . . there really is a book in everyone . . . I am proof of that. 'Thanks' seems an inadequate word to all that have been there and helped this happen.

My book is dedicated in memory of Fran.

Contents

Publisher's Statement

Sophie Andrews is a pseudonym. All names and other identifying details have been changed to protect the privacy of Sophie's family.

I

Falling Apart

I kept on telling my friends that I was well, but they wouldn't listen. I kept on telling my social worker that I was fine now, but she wouldn't listen either. I told my family that I was feeling great, but they ignored me too. I felt the world had turned against me and I wished I was dead. Even dying had to be better than being sent to a nuthouse. And that's where they were sending me.

My mother took me there. It was a huge building on the top of a hill, set back from the road in enormous grounds. I had often passed it as a child and wondered what was inside. Now I knew it was full of people like me. They called it a psychiatric hospital but I knew that was just a posh name for a place where nutcases were locked up.

The thing was, I wasn't a nut. Just a scared, lonely sixteen-year-old. But no one would listen to me, and on that sunny morning in early June I found myself following Mum in through the main entrance to the darkness of a large foyer.

Mum spoke to a woman sitting at a desk and then walked briskly along a corridor leading off the foyer. I almost had to run to keep up with her. There was a smell of disinfectant and a faint sound of people bustling around behind closed doors. Several wheelchairs lined the corridor and porters rushed past us pushing trolleys carrying patients wrapped in bandages.

As we walked on, towards the furthest part of the building, gradually the smell of disinfectant faded and the corridors became quieter and darker. I concentrated on the sound of my mother's heels clicking on the floor until we reached a heavy metal door with a sign that said Department of Psychiatry.

By this time tears were streaming down my face. 'Please don't leave me, Mum,' I pleaded. 'I'm better now. I don't need this, I really don't.'

She stared at the door in front of us, her face expressionless. 'You know this is the only answer, Sophie. There's no one who can help you now, except the doctors here.'

I wanted to scream and tell her she was wrong and that this was a huge mistake. I just wanted to go home. But I stayed silent. Mum never listened to me anyway.

My face felt swollen with tears. I felt so alone and scared. I longed for someone – anyone – to hold me and tell me that everything would be OK. Mum pushed open the metal door, which slammed shut behind us. Ahead was a set of grey, concrete steps. My social worker had told me that the ward where I would be was on the second floor.

I looked at Mum again and thought I saw tears in her eyes as she squeezed my shoulder and pushed me ahead of her. There was no natural light and a fluorescent bulb flickered as we made our way up two flights of steep, narrow stairs. The walls on either side of us had flaking cream paintwork.

At the head of the stairs another metal door stood before us with a glass panel set in the top and a row of locks along the edge. Mum rang the bell and we waited in silence. This is it, I thought. I am about to be locked away and there is nothing I can do. They might as well throw me in prison.

A woman looked through the glass panel and then the locks clicked one by one and the door was opened. We stepped into a long corridor, empty apart from a row of plastic chairs.

'You must be Sophie,' the woman said. I nodded. 'We've been expecting you this morning,' she went on. 'My name is Dawn and I'm a staff nurse on the ward.'

I guessed she was in her thirties; she was attractive and wore lots of make-up over a deep golden tan. She had no uniform on, which I thought was strange.

I stood in silence, staring at the floor, transfixed by the patterns on the threadbare carpet, as Dawn said, 'Come and meet some of the staff who will be taking care of you while you're here.' She put her hand on my shoulder and led me towards a door on the right-hand side of the corridor. I tried to turn my head away to hide my tears and began counting in my head. That usually worked when I wanted to block things out.

'Don't worry,' Dawn smiled. 'We don't bite, you know.'

Dawn opened the door and ushered me into a large room full of people, all chattering and clinking cups and saucers. Mum followed us inside.

'This is Sophie,' Dawn announced.

I looked at the sea of faces staring at me. I felt nervous and scared and started to count in my head again.

'Sophie is new on the ward today,' Dawn continued. 'She will be our youngest patient, so she might be feeling extra vulnerable. She is going to be under the care of Dr Harvey and his team.'

I looked down at the floor again. It felt strange to hear the words 'extra vulnerable'. I had always thought of myself as strong.

A stocky man with a kind face and a mop of black shiny hair stood up and shook my hand firmly. 'Hi Sophie,' he said. 'My name is Raj and I'm one of the charge nurses. A charge nurse is the equivalent of a sister; I expect you're more familiar with that expression aren't you?' I nodded.

Like Dawn, he wore no uniform. In a timid voice I asked why. Raj smiled. 'None of the nursing staff on this unit wear a uniform. It's much more relaxing for everyone like this and we hope it will make us more approachable.'

What sort of place had they sent me to, with nurses without uniforms? I felt even more scared than before. It didn't seem like a hospital anymore and I had no idea what would happen to me.

Raj introduced me to the rest of the staff, but it was impossible for me to take in their names, or remember who did what. There were nurses, doctors, psychiatrists, occupational therapists, social workers, probation officers and even a teacher from the Local Education Department.

'OK, Sophie,' Dawn said. 'I think it would be best if you said goodbye to your mum now. Then I'll show you around the unit. The rest of the patients are in a community meeting and they'll be out in a few minutes, so you can meet them.'

I wasn't close to Mum but at least she was familiar, and I didn't feel ready for her to go. She hugged me and I began to sob loudly. As she tried to pull away from me I clung to her.

'Please take me away from here, Mum,' I pleaded. 'Please don't leave me.'

But she fastened her jacket, pecked me on the cheek and

began to walk towards the door. 'I'm so sorry, Sophie,' she said, as she left.

No doubt she thought it was for the best, but I didn't see it that way. When things got tough, she always left me. That's what she had done when she left me with Dad and now, when she had a chance to be there for me, she was leaving me again.

'Come on, my love,' Dawn said. 'Let me show you where you'll be sleeping tonight.'

There was a calmness about Dawn that I found strangely reassuring. I wiped away my tears with my sleeve and followed her out of the staffroom and down the corridor. There were glass cubicles on either side, each with enough room for a bed, a locker and a couple of chairs. I could see that there was someone in each cubicle. Was I going to be put in one of these, like a goldfish in a bowl? We had reached a large room at the end of the corridor.

'This ward is where you will be sleeping for the time being,' Dawn said. 'Unfortunately the female ward is full at the moment, so you're in the male one, but you and two other girls from the unit will be sharing a separate cubicle.'

We turned into a room off the main one, with glass walls on all sides, and three beds in it. I stared in horror. Not only was I being put in a goldfish bowl, but it was in a male ward, which scared me even more.

In the first bed there was a girl lying on her side reading a magazine. Dawn led me over to her and the girl put the magazine down and looked up. She looked like a skeleton with just a thin covering of skin, almost transparent in appearance. I had never seen anyone as thin as her before and her gaunt features made her look elderly and frail. Her bones protruded through her skin.

'Sophie, I'd like you to meet Anna,' Dawn said.

I stepped forward and shook her outstretched hand, very softly so as not to hurt her. I felt sure I was in the wrong place now. Anna was obviously ill and there was no way I was as bad as she was.

'Hello,' Anna said. 'How long will you be here for?'

If only I knew, I thought. I smiled back at her and shrugged my shoulders.

'OK girls, you'll have plenty of time to get to know each other later. First I want to get you settled in, Sophie.' Dawn moved on, past an empty bed with a large teddy sitting on the pillow, to the third bed. Like the others it had a locker next to it and blue plastic curtains that could be drawn around it.

'This is where you'll be sleeping,' Dawn said. 'But before you put any of your stuff away I'd like to have a look through it.' I looked horrified. 'It's a formality that we have to go through with every patient when they're admitted,' Dawn explained. 'We have to make sure that you haven't brought anything in with you that might harm yourself or others.'

She took my holdall and tipped my clothes and belongings all over the bed, then began to sift through them. I felt exposed and embarrassed.

A moment later she found the razor blades that I had hidden in the lid of my deodorant can and put them in her pocket. I felt devastated. I needed the blades more than anything else in the world. Without them I knew I would be lost. In the past few years they had given me a way of coping with everything that was happening to me. With the blades I had some kind of control in my life, when I couldn't control anything else. They gave me a sense of security.

I wanted to beg Dawn to let me keep them, but I knew she wouldn't, so I said nothing.

Dawn told me to follow her to the medical room. Inside there was a large window looking on to the grounds. It was slightly open and the breeze felt nice on my face, especially as there was a strong smell of disinfectant in the room. There was a single bed with a curtain around it, and a large locked cupboard.

Another nurse joined us. Dawn explained that Amy was the staff nurse assigned to look after me.

Dawn asked me to strip to my underwear and Amy wrote on a chart as Dawn weighed and measured me and asked lots of questions about my health. Amy did a blood test and told me they would be doing a urine test in the morning.

Then Dawn asked me about all the scars on my stomach, arms and legs. She took the dressing off my left arm, revealing the parallel lines of fresh, deep cuts.

'So this is what you had the razor blades for is it?' she asked. I nodded. 'I'll leave you with Amy now,' she said. 'You'll need a few stitches in your arm. Afterwards you can come into the day room and meet some other patients.'

I sat in silence as Amy repaired my damaged arm. She was talking to me all the time but I didn't hear what she was saying. My head felt as though it was spinning around. I wanted to scream at the top of my voice. I wanted to cry. I wanted to be held tightly. I wanted to get out of his awful place.

I tried to concentrate on what Amy was saying to me. 'I know everything seems a bit daunting at first,' she said. 'But I'm sure you'll get on with all the other patients. Have you met the girls in your cubicle yet?'

'I've met Anna but I haven't met the other girl yet,' I said quietly.

'The other person you'll be with is Simone. I'll introduce you to her. Right, that's your arm dressed for now; I'll check it again tomorrow. Get dressed now and I'll take you to the day room.'

I pulled my jeans and jumper back on and followed Amy. As we walked I noticed that there were lots of paintings and poems attached to pinboards along the length of the corridor. We stopped outside a closed door which had holes in the top panel, as if someone had been punching it. There was a large tea trolley outside the room with a huge metal urn, several milk jugs and a pile of blue crockery. From inside came noisy chatter and laughter.

As Amy led me in a strong smell hit me – a mixture of perfume and urine. The walls were painted in bright colours and there was a big window at the end of the room with a steel bar across the centre of it, making it impossible to open. There were brightly coloured armchairs around the outside of the room and a large wooden table in the middle, badly stained with cup marks and words written with a marker pen. A large television sat against the wall in the corner. Like the table, it was bolted to the floor.

The room was full of people, some drinking from the blue cups, some talking, others staring at the TV. One man rocked backwards and forwards in his chair, shouting at the television from time to time. I felt totally overwhelmed.

An elderly lady slept in a chair in the far corner and Amy told me to sit next to her while she went to get me a drink. The smell of urine became stronger as I moved towards her and the only empty seat in the room. The seat looked stained – I took a deep breath and sat down.

I hoped Amy wasn't going to force me to make conversation

with anyone. A few of them looked at me and smiled while others didn't seem to notice me.

I sat in silence with my head down. I felt utterly alone, abandoned by my family and friends, dumped in this awful place without any idea how long it would be before I was allowed out. How could they think being shoved into a madhouse could possibly help me? No one cared; I was certain they would all just forget about me.

More than anything I wished I could be back home with my dad. He was the only one who really loved me. He never meant to hurt me, I knew that. All I wanted was to be with him, but they would never allow that now. They wouldn't even let him bring me to the hospital, or say goodbye.

They had taken away everything and everyone that mattered to me.

2

The Nuthouse

Somehow I survived my first night.

I'd hardly slept at all, but then I hadn't slept properly for years, so that wasn't unusual. What amazed me was that no one else here seemed to sleep either. It had been quite reassuring to be surrounded by other people who were the same as me.

The hospital seemed to come alive at night. Patients who slept all day got out of bed in the evening and spent the night sitting in the corridor chatting to each other and the night staff. In the day room, some people had slept on the floor and others curled up and slept on the chairs. Only the elderly patients had appeared to go to bed. Most of the beds in the ward were empty, and the place seemed eerily quiet.

I had talked to a few people. The anorexic patients, who weren't allowed to leave their cubicles, had come to their doorways and sat looking out on to the corridors. This was their social time and the other patients sat in the corridor to talk to them.

The only scary part had been when a couple of girls managed to get some glue from the office, sniffed the lot and then went on the rampage. They tore down posters and smeared mustard all over the walls – although they carefully avoided damaging the patients' poems and artwork pinned up along the corridors.

Eventually they had been contained by the staff, given strong sedatives and put in solitary confinement. The tablets must have been real knockout drops judging by the state of them at the breakfast table the next morning. They were in virtual comas, unable even to keep their eyes open.

Breakfast was in the dining room – a long dark room – around a large metal table that was bolted to the floor. The window was boarded up, so the only natural light came from a skylight above us. There was an overwhelming smell of frying and the carpet was mottled with trodden-in food. I soon realised why: quite a few of my fellow patients were throwing food and plates on the floor. It was like feeding time at the zoo. The nurses stood behind us in a line, and pushed plates back on to the table as they were pushed off. Patients were told not to pass food to each other, but it was clear from the piles of bacon on some plates that this rule was almost impossible to enforce. The table was covered in food. One woman was trying to make herself sick and had to be whisked away by a member of staff.

Simone, my room-mate, sat next to me. 'What's with all the blue plastic crockery?' I asked her, making an effort to sound far more cheerful than I actually felt.

Simone laughed. 'It's meant to be unbreakable, so that we can't use it to hurt ourselves or others with. Haven't you noticed the cutlery as well? You couldn't cut a jelly in two with one of these knives.'

I laughed and looked down at the bacon that I had been sawing at for quite some time. The knife had barely scored the surface.

I wasn't hungry anyway; I was still too upset about being in this place and my stomach was churning. The food I left on my plate was quickly disposed of by a nurse, in case someone grabbed it to binge on later. I wanted to leave the table but I had been told I must not – the staff couldn't cope with us all wandering around unsupervised, and mealtimes took up a lot of their resources.

I looked around at my companions.

I had learned that the two doped-up girls who'd caused such a commotion during the night were called Mary and Gina.

Mary was nineteen, slim and attractive with blonde hair spiked up into points. She wore dramatic make-up, lots of silver chains and rings and luminous, brightly coloured trousers. Her arms were totally wrecked where she had cut herself over and over again. She had told me in the night that she filled the cuts she inflicted upon herself with anything poisonous that she could find at the time – even the carbon out of a sharpened pencil. That was why the scarring on her arms was so severe. I made a mental note to try it when I next got the opportunity.

Gina was a larger version of Mary. She was twenty and wore identical clothes, jewellery, hair and make-up to Mary. She also had matching scarred arms. They could have been sisters, but in fact they had only met when they were admitted to the hospital six months earlier. I wondered whether they had been similar before they met, or whether one of them had modelled herself on the other. Whichever it was it was clear now that they had formed an emotional and physical bond which was so strong they were almost one person.

I was fascinated. For the first time in my life I was seeing people who abused and mutilated themselves the way I did. I had always felt such a freak for doing it. I'd kept it hidden as much as I could, afraid of others' disgust and condemnation. But these girls understood why I couldn't stop myself doing it.

I wanted to ask them all kinds of questions, but the aura around them was aggressive. I felt that nobody else would be let into their private world and decided to back off until it felt safer.

One thing really did worry me: they had been here a long time already and were clearly still intent on destroying themselves. From what I heard, most of the time they were either totally out of control and smashing up whatever they could get their hands on or they were sedated. If this place didn't work for them, then why should it work for me?

While I was cautious around Mary and Gina, I had found Simone more welcoming. She had come to the hospital suffering from bulimia, alcoholism and self-abuse and had attempted suicide several times. What surprised me was that she was in her thirties, very well educated and well spoken, with a highly paid job in central London and a flat she shared with her boyfriend in Brighton. If there were prizes for the best-dressed patient she would have won every time. Simone had so much going for her, yet emotionally, it seemed, she was as screwed up as everyone else. That's the one thing we all have in common, I thought. Irrespective of age, race, gender, sexuality and class – at the end of the day we are all crazy.

When we were allowed to leave the table, I returned to my cubicle. I had been told the day before that I would be attending compulsory group therapy sessions and I had half an hour until the first one. Even thinking about having to talk about myself with a group of complete strangers terrified me. I had never been able to talk about what had happened to me. In the past I hadn't been able to tell my teachers, my mother, Social Services or my doctor. So how was I going to tell complete strangers? The idea made my stomach churn around again. Maybe if I pretended to be sick I wouldn't have to go.

Anna was on her bed reading again when I returned to the cubicle.

'How was your first hospital breakfast then?' she asked.

Once again I put on my polite, cheerful mask. I was a master at it. I'd been brought up to be polite no matter what, and I'd also spent the past few years trying to persuade social workers and teachers that everything in my life was OK, despite the fact that it clearly wasn't. So I knew how to put on a brave face.

'I couldn't face it I'm afraid – I just feel so nervous. Mind you, hospital food isn't that good anyway is it?' I smiled.

'I understand it gets more palatable as the months go on. You might get to like it in the end,' Anna joked. 'Anyway don't ask me about food, it's not exactly my strong point.'

Self-deprecating humour, as I was to discover, was what kept everyone going. It got them through the day, when all else failed. It seemed to be a way of coping, and surviving the awfulness of their daily lives.

The night before, Anna told me of her battle with anorexia, which she had nearly lost on several occasions. When she came to the hospital she had weighed only three and a half stone and had had to lie on a special waterbed, as a normal bed bruised her every time she moved. She had put on some weight in the year since then, but was still on permanent bed rest, as were all the anorexic patients.

Their meals were brought to them, and they were supervised to make sure they ate. They stayed in bed all the time, unless there was a meeting, and they would be escorted to that. Anna was accompanied when she washed and all the anorexic patients had to use commodes beside their beds as they couldn't be trusted in the toilets alone in case they vomited their food. The idea of living like that horrified me, and as I looked down at my own rather overweight body I thought, I may have all sorts of problems, but at least I'll never have anorexia.

Anna had explained, with the black humour that I was soon to discover was typical of most of the patients, that the only benefit of being anorexic was that they each had a portable television in their cubicles. They weren't allowed to watch the main one in the day room until they had reached their first target weight. This was a big thing, because in the day room there were fights over which TV channel should be on and quite often the TV was smashed. Apparently the hospital relied on local charities for regular donations of televisions.

While the anorexics were watched at all times, Anna explained that the rest of us could use the shower and go to the loo without being accompanied but it was forbidden to lock the doors. Staff had to monitor all bathroom visits, in case anyone tried to commit suicide, self-harm or have sex. I was horrified by the idea of someone walking in on me in the toilet. As we spoke I felt my swollen stomach, wondering just how long a human being could last without going to the toilet. I intended to put the record to the test.

This morning Anna asked me why I had been admitted, but it was still far too painful to think about, let alone talk about.

'I have to go to this meeting, Anna.' I got up to leave.

'Before you go, Sophie,' Anna said, 'do you think I could be a pain again and ask you to get me a cup of tea? Sorry to be a nuisance, I'm just so thirsty.'

'No problem,' I said, and set off down the corridor towards the kitchen.

Although I had been on the ward for less than twenty-four hours I had already made Anna countless cups of tea. I was surprised she wasn't on her commode all day. I took the tea back to her and then hurried off to the meeting.

By this time I had learned that there were four Consultant Psychiatrists on the unit, each specialising in different areas: Professor Hill specialised in anorexia patients, Professor Grant took care of the bulimics and alcoholics, Professor Roberts was responsible for those inmates suffering from schizophrenia, senile dementia and depression and Professor Harvey was the psychiatrist who specialised in young people, victims of abuse, complete psychopaths and anyone who didn't fit into any other category.

I was in his group.

We were ushered into a room where plastic chairs had been arranged in a semicircle. There was a big mirror on one wall which I was told was a one-way window. Behind it was a small room, from which various experts observed and monitored the patients. A microphone dangled in the middle so they could hear us as well, and a phone sat on a desk in the centre of the room. The two nurses, Dawn and Amy, were running the group, along with a social worker called Helen.

I had spent two years having weekly counselling sessions with a social worker, but this was very different. It all seemed a bit Big Brother to me; I found the idea of being watched by unseen people scary and sat on the seat nearest to the door, so that I could bolt if it got too much.

I looked around. There were several other patients, most of whom I didn't know. Then Mary and Gina burst into the room and threw themselves down on the seats opposite me.

'Why don't you two sit apart from each other today, just as a trial?' suggested Helen.

Mary and Gina gave her a look that could have cut her in half and Mary threatened to leave the meeting if they couldn't sit together. The idea was rapidly dropped.

It seemed to take an age for people to drift into the room and Dawn, who kept looking at her watch, began to get agitated.

Finally, all Dr Harvey's patients arrived.

'Right,' began Dawn, 'who would like to start the meeting by telling us how they feel today?'

Silence.

'Any volunteers?'

Silence.

'Sophie, why don't you start by introducing yourself to the group and telling us how you are feeling on your second day here.'

I felt my stomach lurch as she spoke to me. All my thoughts became jumbled and my mind went totally blank.

'It's OK, take your time. Just say the first thing that comes into your mind,' Dawn said.

'Shit,' I said, without even thinking. 'Shit, shit, shit.' There was no stopping me now. 'My name is Sophie, I'm sixteen years old, I don't know what I'm doing in a place like this and I feel like shit . . . that's it.'

'Join the club then, so do I,' agreed Mary.

'I feel terrible as well,' added Gina.

A ripple of laughter swept around the room.

'I think we all feel like shit most of the time in this place,' said a man to the left of me.

'Yeah, but you look like shit, Harry,' Gina piped up.

'Taken a look at yourself today, Gina?' Harry replied. Gina looked around and laughed. There was an air of tension around her, and a sense that she might erupt at any minute. She stood up. 'Look,' she said, 'I really don't need all this crap today, I'm knackered, so I'm going back to bed. Have a lovely meeting all of you.' She moved towards the door.

'I expect you're both tired after all the damage you caused last night,' Harry said. 'Have you two got shares in Bostick? You should, with all the glue you get through.'

Gina was now leaning against the door. 'Can somebody let me out of here please?' she asked. It was only then that I realised there were no handles on the inside of the door, making it impossible to leave the room. I felt scared and trapped. I wanted to leave too, but I felt rooted to my seat. Gina had become agitated. She stomped back into the room and pressed her face against the one-way mirror.

'*Can somebody let me out of here please.*' The room shook as she screeched at the top of her voice. Amy jumped up and put her arm around Gina's shoulders, and at the same time the door was opened from the outside.

'Calm down,' Amy said. 'The door is open now. Please try to stay though. We all want you to stay.'

Gina pushed past Amy, towards the door. Mary had also

stood up and was one step behind her. They stormed out of the room together and Mary swung the door shut with all the force she could. There was silence as the rest of the group sat, expressionless.

The phone on the desk rang. Amy picked it up and said 'yes' a few times before replacing the receiver.

'How does everyone feel about what just happened?' Helen, the social worker, asked.

'I'm sick of those two, they spoil the meetings all the time,' said a middle-aged woman called Jane. 'After all, none of us wants to be in this place. They're not the only ones who are fed up and they don't seem to want to be helped. What's the point in them being here with us?'

'I know it's frustrating, Jane, but everyone here is at a different stage in their treatment and not everybody finds group work easy,' said Helen. 'As a group though, I hope we can support them, so that eventually they'll feel they can trust us, and use the group as they should.'

'When is this meeting going to finish?' I asked quietly. I was finding it hard to take.

'Are you finding this session difficult too, Sophie?' asked Dawn.

'It scares me to sit here and talk. I don't trust anyone,' I said.

'Not even yourself?' asked Dawn.

'Especially not myself,' I answered.

'That's really sad, love,' said Jane. 'I'd hate to think that any of my kids felt that bad about themselves. You're too young to have to feel like that.'

'I feel like Sophie does,' said a girl named Katie, much to my surprise. 'I scare myself sometimes when I see what I do

to myself, but I just can't stop it. I hate myself. I really do.'
Katie carried on speaking about her feelings and her past and
how hard it was to live with herself and as she talked I sat
and stared at her, transfixed.

Other people joined in, but I barely heard what they said.
Katie's words had affected me so deeply. I just couldn't believe
that there was someone who felt the same as me, and who
seemed to have gone through many of the same things. It was
as though she could see inside my head. I was suddenly
conscious of Dawn's voice.

'Right everybody,' she was saying, 'I think we should wrap
this meeting up now. We've achieved a lot today and I'm pleased
that some of you were able to open up to the rest of us and
talk about how you feel. Remember, there is a community meeting today at 2 p.m. for everyone and I've also been asked to
remind everyone that the writing therapy class is at 4 p.m. in
the occupational health unit. Is there anything else that anyone
wants to add before we finish?'

'Just one thing,' said Helen. 'Please remember that today
is weighing-in day for the anorexic patients. Feelings will be
running high, as they always are at this time. Bear this in
mind. Thanks.'

'I'm sorry,' I said. 'I don't understand. Why will feelings
be running high?'

'Every Tuesday the anorexic patients are weighed. There
is tremendous pressure on them to achieve target weights and
any weight loss is dealt with quite severely. So it can be quite
an emotional time and patients can become very distressed.'

'It seems very harsh to deal with people severely if they
lose any weight,' I said.

'I know, Sophie, but the doctors have great success with

treating anorexia here, all food and drink intake is carefully monitored and . . .'

'Sorry to interrupt you, Helen, but did you say drink intake was monitored too?' I asked.

'Yes,' she answered, 'why?'

'Oh, it's nothing, I just wondered.'

I smiled. So that was the reason for Anna's endless requests for cups of tea. No wonder she kept apologising to me. I couldn't help but admire her nerve.

3

The Truth Hurts

That afternoon in the writing therapy group I plucked up the courage to read out a poem I'd written about how lonely I felt. As always, all my feelings had come pouring out when I started to put pen to paper. I had always found writing much easier than talking.

'Thank you, Sophie, you've taken a big step in sharing that with us,' said Claire, the occupational therapist who was running the group. 'I hope you'll find the support you need here.'

I nodded, and forced a smile.

'We're all here to help and support each other,' said a middle-aged man called Frank. 'I've made some very strong friendships since I was admitted, and I'm sure you will too.'

I looked around the room and wondered if the others all felt as lonely and isolated as I did. I wished that I had never read my poem; no one was saying anything and I felt the walls were closing in on me.

'Would anybody else like to share what they've written today?' asked Claire.

Silence. I bet I'm the only mug daft enough to do that, I thought. Never again.

Then I heard someone speaking and looked round to see Mary fumbling with a piece of paper.

'I'd like to read my poem,' she said nervously. 'It's quite a long one so tell me to stop when you get fed up.' Claire smiled and Gina held Mary's hand tightly as she read out, in a shaky voice, a deeply moving poem about the frightened little girl she saw looking back at her from the mirror.

I thought back to the earlier meeting in the morning when she and Gina had stormed out, and to the night before when they had gone on their glue-sniffing spree. Could this really be the same person?

As she came to the end of her poem Mary started to cry. Gina held her tightly, rocking her gently like a baby. She sobbed quietly on Gina's shoulder.

The group ended soon afterwards and we made our way back from the occupational health unit to the wards. I felt numb and longed to be alone. When I got back to my cubicle, Simone wasn't in her bed and Anna was asleep. Gratefully I pulled the curtains around my bed, then lay down and buried my head deep into the pillow.

I must have fallen asleep, as I awoke with a start when Dawn tapped me gently on the arm and told me it was time for dinner.

'I'm sorry,' I said, 'but I'm just not hungry tonight. Would you mind if I just stayed in bed?'

'You're not fed up with hospital food already are you?' Dawn joked. 'I'll come back and check on you later.'

I reached into my locker and pulled out my diary.

My diary had always been my most trusted friend. I had told my diary everything since I was twelve and my life had started to go wrong. I turned to the fifth of June and began to write.

I've settled down now. Yesterday it was all a bit of a shock to the system. I felt scared of the other patients, but I'm getting to know some of them a bit better now. I've talked to somebody here called Katie. She's been through the same as me. Last night I wanted to cut myself. I want to have my blades back that were taken off me. It's such a release when I can see the blood running away from me, I'm not sure that I can cope in any other way. I'm feeling so confused. I know that I can't sort all this out on my own and that I am not strong enough to do it. I'm scared that I'm too screwed up for the professionals to sort out. Oh God, I just wish that I could be punished for what has happened. I'm scared of living and scared of dying, it's all such a mess. I've got to see Dr Harvey in a ward round tomorrow and I'm dreading it.

My mind was racing faster than I could write. Panic swept through me, as my feelings tumbled out. I felt so scared and so alone. I couldn't write anymore. I felt like screaming at the top of my voice, but I had no words inside me to scream. I wished that I could hurt myself; that was the only thing that I was good at.

Dawn appeared by my beside.

'How are you feeling?' she asked.

'OK, thanks,' I lied.

'Do you feel that you want to talk to me about anything that's happened?'

'No, I'm fine at the moment,' I said, attempting to sound cheerful.

Dawn didn't press me any further and said she'd be there for me, whenever I was ready to talk to her. There was a loud scream from the corridor outside the ward so she hurried out, telling me she'd return later to check on me. I wished she wouldn't, I was beginning to feel claustrophobic.

I shut my eyes. My head was still spinning and the thoughts in my head felt trapped inside. I wished that I could trust someone enough to be able to tell them how I felt, but the thought of doing that was just too scary. I was terrified that I wouldn't be believed and that instead I'd be judged, and blamed.

I thought back to the writing therapy class and how easily the words had flowed on to the paper. Maybe writing is the answer, I thought to myself. Maybe if I get it all out on paper, I won't need to stay in hospital. I pulled my writing pad out of my bag and lay on my stomach with my notepad in front of me, and after a few minutes the words began to flow.

Sarah felt cold and scared in her bed, even though she was curled up into a ball with her quilt wrapped tightly around her. Through the gap in her bedroom curtains the stars shone brightly. Sarah usually felt safer when she saw them smiling down on her, like bodyguards. But tonight, they didn't seem to help.

She looked around the room, desperately searching for something to focus on. That always helped her to cope. Questions raced around in her mind. Would she fight? Would she tell in the morning? No: if she told she might lose him, and that would be worse than what was happening. There was no one to tell now, anyway. It was just the two of them, it was their secret.

She was crying now, silent tears that she wiped on the edge of the quilt. I'm worrying about something when I don't even know it will happen, she thought.

But she did know. There was something about the way he had spoken to her and looked at her as she said good-night. It had made her feel nervous and cold inside. She knew what it meant. But at least he loved her – that's what he had said.

Sarah looked up at the stars. 'Please protect me tonight,' she whispered softly. But the stars seemed a million miles away.

It was some time later when the handle on her bedroom door slowly turned. The light from the landing outlined his silhouette in the doorway. 'Turn your light on, Sarah.' He closed the door, and leaned back against it. She didn't look at him – she stared through the small gap in the curtains. He moved to the window and stared up into the night sky, following her gaze. Then he turned back to her and smiled. He was unfastening his trousers now. Sarah sank back into her bed and closed her eyes. She smelt his aftershave, that smell that had been so reassuring to her for so many years, until it all changed and he started to hurt her.

She heard the curtains being drawn tightly together. A moment later his footsteps padded towards her over the carpet. She kept her eyes tightly closed.

'You're going to be good for me tonight, aren't you?' he said.

Sarah didn't answer. She thought he might leave her if he thought she had fallen back to sleep. But he grabbed her roughly across her shoulders and pulled her up.

'You will be good,' he barked. He wasn't asking her this time, he was telling her. He was naked now, and climbing on to the bed. Sarah looked at her bedside lamp.

'No,' he said sharply. 'We'll keep the light on tonight, you're going to see every bloody bit of this.'

The quilt was ripped from her, and her nightdress pushed up above her head. Then he was upon her – his legs pushed hers apart until she felt that they would break off. Sarah started to count, it was something to focus on, until it was over.

She felt a burning and tearing sensation as his penis entered her body. She wanted to scream, but no scream came. She was paralysed. He was inside her, pushing himself further into her, so that her arms and legs felt nailed to the bed. Then he withdrew and she felt something cold and sharp being pushed into her and knew it would be the blade of his favourite kitchen knife. There was a burning, agonising pain deep inside and she felt the blood trickle out of her.

She tried to count – anything to take her mind off the pain. It felt like her body was being cut into pieces. Just as she thought she would pass out he took out the knife and entered her with his penis again. He liked blood; it excited him. If she didn't have a period then he would make the blood come himself.

Eventually he finished and lay exhausted on top of her, breathing heavily on to her face. Sarah couldn't move; she felt numb all over, but it was better than the pain. She tried to move her legs, but his bulk pinned her down. She smelled his stale breath and the sweat that had now dripped on to her body.

Her once warm and safe bed now felt cold and wet. Sarah prayed that it was only semen or urine that had soaked the bed, and not too much blood. She struggled *to hold back her tears. Then he roused himself and smiled down on her.*

'That was good,' *he laughed, as he climbed off her. He looked down at her torn body and then kissed her cheeks gently. She liked it when he did that, it meant she had done well. He turned off the beside lamp and whispered,* 'I'll see you in the morning.' *Then he went over to the window, drew back the curtains and left her, staring out into the night sky.*

The stars weren't shining now, her protectors had gone and Sarah was left in darkness.

She felt so dirty – worse than she'd ever felt before. She sat up and tried to get off the bed. She hurt so much. Crying, she made her way into the bathroom. She turned on the bathroom light and looked down at her herself. When she saw the blood she began to fill the bath with water – the hottest water that she could run from the taps.

Sobbing and shaking, Sarah climbed into the bath. The steam rose and she could feel her skin being scalded. She scrubbed herself until her skin was raw. It was good being so red, she thought, the scars on her arms and legs looked so vivid.

She sat in the bath, crying, until the water went cold. Then she pulled the plug out and watched the red water drain away. She still felt dirty, and she knew that she would never feel clean again.

'Why am I so bad?' *she said out loud.* 'No one is as bad as me. I need to be punished.'

She felt calm and determined now. She was going to do what she had planned to do, since she'd first started to do bad things with the night figure. Sarah reached up to the bathroom shelf and pulled out a packet of razor blades from the lid of her deodorant can where she kept them hidden. She knew then that it was the only answer – the only way she would ever stand a chance of being clean again.

Calmly she ran some more hot water into the bath and took a razor blade from the packet. This would be the final pain, the final time that she would be hurt, and then she would no longer be bad.

She pushed the blade deeply into the veins in her wrists. Then she put her hands and arms into the hot water and slowly watched the badness flow away from her soul.

'No more hurt now,' she said as the blood flowed away. A sense of relief swept over her as her life slipped slowly away.

There were different tears in the morning. Not Sarah's tears any more. They were her father's tears as it dawned on him what he had done to his daughter. Now it was too late though – too late to put things right. Too late for Sarah.

That was the only way I could write about what had happened to me, as if it happened to someone else. Sarah was me, and the man who violated and abused her was my dad.

I always imagined the same ending. With me dead and my dad sorry for what he had done and full of remorse.

The reality was very different, though. I did get in the bath, but I didn't die. I cut myself, over and over again, trying to punish myself and blot out the pain and hurt.

But my dad was never, ever sorry.

The feelings welled up inside me – pain, anger, fear, hurt. I felt the pressure build up inside my head as if it was going to explode. I had to do something to relieve it. But my blades had gone. Desperately I looked around for something, anything, to take the pain away. There was nothing. But then I remembered the small kitchen, down the corridor. In a state of near-panic, with tears rolling down my face, I got off the bed and ran out of the ward.

4

Under Control

'Morning, Sophie,' Dawn said. 'You're next in the ward round today, so can you come with me.'

I nodded and followed her down the corridor to a bench situated against the wall, next to a closed door.

'Wait here,' she said. 'I'll come and get you when we're ready.' She disappeared into the room, shutting the door behind her.

I sat on the bench, staring down at the swirling circles in the pattern on the carpet.

'Hiya.'

I looked up. It was Katie, the girl who had spoken in the therapy group the day before. She sat down on the bench next to me.

'First ward round today?' she said. I nodded. 'Do you know what they call this bench?' she said. 'It's called the distress bench – I suppose it's obvious why, you look pretty distressed.'

I smiled and she grinned back. The moment she began talking in the group I had felt drawn to her and hoped we might be friends. She was nineteen and very slim, with short, spiky reddish hair. She had quite sharp features and looked tough, yet when she smiled, her eyes lit up and a real warmth seemed to radiate from her.

Katie told me that she was from Colwyn Bay in north Wales, which explained her strong Liverpudlian accent. She had been sent to this hospital as her 'last chance' to be sorted out. Hours of counselling and therapy and committal to a psychiatric unit in Wales had done nothing for her and the professionals were running out of ideas. Now she had been told that if Dr Harvey couldn't sort her out, then no one could. She'd arrived two months earlier, but so far she was still as intent as ever on destroying herself.

Katie stopped speaking as the door opened behind us, and Dawn appeared. 'Come on now, my love,' she said to me, 'you're wanted.'

'Can I see you later?' Katie asked Dawn.

'Of course,' Dawn said, as she put her arm around my shoulders and guided me into the room.

Inside there were half a dozen staff members, seated in a semicircle, with an empty chair in front of them. I sat down rigidly in the chair, wishing I could escape from the room. I glanced towards the door – there was no handle on the inside. My heart sank.

I recognised some of the people, but not all. Most had been introduced to me on my first day on the ward, but this was my first meeting with Dr Harvey, my consultant.

He got up, reached out his hand to me and introduced himself. He was tall, heavily built and black, and his hand engulfed mine as he shook it. I felt totally in awe. He smiled at me as he sat back down in his chair.

'Welcome, Sophie,' he said. 'I'm pleased to meet you at last. I've been hearing and reading a lot about you.'

I tried to smile back, but I was too nervous.

'Do you want to begin by telling me about what happened last night?' he asked gently.

'Not really,' I replied.

'I'd like to hear your interpretation of what happened,' he said.

I thought back to the night before and the writing that I had been doing while lying on my bed, and the way it had made me feel.

'Just start at whatever point you like,' he encouraged.

I took a deep breath. I knew I had to get this over with, and tell him what he wanted to know, so I forced myself to talk.

'I decided to write down some of my thoughts last night, Doctor,' I began. 'And, well, I became a little upset afterwards. I got a little out of control.'

I looked around the room for some reassurance. Amy smiled at me.

'Well, the thing is, Doctor, I got very upset when I had finished writing and I read it back to myself and I felt pretty out of control. It was a strange feeling because I hadn't got the razor blades anymore, as they were taken off me when I came in. It was the first time that I haven't had them. I felt that my security had gone, in a way.' My voice was shaking as I spoke and I looked around the room nervously. Everyone's eyes were on me. Dawn gave me a reassuring smile.

I looked down at the floor. 'I was in a panic and I wanted to hurt myself. I remember running along the corridor into the kitchen. I saw a cup that wasn't one of the unbreakable ones and threw it on to the floor. It smashed, and I picked up a piece and began to cut my arm with it.' My voice began to falter.

Dr Harvey broke in. 'Carry on, Sophie. You're doing very well.'

I looked up towards Dr Harvey. 'I just couldn't stop myself, and the feeling that I got when I saw the blood just made me feel so much better. I know that what I did wasn't good, but it's the way I've always coped.' I paused. 'I don't remember much more than that, only going to the medical room and having my arm dressed. Then the medicine I was given made me feel very tired, and I must have just gone to bed and fallen asleep. I don't remember any more until this morning.'

I was relieved to have finished the story. Talking about it had been an ordeal.

Dr Harvey looked intently at me. 'We're all very conscious that you were out of control last night, Sophie,' he said. 'I hope that eventually you will be able to come to us when things get too much. I know it won't be easy for you, but we are here to help you. Do you think you could read to us or let us see what you wrote last night?'

'No. I'm sorry, I really don't feel that I can share that with anyone yet.' I felt sick inside at the thought of anyone knowing what I had written.

'OK,' he said. 'But remember you are safe here and all the staff are here for you when you need them. Claire tells me you shared your poem in the writing group. You obviously find it easier to express yourself on paper.'

'Yes I do, words on paper are safe, aren't they?'

He smiled. 'I hope you'll find it a safe enough environment here in the end not to need to put it all on paper.'

I nodded. 'Thank you,' I said.

'I'm going to prescribe some medication for you, chlorpro-mazine, to take daily for the time being, just to calm you down a bit. It's a very effective drug that we use with great success. Hopefully it will help you stay in control as you begin to share those painful feelings with us. And in time we'll be able to reduce the medication.'

'How long will I be here?' I asked. I was desperate to know when I could leave.

'At least six months, maybe a year, maybe more,' he said. 'Everyone needs a different length of time to heal.'

I was horrified. I couldn't imagine surviving in this place for six weeks, let alone six months, and a year just didn't bear thinking about.

After the meeting Amy took me to the medical room. I waited for her to let herself in and followed her inside. After three visits to the medical room in three days I was beginning to be familiar with the routine.

She handed me a capsule to swallow. 'This really will help,' she said. 'You were a danger to yourself and others last night.'

'I would never hurt anyone else,' I said hotly.

'You don't know that, Sophie,' she replied. 'When you're that out of control, anything could happen.'

'I would never hurt anyone else,' I repeated, choked to think that she thought that I was some sort of danger to others.

'There's an art therapy class this afternoon at 2.30,' Amy said as we left the medical room.

'I might just go and have a lie down for an hour first,' I said. 'I still feel quite tired.'

Amy said she'd see me later and I walked back to the gold-fish bowl that I slept in.

Anna was on her bed. 'You survived your first ward round then,' she said. 'Was it OK?'

'I suppose so,' I replied. 'I'm glad they're only once a week though.'

Anna smiled, her skin stretching itself over her gaunt face. It put my problems in perspective every time I looked at Anna. She really was ill.

'Do me a favour, Anna,' I said.

'On one condition,' she replied.

'OK, I'll get you a cup of tea,' I laughed. 'Can you wake me up for my art group at 2.30? I'm feeling pretty knackered.'

It seemed only a minute later that she woke me. I opened my eyes – but it was a bad idea. The room was spinning.

I tried to reply to Anna. Another bad idea – my mouth was totally dry and my words barely croaked out. I moved my legs out of the bed to try to sit up. They felt heavy and numb, as if they weren't mine.

I tried to stand up but my legs wouldn't move, they were like lead weights. I fell heavily back on to the bed and shut my eyes tightly to stop the room from spinning.

'Sophie, are you OK?' Anna asked from the other side of the curtain.

'No, not really,' I croaked back. 'I don't know what they've done to me.'

'They've got you on chlorpromazine haven't they?' Anna asked.

'Yeah, they have,' I croaked. 'Is this what it does to you?'

'I'm afraid so,' she replied. 'They put loads of people on it in here. After a few weeks though, you'll be back to normal and you won't even realise you've taken it.'

I closed my eyes tightly and thought about what Anna had just said. The idea that I wouldn't even realise I'd taken it in a few weeks' time really worried me. I didn't want to get that used to a knockout drug.

I didn't make it to the art therapy class or anywhere else that day. I felt so tired I wanted to sleep for weeks or even months. I wished that I could sleep for a year and wake up to find that this was all over and I was free again. I wanted to be somewhere else – anywhere – away from this madhouse.

And I missed Dad. I couldn't help it. Even after everything that had happened, I still missed him. I wanted to be a little girl again, like I was before all the horrible stuff happened. Daddy's little girl.

5

Daddy's Little Girl

Right from the start it was always Dad and me, with Mum somewhere in the background. Dad treated me like the one who mattered to him, the one who was important, while Mum was on the outside.

I always knew I was adopted. They told me I was special because they had chosen me. Or to be accurate, Dad had chosen me and Mum had gone along with it. I was a few months old when he picked me out as the child he wanted.

Social Services must have been delighted. My parents were a very respectable middle-class couple. Dad was an accountant and Mum was a secretary. They had been married for ten years and no children had come along. Tests had shown that Mum would never be able to have a baby so they had decided to adopt.

It was Dad who, having picked me, gave me my name. Later, when I was older and Mum was angry with me, she used to shout, 'I never picked you anyway; I wish I could take you back.'

Looking back through the photo albums there are thousands of photos of me and Dad, but it's hard to find one of me with Mum. From the start Dad was the one who did everything with me.

We lived in a comfortable three-bedroom semi in south London and I wanted for nothing. I was surrounded by toys, I had a lovely bedroom and a doting father who dropped everything the minute he got home to play with his little girl.

Mum went back to work full-time soon after the adoption and I was cared for by my grandparents while my parents were at work. When I was old enough to start school I went to my grandparents' house to have my tea. My nan and grandad – Mum's parents – were lovely. Nan would bake cakes with me and see that I did my homework, while Grandad was a quiet and loving man who was always kind. I loved my time with them and Dad would collect me on his way home from work.

He'd take me home and for the rest of the evening he concentrated on me. Mum would get back from work and make dinner, while Dad played with me and then put me to bed.

On Saturdays Dad would take me to visit his parents. His mother had suffered a severe stroke and was paralysed and permanently in a nursing home. We'd visit her there, sitting with her for a while, before going round to see his father, who still lived at home.

On Sundays Mum would cook Sunday dinner while Dad and I went to the park with our dog – the one he had bought for him and me – or played together. Then he'd take me to the sweet shop and buy me bags and bags of sweets, as many as I wanted. Not surprisingly, I was a plump kid. I thought of Dad as my best friend. That's what he said he was. I had other friends, children from school who I would sometimes play with or have over to tea. But most of the time it was just me and Dad. He said we didn't need anyone else.

Materially I had everything. A Barbie doll with dozens of outfits, plenty of dolls, a train set and cuddly toys. Later on I had a CB radio, which was the latest gadget. Dad and I would play with all of them. But his favourite game was play-fighting. He would chase me round the house and when he caught me he would roll around the floor with me, pretend wrestling and pinning me down. I would shriek with laughter, although sometimes when Dad was on top of me I had to yell at him to stop.

I didn't think there was anything odd about the amount of time Dad spent with me. I didn't know that it was any different for anyone else. I felt lucky to have a daddy who loved me so much. And Mum just didn't seem to be part of anything – I have barely any memories of being with her. As I grew older Dad treated me more and more like an adult. When we went out in the car I sat in the front with him, and if Mum came along she sat in the back. They weren't getting on very well by this time; they would argue a lot and Dad would confide in me that things were very difficult with Mum.

Dad sent a valentine to me each year, and he made a huge fuss of me on my birthday, showering me with presents. He and Mum didn't seem to enjoy being together at all.

If I heard them arguing I always jumped in on Dad's side, even if I knew he was wrong. It must have been very hurtful for Mum, but I didn't see that then. I blamed her for every row and for making Dad unhappy.

When I was nine or ten I got a Purdey haircut. I think just about every little girl did. Actress Joanna Lumley played Purdey in *The New Avengers* and I thought she was great, with her short blonde bob that framed her face. Dad had bought a motorbike around that time, and he would take me on the back of it. I felt so grown-up, flying along with my arms wrapped round him and my grown-up haircut.

When I was eleven I started at the local comprehensive. I was a bright kid and Dad wanted me to do well academically, so he bought me lots of books and spent hours helping me with my homework.

Dad had always been relaxed about his body, often walking around the house naked, while Mum never did. Of course, as a small child I wasn't worried about privacy or nudity. But as I got older and began to approach puberty, I wanted to be more private. Dad was always coming in while I was in the bath and I began to feel a bit embarrassed. So one day I locked the bathroom door.

Dad came and tried to open the door and when he realised I had locked it he went mad, shouting and banging on the door so that I had to get out of the bath to open it. He said he needed to use the loo. He was so angry that I didn't dare ever lock the door again. He carried on coming into the bathroom and he would make little comments like 'I can see you're turning into a woman.' I felt terribly uncomfortable, but I didn't know how to stop him.

It was Dad who bought all my clothes. I never went on girly shopping trips with Mum. Dad took me, and he advised me on what to wear and made me try on my new clothes for him.

Dad had always liked a drink in the evening. He had a bar in the living room and would pour himself a whisky after work. And from a very early age he gave me alcohol too. He'd pour me a miniature version of whatever he was having. I didn't like the taste, but I was pleased that he thought I was grown-up enough to have it, so I drank it. By the time I was ten it was our evening ritual – a drink together. Mum was often out; she liked to keep fit and she was a member of a local bowling club. So often it would be just me and Dad at home in the evening.

In the holidays I would go round to Nan and Grandad's. Sometimes, as a treat, Dad would take me to his office with him. He worked in a big office in central London and I loved seeing it. He'd show me off to the people he worked with, and although I squirmed at all the attention, it was fun.

Dad was always very flirtatious. He wasn't a hunk – just five foot seven, slim, with neat dark hair and dark-framed glasses – but women seemed to like him. He was always smartly dressed – in a suit during the week and smart trousers and shirts at weekends – and he'd flirt with the women in his office, with the teachers at my school and even with my nan when he came round. Nothing too over the top; he never caused offence, he just laughed and chatted and was very at ease with women. I think my nan found him amusing, and I imagine the others did too.

All except Mum, it seemed. Their fights were getting more frequent and as the distance between her and Dad grew greater she spent even less time with us. I didn't care, though. Mum was the stern one, the one who wasn't fun. Dad was the one I wanted to be with. He said we were special to each other.

Dad and I used to play tennis together. Both my parents played, but as I grew bigger and stronger I became a good player and replaced Mum as Dad's regular partner. I also played for my school, and they recommended that I join a local tennis club where Dad and I played as a doubles pair.

It was Dad who prepared me for my first period. That's something a mother would normally do, but with things the way they were in our family, I wasn't surprised that he did it. He asked me if I'd been told about it at school and bought some sanitary towels for me to have ready. I was twelve when I got my first period. It happened at school. I felt a strange mixture of pleasure at becoming a woman and fear at something that felt so odd happening to my body. Most of all I wanted it to be private. Like any young girl I squirmed at the mention of bodily functions, especially mine.

That evening I told my parents. I felt very awkward and Mum was awkward too. But Dad was elated. He insisted they take me round to Nan and Grandad's so that we could all have a party to celebrate. Nan was a little surprised and Grandad looked rather embarrassed, but Dad worked his charm on them and Nan got out the sherry so that everyone could drink to me becoming a woman. I couldn't have known it then, but getting my period marked the end of the life I had known until then. Everything was about to change.

It was about two months later that Mum went away for the weekend with her bowling club.

That night after dinner Dad and I had a drink, as usual, played for a bit and watched some television. I stayed up late, but that was normal; I often went to bed at the same time as my parents. But as we were about to go up, Dad said, 'As your mother's not here, why not come into my bed?'

I didn't think this was strange. No alarm bells rang. There had been plenty of occasions in the past when I'd got into bed with my parents for a cuddle in the mornings. I just thought he was being nice.

Dad always slept naked, so I was used to that. We both got into bed and said goodnight. I turned to go to sleep, but the next minute, with no warning and without saying a word, he pulled me towards him, pushed up my nightie, got on top of me and had full, penetrative sex.

I was scared and in terrible pain. It hurt so much that I thought I was going to die. I knew what was happening – I had learned about sex – but I didn't understand why my dad was doing it to me.

When it was over he held me close and told me how much he loved me. I felt so confused. I knew, deep down, that what he had done was wrong. But I so wanted to make him happy, and there was a part of me that felt special, too, because he told me that whatever happened we had each other, and that I was his special girl. So I shut away all the scared feelings and the pain and kept telling myself, this is Dad, so it must be OK, he loves me, he wouldn't do anything wrong.

From that time on, a couple of times a month, when Mum was out, he would take me into his bed and have sex with me. I was glad that it was always his bed, because that way mine still felt safe. After he had done what he wanted I would pad down the hall to my room and curl up in the warm comfort of my own bed, trying to blot out my unhappy feelings. He didn't have to tell me not to say anything to Mum. He knew I wouldn't. I understood from the start that this was our secret.

Besides, I didn't get on with her at all. She seemed to disapprove of whatever I did. When I was twelve I found my old baby book. In the back of it she'd written in it that she couldn't relate to me and that she was very disappointed in me. That hurt so much.

Looking back I can see that my behaviour had probably worsened, as a result of the abuse. I was no doubt trying to draw her attention to the fact that something was desperately wrong. But she had no idea what was going on, and simply thought I was being difficult and distant with her.

For a year Dad continued to have sex with me in his bed. Then one night he appeared in my room when I was doing my homework, and made me lie on my bed so that he could have sex with me. After that he would come in whenever Mum was out and I was in my room, even during the day. And he began doing it more and more often. My bed wasn't safe or comforting any more.

Although I prayed that he would stop, I felt powerless against him. I had no choice. I felt he was all I had in the world – I had been rejected by my birth parents, Mum didn't care for me, so Dad was everything. I wanted to please him so badly. When he was pleased with me everything was good, he would cuddle me and give me treats. But when he was angry I felt so afraid, terrified that he would reject me, tell me I wasn't good enough and that he didn't want me any more. I couldn't bear the thought of that, anything was better than that. So I put up with whatever he did and tried to believe that it was because I was special, his girl, the one he loved. Awful as the abuse was, I felt I could manage it – until Mum left. She didn't even tell me she was moving out.

I had been invited to go to America for three weeks during the summer holidays by a cousin of Mum's. I was so excited; it was the biggest adventure I'd ever had. When I left, Mum, Dad and Nan all came with me to the airport. When they said goodbye I couldn't understand why Mum was crying so much; she seemed distraught, as if her heart was breaking. 'I'm only going for a holiday, Mum,' I said. 'I'll be back soon.'

But when I got back only Dad was there to meet me, and

in the car on the way home he told me that he and Mum had split up and she'd moved out. 'She'll be in touch,' he said.

I wasn't sure what to feel. I wasn't close to Mum, but that didn't mean it was OK for her to just disappear. I was angry and hurt. And what was going to happen now? An icy fear gripped me as I realised it would be just me and Dad – all the time.

Had she known what Dad was doing, I wondered? She had been too weak, I thought furiously. She had run away, instead of facing the truth and doing something to protect me. She hadn't even left an address. I felt I would never forgive her.

It was the summer of 1983, I was fourteen and within days of Mum leaving my life had transformed. From the start, Dad expected me to take over all Mum's jobs. So after school I would clean the house, iron his clothes and make his meals. Before Mum left she and Dad both cooked, but after she went he told me to cook every night. But that was the easy part. Once Mum had gone Dad expected me to go into his bed for sex every night. Only after he had finished could I slip back to my bed and struggle to go to sleep.

At school I had always done well, but my schoolwork began to slip. I had no time to do any homework, and besides, Dad was giving me more and more alcohol, and I wanted it – that way I could try to blot things out. I was drinking every night and sleeping badly. I began to arrive at school exhausted and hungover, so I could barely concentrate on my books any more.

My teachers noticed my work slipping, but put it down to my mother going. One young, newly qualified English Teacher, Miss Thomas, was concerned about me. 'You've changed,' she said. 'What's happened?' I told her my mum had left and she accepted that.

My friendships suffered. I could never see my friends because I was too busy looking after Dad and the house. They said I was turning into a housewife, but I took this as a compliment. I felt important and needed; Dad couldn't manage without me. I felt my friends' interests were trivial compared to my life.

But the truth was that I was feeling increasingly terrified and trapped. By now, Dad's parents had both died, so we no longer went to see them on Saturdays. Instead we spent the weekends at home together. We would do the shopping on a Friday evening and then spend Saturday and Sunday drinking and having sex.

I couldn't see a way out. More than anything I was terrified of losing Dad. He was all I had, my whole world. Yes, he was responsible for the bad things that were happening to me, but all the good things came from him too. He loved me, he told me that all the time. 'We've got each other,' he'd say, 'we don't need anyone else.' He behaved as though life was idyllic – just the two of us, happy and cosy in our own little world.

It was a little world that was rapidly closing in on me. I struggled to cope, but increasingly I couldn't. Dad told me I mustn't be weak, that it was a test of character and that I should be able to carry on at school and do well, despite having to do more jobs at home. The abuse was never mentioned.

I felt there was absolutely no one to turn to. I still went to my nan's after school sometimes, but by this time Grandad had died and she was getting old and frail, so I didn't want to worry her. And besides, if I told anyone I would be betraying Dad. I would lose him, lose my home, lose everything. He had told me that.

Mum had phoned a couple of times, but I didn't want to speak to her. I was rude to her and just wanted her to get off the phone. She wasn't going to help me. She would say, 'Do you miss me?' and I would say 'No.' Within a few weeks of her leaving I was in pieces. I couldn't be the 'wife' Dad wanted me to be, and manage school and the life of a fourteen-year-old as well. Increasingly I felt a build-up of pressure in my head. I was angry with myself because I couldn't manage. I felt I should be able to. Dad needed me to. But how?

6

Runaways

Life in the unit during that first week felt almost unreal, as if it was happening to someone else, and I longed to get out. The only thing that kept me going was getting to know Katie. We liked one another from the start and I felt I had never had a friend like her. Unlike my school friends, whose lives were so different, Katie's past had been very like mine. She too had been sexually and mentally abused by her father and grandfather and had started self-harming as a result. Katie and I understood one another and we soon started spending most of our free time together. She called me her 'little sis'.

One day, just over a week after I had arrived in the hospital, Katie was told that her grandmother back home in north Wales was terminally ill. Her grandmother was the only member of her family Katie felt close to, but she wasn't allowed to leave the hospital to go and see her. Katie took it badly.

Meanwhile I had attended my second ward round, in which I was told by Dr Harvey that he was arranging a family therapy session for the following Wednesday, with me and my parents, and the thought of this terrified me.

Dr Harvey knew I had been abused by my father, though

not the full extent of it, but this kind of 'get everyone round
the table' meeting – insensitive as it undoubtedly was – was
part of the hospital's treatment policy at that time. They tried
it with every new patient, and not surprisingly it caused a
huge amount of anxiety to those who had been abused, who
would do whatever they could to get out of going. The idea
was to agree together a care plan for the patient, but even
when the meetings actually happened, they seldom did any
good.

I knew I couldn't possibly go through with it. I told Katie,
and we decided that we had to get away. Neither of us could
stand being in the hospital any longer. The next day was
Katie's twentieth birthday and she wanted to spend it out of
the hospital.

We took a large plastic bin bag from a cleaner's trolley and
hid it in Katie's bedside locker. We each returned to it during
the day, putting essential supplies in it for later: a hospital
blanket, some toiletries and some biscuits from the kitchen
cupboard. Then, after supper, when the staff were changing
shifts, we managed to slip through the ward door when it
was unlocked and escape.

As soon as we got out of the unit we ran as fast as we
could, through the rest of the hospital. Even after we'd left
the hospital, we carried on running for at least half a mile,
constantly checking behind us, in case we were being followed.

It wasn't until we had reached the Underground station
and got on to the first tube that came along, that we finally
relaxed. When we realised we'd done it our mood changed
from anxious to euphoric.

Neither of us had a clue about what we were going to do,
where we would go or what viable alternative there might be

to hospital. We weren't being rational, and over the following hours our mood swung between relief at getting away, excitement at the adventure and depression because we actually had nowhere to go and no money.

Katie didn't know London, but I knew it well, so I told her about the places we passed on the tube and suggested a place where we should spend the night. We jumped off the tube at Charing Cross station and raced from there to Trafalgar Square and the church of St Martin in the Fields.

We were both excited; it seemed like an adventure we could share. I had slept rough before – in the two years before I came to the hospital I had run away from home many times – and I knew that St Martin in the Fields was a place where we'd find other homeless people, gathered on the steps outside.

We found a spot and sat down on the wide stone steps, huddled together for warmth. All around us people were strewn across the steps, many in makeshift cardboard homes and wrapped in blankets.

I looked at my watch. It was one minute past midnight.

'Happy Birthday, Katie,' I said, as I put my arms around her and hugged her warmly.

'First birthday I've ever had in London,' she replied drily.

In the distance the lights of clubs and theatres glowed. We watched groups of glamorously dressed people as they walked past, laughing loudly, on their way home from an evening out. They seemed to look through us, as though we didn't exist.

Katie began to shake; even though it was a summer night it was bitterly cold. I rummaged through the bin liner for our blanket and we sat together and put it over our legs.

Looking through the bag, I started to realise that Katie had absolutely no idea what living on the streets would be like.

I pulled shampoo and conditioner out of the bag and began to laugh. 'Where's the bathroom then, Katie?' Katie grinned and pointed to the fountain in the centre of Trafalgar Square. 'It may not be hot, but it's running water.' We were both laughing as I put the toiletries back into the bag. Then my hand rested on what felt like a plug. I pulled it out and looked in disbelief at the hairdryer which emerged from the bag on the end of it.

'Katie, you didn't pack this, did you?'

'I never thought,' she replied, embarrassed.

'Where did you think we were staying? The Hilton?' I asked. 'You may have sockets in the streets in Colwyn Bay, but we don't have them in London, sorry!'

We both began to laugh hysterically. What made it even funnier was the fact that our arms were cut to shreds and we didn't care about that at all, but our hair, well, that was different – we had pride in our hair, which was why Katie had packed all the hair things.

'You two will be cold like that,' said a gruff voice behind us. We turned to see an old man, lying on the steps behind us, under a cardboard shelter. At least I thought he was old. With his weathered face and long beard, it was hard to tell.

'There's cardboard around there,' he said pointing to a street that ran along the side of the church. 'It's left there by the market traders at the end of the day. Go and get some.'

I knew where the cardboard was from previous visits, but we thanked him anyway.

We stood up and picked up our belongings.

'I'll mind your place for you,' the old man said.

Katie looked at him in disbelief. 'Can you believe that?' she said as we made our way down the steps. 'I didn't realise this place was all that sought after.'

'It is,' I assured her, grinning. 'It's one of the better places to doss down.'

Katie was learning fast.

As we made our way across the road we saw a large group of people with brightly coloured flags and banners standing outside a building. We decided to go and see what they were up to. As we got closer we could hear them chanting and singing. Some were waving flags and others were holding large boards with the word 'Mandela' on them.

When we reached the edge of the group, a woman turned to us. 'Hello girls,' she said, 'have you come to join us?'

'What do we do?' Katie asked.

The woman explained that this was the campaign group to free South African political leader Nelson Mandela from prison. They had camped outside the South African Embassy, which was where we were standing, twenty-four hours a day for several months. Extra support, especially at night, was welcome.

'We sing songs to keep ourselves awake and drink lots of coffee,' the woman said. 'I was just going to get some coffees now. Would you two like one?'

Katie and I began to search through our pockets for money. Katie produced a pound from her pocket. 'That's all I have,' she said

'Don't worry about that,' the woman replied, 'it's free. We use some of the donations we get for coffee.'

'Nelson who?' Katie said, as soon as she was out of earshot.

We began to laugh. Admirable as it seemed joining an all-night vigil to free Nelson Mandela, we both knew we were really there for the free coffee. We went on to spend most of the night with the demonstrators, drinking coffee, listening to stories and singing songs. By sunrise we had learned most of the songs and knew a lot about Nelson Mandela. We were also very tired and very dirty.

We made our way over to the fountains in Trafalgar Square where the people of the night were washing. We splashed the cold water over our faces. It didn't smell too good, but at least it was cold and wet and it made us feel more awake.

London was waking up and people were on their way to work. Smart office workers walked briskly through Trafalgar Square. Most of them kept their heads down as they passed by us, pretending that we didn't exist, though we got the odd disdainful look.

We made our way back to Charing Cross station and used the toilets there, paying 10p for the privilege. We tidied ourselves up a bit in the toilets, until the attendant saw us and told us to get out.

We spent the rest of Katie's birthday in St James's Park, lying on benches trying to get some sleep. By the afternoon we had eaten all our biscuits. All we had left was £1.50 between us.

At about three in the afternoon we made our way back to Trafalgar Square. We got back to the steps of St Martin's just as an afternoon service was due to begin.

'Shall we go in?' I asked Katie. 'This is a beautiful place.'

I had been in quite a few times before and knew we wouldn't be thrown out, even though we looked dirty and bedraggled.

As we entered the church we were given a friendly smile and directed towards a row of pews at the front.

Katie and I went through the motions of praying and singing hymns and even though we were both very cynical about God and religion, there was something comforting about it. For that short while we were just the same as everybody else, our pasts didn't matter and everybody around us seemed warm and friendly and at peace. I had always felt something reassuring there, a sense of unconditional love that I had never found anywhere else.

After the service we sat for ages watching the world go by, playing a game as people went past, guessing which names we thought suited them and what sort of lives we thought they had.

When evening came we decided we couldn't face another night of singing. We were both tired and cold and the euphoria at escaping was giving way to fear and anxiety about what we were going to do. Around us, people started to construct their shelters for the night, cocoons made from cardboard and blankets.

Katie waited on the steps while I went to get some cardboard from behind the station. I returned with a couple of large flat boxes, but we decided it was too early for bed, so we just sat on them, with our blanket over our legs to stay warm.

An hour later Katie turned to me. 'I want to go back,' she said resolutely. 'It's no good staying here any longer; I won't be able to survive on the streets and we'll have to go back sooner or later you know.'

I was shocked. Despite feeling down, I had no intention of going back. 'What's happened to your fighting spirit?' I said. 'You've survived worse than this.'

'I feel scared here, there are so many weirdos. We might as well go back and be with the weirdos we know in the hospital.'

Katie was crying. I put my arms around her and we held each other. Too tired to talk any more, we sat on our cardboard, holding hands under our blanket for the rest of the night.

In the morning, Katie went to a payphone, rang the hospital and spoke to Dawn, who said she would come out and get her immediately. I asked Katie to say that we had gone our separate ways earlier and that she didn't know where I was.

I had no idea what I was going to do next. There was nowhere I could go and no one I could turn to. But I wasn't ready to face going back to the hospital; I'd rather try to live on the streets than in the nuthouse. Saying goodbye was the hardest thing in the world to do. The best friend I had ever made was leaving me and I didn't know if I would ever see her again. In the short while we had known one another Katie had become like a sister to me. We held each other tightly and promised to keep in touch.

'Take care of yourself,' I said.

'I will,' she said. 'Remember I love you.'

I watched from Trafalgar Square as Katie stepped into Dawn's car. I wondered, for a moment, if I'd done the right thing. Part of me wanted to run out and stop the car and go back with her.

Without Katie I felt lonely and desperate. I had absolutely no idea what to do and I wasn't rational enough to make a plan. I believed fate would decide whether I got help, lived rough or died, and I didn't much care which it would be.

I walked around for hours, with no idea where I was going. By four in the afternoon I was outside Victoria station. Exhausted, I sat down on the cold floor outside the station, leaning against the wall of the bookstore behind me. The entrance to the Underground was opposite me and I watched as droves of people swarmed in and out, like ants.

I pulled out the cream blanket with the large blue letters NHS embroidered on it and wrapped it tightly around me. My eyes felt heavy and sore and I fought to keep them open.

I was awoken with a start by a sharp pain in my foot. People were rushing past and someone must have stood on it. I looked at my watch. I had only been asleep for half an hour.

I became aware of someone watching me. I looked over the road and saw a man standing outside the Underground station, staring at me. As my eyes met his, he smiled.

He began to walk towards me. He was smartly dressed, with a black moustache and shoulder-length black hair.

'Hello,' he said. 'You want come with me to my house? I make you happy.'

His English was very broken, but I knew what he wanted. I had met men like this before. Without saying a word I got up and began to follow him into the Underground.

Most people would be horrified by the idea of going home with a strange man for sex. But I was in a state where, almost robot-like, I simply went along with whatever happened next. I had no self-regard and no sense of looking after myself. I wasn't afraid, because nothing he could do to me would be worse that what I'd already been though at home, and in any case I didn't care whether I lived or died.

I believed that if I was meant to live then I wouldn't be killed by a stranger.

He bought two tickets and led me on to a District Line train. He told me that his name was Dalip and that he had only recently come to this country from the Seychelles.

I told him nothing, apart from my first name.

He said he lived near, so at every stop I waited for him to make a move, but he remained seated. I was getting nervous. Where was he taking me? Finally, near the end of the line, at Barking, we got off.

A taxi took us to a quiet residential area, with large detached houses on either side of a tree-lined avenue. As we walked along it Dalip suddenly pushed me down behind a parked car.

I fell to my knees, with Dalip leaning hard on my shoulder. A few seconds later he released his grip on me and I got up. 'Sorry,' he said. 'My cousin. She must not see you.'

I followed him into a large house nearby and stood in the hallway, awaiting my instructions.

'Do you want a drink?' he asked.

'Yes please,' I replied.

'Vodka, whisky, gin? What do you want?'

'Anything.'

'OK,' he said. 'Come with me now.'

At the top of the stairs we went into a large, bright bedroom. Dalip moved to the window and drew the curtains tightly, then gestured towards the bed. 'You get in, I get drink, OK.'

I began to undress, almost robotically, as he left the room. It would soon be over and he seemed OK. I hoped he would let me have a shower afterwards.

Dalip returned carrying two glasses and a bottle of whisky. He sat down on the bed and handed me a glass, which I gulped down. I reached for the bottle to refill my glass.

'I no bad man,' Dalip was saying, 'you no need more drink.'

'I do,' I replied, 'believe me.'

I lay on the bed, motionless, while he had sex with me. I wasn't even thinking about what was going on. I had long ago learned to shut down my body and mind completely.

After Dalip had finished, he tried to talk to me, but I didn't want to know. He was looking at my arms and it made me feel nervous.

'What has happen to your arms, Sophie? Accident?'

I ignored him and began to get out of the bed. 'Can I wash please before I leave?' He nodded and got out of bed to show me the bathroom.

I washed and scrubbed at myself for ages and then pulled my clothes on again. When I came out of the bathroom, Dalip, dressed again, was waiting.

He reached into his pocket for his wallet and produced some bank notes. 'No, please,' I answered. 'Just the fare will be fine.'

He looked confused, but accepting money for sex was the one thing I had never done. I felt that to take money would make me a prostitute, which I wasn't.

Dalip was speaking again. 'I work in clothes industry. Meet me next week, I get you some clothes.'

'OK,' I replied.

Dalip seemed pleased. He phoned for a taxi and gave me ten pounds, to cover the taxi fare and tube back to Victoria, still insisting I meet him there the next week.

I was soon back in central London, where I caught a tube to King's Cross. It was ten thirty and I needed to find a place to spend the night.

King's Cross was a place I knew well. I had first run away from home when I was fourteen. Desperate because of the escalating abuse at home, I had taken off and found myself at King's Cross, where I slept rough for two nights. When I went home again Dad hadn't even called the police. He didn't want anyone asking questions, so he had simply waited for me to show up again.

After that I regularly ran away and slept rough for a couple of nights, usually ending up at King's Cross or St Martin in the Fields. Frightening, cold, dirty and dangerous as it was, it was my only way of escaping from what was happening to me and a slab of filthy concrete felt safer than my bed at home. During those nights on the streets I used to talk to runaway kids from Scotland and the north. And more often than not I was picked up by men wanting sex.

Most of them were businessmen who were often nervous and who treated me reasonably well. But there were others who wanted rough sex, which only reinforced my sense of worthlessness and led to even more self-harm.

Bad as I felt about myself, I still clung to certain values. I never took money for sex, which allowed me to feel that I wasn't a prostitute. In my desperate and lost state, I was looking for love.

That day, after returning from Dalip's house, I made my way to the walls at the far side of the station as I had so many times in the past. Although the station was still buzzing with activity, people were already settling down for the night. I saw a space available and made my way towards it. Then I slumped on to the ground, pulled the blanket from my bag and wrapped it around me tightly.

Not far from me prostitutes were touting for business. I watched as smart-looking businessmen picked them up, respectable-looking men, who could be your friendly bank manager or doctor between nine and five and who were no doubt on their way home to a wife, a semi and two point five children.

A few years ago I would have been shocked, but sadly nothing surprised me anymore. I knew only too well how many 'respectable' men were happy to have sex with prostitutes – and with young girls.

The last time I had eaten was when Katie and I had shared the biscuits the day before. I felt in the bottom of the bag to make sure that we hadn't dropped any. My hand rested on what felt like a bottle. I pulled it out – it was a bottle of whisky. Dalip must have slipped it into my bin bag. For a moment I felt quite touched by his kindness.

For a split second I hesitated. Did it make me a prostitute if I drank this? Was it a kind of payment? I hoped not. It would help me sleep.

Within moments a group of people had joined me, all hoping for a swig. I felt scared and gave it to an old woman, who hurried off with it, across the station concourse.

I was desperately tired, yet I didn't feel safe enough to go to sleep; there were too many strange people around. It was half past twelve, the last trains out of London had left and a few bedraggled-looking travellers stood staring at the railway information board, hoping for a miracle to happen. Eventually most left, but a few decided to spend the night at the station. Unlike the dossers the stray travellers sat on benches, bolt upright, with newspapers in their hands. Unfortunately this only made them targets for beggars, and as the night went on, most of the travellers gave up and left.

At one thirty I saw a policeman making his way around the edge of the station, speaking to each person. I gathered my belongings and slipped quickly out of the station.

Out on the Euston Road I looked around and spotted a café that was still open. I had enough money left for a drink, so I went in and bought a coffee and a pack of three biscuits. It was a busy place, with a mixture of nightclubbers, tramps and cab drivers. I sat at a small table near the window and wiped a small circle in the steamed-up window so I could look out. I finished my drink and sat in the café for as long as I could, but I was soon told by the owner to get out.

Back on the Euston Road a car slowed down and stopped next to me. The driver wound down his window. 'How much?'

'Sorry, I'm not for sale,' I replied.

I strode up the road as confidently as I could. I knew he was still watching me and I felt terrified.

'Don't play hard to get with me, you bitch.' He had parked his car half on the pavement and, having jumped out, was now behind me. I started to run, but he grabbed my arm and pulled me back.

'I know you're playing games,' he hissed, his foul breath engulfing my face. He began to pull roughly at my shirt. I managed to summon enough strength to kick him hard on his shins and as he yelped and let go of me I ran.

When I got into the station and was among people again I looked round. He was gone. I fell to the floor in a crumpled heap and began sobbing. People were waking and staring at me, so I made my way to a far comer of the station, sat down on the floor and cried uncontrollably. I just didn't know what to do anymore. I felt as though I was walking through a long dark corridor, with doors that led to brightly lit rooms on either side of me. I could see people entering these rooms, yet every time I got near one, the light went out and the door was shut on me. I felt that I couldn't go on much longer.

I sat on the floor, shaking violently, for what seemed like hours. I had dropped my bag when the man had grabbed me, so I now had no blanket to keep me warm. I knew there was no point going back to look for it, my belongings would be long gone by now.

I felt dirty and cold and absolutely desperate. I looked down at myself. The man had ripped the front of my shirt in the struggle. I hated my body so much, it had caused me so much trouble. The hate I felt towards myself was overwhelming. I had to hurt myself; that was the only way to relieve the awful, painful feelings.

Then I saw it, an empty sherry bottle lying next to me on the ground. I picked it up and smashed it against the wall. People stirred, but I didn't care who heard me.

I picked up a piece of glass and attacked myself viciously with it, ripping at my arm, reopening all my existing scars. The blood began to pour and a sense of relief began to wash over me. Still, it wasn't enough; I deserved more pain than this.

I tore into my arm again, until there was no flesh left without blood on it. I felt no pain any more. I pulled open my shirt and began to cut my stomach, fresh skin, that I hadn't touched before. I dragged the piece of glass across my skin, pushing down hard as I did so, making long parallel slashes.

I was crying uncontrollably again. The panic I felt was unbearable. I was so scared. Every terrible memory came back to me as I slashed at myself and sobbed. I just wanted to be dead.

7

Numbing the Pain

The first time I hurt myself deliberately was two years before that dreadful night in King's Cross.

I had been in the kitchen making dinner and my head felt as if it was going to explode with frustration and misery. Suddenly, almost without thinking, I stuck the blade of the tin-opener I was holding into my hand. As I watched the blood spurt out of the wound I felt an instant rush of relief. It was like taking a cork from a bottle; all the pressure that had been building up in my head dissolved and I felt strangely calm. I didn't even feel the pain of the wound. I just felt so much better.

Later on, the cut in my hand hurt a lot. I had bandaged it and it throbbed with pain. But I didn't care: the relief had been worth it.

I told Dad it had been an accident. But a few days later I lit one of his cigarettes and stubbed it out on my upper arm. As my skin began to singe and blister, I felt the same enormous relief. I lit the cigarette again and stubbed it out on my stomach.

I felt that at last I had found a way to cope. If hurting myself got me through, then the pain seemed a small price to pay.

Within a couple of weeks I had several blisters and cuts on my body. Dad saw them and I told him I'd hurt myself. I explained that it felt like a release, when things built up inside me.

Dad was fascinated. 'You like hurting yourself do you?' he asked. I was puzzled by the excitement in his voice. But then he offered to help me, and I understood. He joined in, putting a cigarette out on me and saying, 'Is that nice?'

That's why I blamed myself for so much of what happened next. By hurting myself I was giving him permission to hurt me too – or that's how it seemed.

He had always liked blood – it excited him. He loved it when I had my period and always wanted sex then. But now he realised he could make the blood come whenever he wanted.

The first time he penetrated me with a knife I thought I would die. The fierce, burning pain was so bad that I prayed I would pass out. But I didn't, and as blood poured out of me Dad had sex with me, doubling the pain and the damage being done to me.

He didn't use the knife every time. But that made it almost worse, wondering every night whether he would or not.

He seemed to want more and more sex. I would go to his bed with him, and then slip back into my own. But later in the night he would come through to my room and want sex all over again. And more often than not he wanted violent, bloody sex, which meant using knives and even bottles on me. There were many nights when I thought he would kill me. I just wished that it would happen soon.

After he had left my room and gone back to his own bed I would get up and scrub myself in the bath. I never felt clean any more, no matter how much I washed.

By this time I had begun self-harming more and more. I had discovered razor blades and after Dad finished having sex with me I would sit in the bath, sobbing and cutting deep parallel train tracks across my arms with a blade. Then I'd start again, cutting downwards across the lines I'd already made, so that my arms had a criss-cross pattern of raw, bloody wounds. When I felt I'd punished myself enough I would bandage my arms, then go and change my bloody sheets and get back into bed. But I barely ever slept, and mostly I got up again and paced around the house for the rest of the night.

The wounds I made on myself hurt, of course they did. But the relief I felt when the blood ran out was more important than the pain. And I'd pass a threshold where I didn't feel the pain any more. It was only later, after they were bandaged, that my arms were dreadfully painful. But even that pain wasn't enough to stop me doing it again. Often I'd just re-open the wounds that were beginning to heal. I felt the more I hurt myself the better it would be.

Sometimes the bleeding from my arms when I'd cut myself, or from my vagina when Dad had cut me, wouldn't stop and I had to go to hospital. Dad would take me, and say that I'd come home in that state, blaming a non-existent boyfriend, or claiming that he couldn't stop me from self harming.

We had three hospitals with accident and emergency departments within reach of us, and Dad would not take me to the same one twice in a row. I went to each one at least three times, but they were huge, busy departments, the staff were different each time and there was never a reference to previous records. Dad was always supremely confident and very plausible. He came across as a professional man, deeply concerned about his daughter, and none of the hospital staff ever appeared to doubt him.

When he got me home again he'd warn me that I had to cope better, and that I mustn't let him down. 'I'm all you've got,' he would say. 'We need each other. You don't want to lose me, do you?'

Numb with misery I would shake my head and he would cuddle me and even put me to bed and make me a hot water bottle.

I didn't understand then, or for a long time, that I was turning the anger I should have felt at my father in on myself. I wasn't able to feel any anger towards him, only towards myself for not being good enough and not coping well enough. Despite what he did to me I loved him and was desperate to please him. I just wanted to make him love me, and to stop him leaving me. I was so petrified of losing him that I felt my life would end if he rejected me.

I thought that Dad had done his worst when he began using knives and bottles on me. But there was more to come. One night he appeared in my room with a second man. The man watched and masturbated as Dad had sex with me. Then Dad watched and masturbated while the man had sex with me. Dad was the one in control, deciding what the other man could and couldn't do, and I could see what a kick he was getting out of it.

After that Dad often brought other men to have sex with me. There were seven of them who came in all. Dad would bring them one or two at a time, though sometimes, especially at the weekends, three or four came at once. He would let them hurt me too, using the knives and bottles on me. He enjoyed watching.

All this had happened in just a few months since my mother had left. I was still only fourteen. But by this time I was a wreck. My schoolwork was non-existent, I was often drunk and I self-harmed almost every day. The school was aware that I was a 'problem' but not why. They thought it was all due to Mum leaving and I was given regular pep-talks about pulling myself together and dealing with my parents' divorce more positively. Most of my friends had given up on me. I was no fun anymore. While they talked about parties and make-up and boyfriends, I just muttered that I had to get home and make my dad's tea.

My best friend was Karen, a really nice girl I had known for a few years. In the past we'd had a lot of fun together, fooling around in class and sharing the same sense of humour. But she couldn't understand what was happening to me, and I couldn't tell her.

I had been round to Karen's house lots of times, and knew her father, Dave. He was a carpenter and seemed to be a nice man. He knew Dad to say hello to, but not well, or so I thought.

One night Dad appeared at my door with another man. I was shocked to see that it was Dave. Like the others, he had sex with me while Dad watched, and then he watched Dad have sex with me. After that he became a regular member of Dad's gang. And I could never look Karen in the eye again. I became very distant with her. It wasn't her fault, she didn't know what her dad was doing, but I couldn't help thinking that because he was abusing me, he wasn't abusing her. I was protecting her, but she didn't know it.

I had always been plump as a result of all the sweets Dad

fed me. But now he decided that I should learn to budget. We always shopped together on a Friday evening, and Dad enjoyed throwing all kinds of things into the trolley. He had plenty of money and he liked to eat well. But suddenly he announced that he would be giving me my own money to buy my food and that he would buy his. He bought all the food he liked, but the money he gave me wasn't enough for my food for the week. When he suddenly told me to plan all my meals for a week, I didn't know what to buy. Dad would leave the supermarket with a loaded trolley, while I had a miserable little pile of food. I would be having an egg on toast for dinner, while Dad had steak with all the trimmings, which I still had to cook for him.

He became obsessive about marking all his food and mine with different coloured stickers and putting it in separate cupboards and parts of the fridge. I wasn't allowed to have anything of his without asking, and when I did ask he'd say, 'I'll think about it.' Then if I was 'good' when he had sex with me that night, he would give me something out of his food cupboard as a reward.

As the weeks went on he gave me less and less money for food, telling me, 'You've been spoilt, you've got to understand the world and learn to manage.' I would run out of food by the time the week was halfway through and have to beg him for some. And he would play games with me, making me wait to see if he'd give me anything. He might suddenly decide to offer me a McDonalds, or fish and chips, and even if I'd just eaten I'd say yes and eat it all, because I never knew when I would get the next meal. As a result I became obsessed with food.

I lived my life in fear. Fear of not eating, fear of being in trouble at school, fear of Dad and his friends coming in the night. Because I never knew when they were coming I lay awake every night, waiting, listening, dread in the pit of my stomach at every sound.

I couldn't have imagined anything more awful happening until at fourteen and a half, four months after Mum left, I got pregnant. In a state of terror I told Dad, who was delighted. He thought it proved that he could have children, and he wanted me to go ahead and have the baby. 'We can do this,' he kept saying. 'Be strong, pull yourself together and have this baby.'

But I felt completely desperate; I couldn't possibly have coped with having a baby.

A few days later I got drunk and swallowed a load of paracetamol before staggering into school. The teachers took one look at me and got me to hospital, where I had my stomach pumped.

Dad was called at work and arrived at the hospital to collect me. When he got me home he was furious with me for drawing attention to myself. He realised then that I wasn't going to manage having a baby, and he took me to an abortion clinic. Before we went he made me practise the story he had made up about me being pregnant by a boyfriend I had met over my CB radio.

When he got me home he told me I had failed him. I wept and begged for forgiveness. 'I'm sorry I failed you,' I sobbed, 'I'll be stronger next time.'

A couple of weeks later I ran away for the first time. Not because I wanted to get away from Dad, but because I felt such a failure. I was afraid that if I didn't get myself together I would lose Dad, so I took off in order to try to get a grip on myself. I slept rough for a couple of nights before going home. When I got back Dad didn't ask if I was OK, only whether I'd told anyone anything. I promised I hadn't.

After that I ran away regularly. That's when I discovered St Martin in the Fields, learned where to get cardboard to sleep under, and got picked up by men. I always went with them; I was programmed to comply with men who demanded sex, I felt that was all I was good for. I knew that one of them might turn out to be a psychopath and kill me, but I felt my life was worthless, so it wouldn't matter.

Dad always waited for me to come home, then got angry and told me I had to be stronger. And I always vowed that I would. But I didn't know how to be stronger. I had no one and nothing – except him. He was all that was good and all that was bad in my world, rolled into one. He would cuddle me, comfort me, buy me treats, then deprive me, threaten me, abuse me and injure me.

My self-harming had escalated to the point where I cut my stomach and the tops of my legs as well as my arms and the wounds often became swollen and infected. Despite this no one knew about what I did except Dad and the doctors who treated me.

Today doctors might investigate further, or at least report the case to Social Services. But twenty-five years ago it seems that no one in authority would act unless I told them what was happening to me, which I felt unable to do.

I was utterly without hope and was certain that, one way or the other, I would be dead soon. Either Dad and his friends would kill me with their brutal and violent attacks or I would kill myself, with razor blades, alcohol, bleach and painkillers.

It was just a matter of time.

8

Samaritans, Can I Help You?

After cutting myself with the broken glass I fell into an exhausted, fitful sleep on the station floor.

Early in the morning the toilets were opened and I got painfully to my feet and made my way over to them. When I saw my refection in the mirror I started to cry. My face was dirty and tear-stained and my shirt was ripped and covered in blood. I looked as if I'd been on the streets for three months, not three days.

I washed myself as best as I could. My arms and stomach were hurting badly. I tried to clean the wounds, but any pressure I applied just started the bleeding again. I wrapped some toilet paper around my arms to try to soak up the blood. I needed stitches, but there was no way I could go to a hospital – they'd have me back to the nuthouse the minute I went through the door and I wasn't ready for that.

I fastened my jacket tightly to cover the blood. My arms were feeling tight and stiff. I looked back in the mirror. I looked little better than before, but I was past caring.

There was only one thing I could think of doing. I went out of the station and found a phone box nearby.

'Samaritans. Can I help you?'

Silence.

'Hello, Samaritans. Can I help you?'

'I don't know.' I was crying.

'What's happened, love? You sound very upset.'

More sobs.

'Why not start with your name. I'm Pam. What can I call you?'

'Sophie.'

Pam's voice was kind and patient.

'Where are you, Sophie?' she asked.

'In a phone box at King's Cross.'

'You sound very young. How old are you?'

'Sixteen.'

Pam continued to ask me, gently, about myself. She rang me back when my money ran out, and coaxed me to speak to her about how I felt. I didn't say much – there were lots of silences, but I knew she was there and just having her on the end of the line was comforting.

After half an hour I became conscious about the length of time we'd been speaking.

'I'd better go now,' I told her.

'You don't have to go, Sophie,' she replied. 'I'll speak to you for as long as you want me to be here.'

'Thanks, but I'd better go.'

'Why don't you try to come in to see us? At least you'd be safe and warm here.'

I looked down at myself. I was filthy and covered in dried blood. I couldn't possibly see anyone in this state.

'It's OK, I'll be OK tomorrow, sorry to have bothered you, thank you,' I stuttered.

'You haven't bothered me at all. I'd like to help.'

Pam was so warm and kind. But I was afraid that if I went to see her she might send me back to the nuthouse.

She was still speaking, giving me directions to their centre in Kensington.

'I can meet you later this evening,' she said. 'At about seven. Will you come?'

'Well, OK, if you're sure you don't mind.'

I hadn't meant to agree. And I still wasn't sure I would go.

I put down the phone and walked along the Euston Road, past St Pancras and Euston stations to Regent's Park, where I decided to get some sleep. I was too tired to worry about who was around; I lay on the first empty bench I came to.

My arms felt sore and painful and my stomach bled every time I moved, so I stayed on the bench all day, utterly exhausted and dozing on and off. Late in the afternoon I got stiffly and painfully to my feet and set off to find the address Pam had given me. In my exhausted state I was slow, and I hadn't a clue how to get there so I had to keep asking for directions. By seven thirty I was still several streets away. I was sure Pam would have left.

At ten to eight I arrived outside a large white door. Heart pounding, I rang the bell. Pam will have gone, I thought, and was about to run away, when a man opened the door.

'I've come to see Pam – I expect she's gone. I'm late.' I turned to go.

'No, she's still here waiting for you,' he replied. 'You must be Sophie. Come in.'

He closed the door behind me. 'I'll just get Pam for you,' he said, disappearing through a door off the hallway.

A moment later it opened and a woman in her early thirties

appeared, smiling warmly. She came over to me, put her arms around my shoulders and pulled me towards her.

I flinched and pulled away.

'Oh, my love, what's the matter?' she asked

The blood was beginning to trickle down my arm. I could feel it running over my wrist and on to my hand.

Pam looked down.

'Oh, my God, let me get a bandage.' She ushered me into a small room containing a couple of old armchairs and a white formica table, and made me sit down.

Pam helped me while I cleaned and bandaged my arms and for the next hour we talked. I told her about running away from the hospital and the past few nightmare days on the streets. And I told her how much I hated myself and that I sometimes wished that I could be dead. She held my hand as I spoke. I felt reassured and the words just tumbled out.

'Where are you going tonight?' Pam asked.

'Don't know,' I replied, 'but not back to that nuthouse, if that's what you're thinking.'

'Wait here a moment,' Pam replied. 'I'll see what I can do.'

As I waited for her I leaned back in my armchair and felt my eyes closing. The room felt warm and safe.

Ten minutes later Pam came back, startling me. 'I've got permission for you to stay here tonight,' she said. 'You'll be much safer here than on the streets and tomorrow we'll talk about what you'd like to do.'

I tried to protest that I was fine and should go, but I was too tired and sore to put up much of a fight. Pam sorted out a mattress and a quilt for me.

'Would you do something for me?' I asked. 'I've called the Samaritans before. I rang my local branch and they helped me when I was at home, before I went into hospital. I had a befriender – that's what you call them, isn't it? Her name was Fran. Would you call her for me, and tell her where I am?'

'Of course I will,' Pam said. 'I'll try to reach her in the morning.'

She knelt on the floor next to me to say goodnight. 'I have to go home now, but someone will sit in here all night with you in case you want to talk,' she said.

She tucked the quilt around me and I felt safer than I had for as long as I could remember. I started to cry as she leaned over and kissed my cheek.

'Sleep well, I'll see you in the morning,' she whispered.

Moments later I fell into a deep sleep.

9

Family Therapy

The first time I had called the Samaritans I was fourteen and absolutely desperate.

It was a few months after my mother left and the abuse I was suffering at the hands of my father and his 'friends' had left me a complete wreck. I was self-harming every day, and missing school or arriving drunk. I was without hope and I wanted to die.

I had seen the Samaritans' number on the wall in a phone box. I had a vague idea that they helped people, but didn't know much more than that. One night I had let myself out of the house after Dad had finished doing what he wanted with me and gone to bed. I was distraught, unable to sleep as always, and my head throbbed with the pressure and pain of not being able to tell anyone what was happening.

I stood in the phone box, looking at the number, and eventually I plucked up the courage to call. The very calm, warm-voiced woman who answered waited while I sobbed into the phone for several minutes.

That first time I said very little, but she encouraged me to call again, and a few nights later I did. It took me weeks to begin to trust her enough to open up and talk, but in time I began to tell her my story. Her name was Fran, and once we were speaking regularly, she told me when she would next be at the local branch, so that I could talk to her if I needed to. Fran became my befriender – the Samaritans' term that was used in the eighties for someone assigned to be there for a person in need. She invited me to come to the branch to talk to her in person, and I did. It was no more than a sitting room with a couple of old sofas in it, but it was a safe place to talk and it became a sanctuary for me.

The Samaritans became my lifeline. I have no doubt that I am alive today because of the support they gave me. Fran would regularly call me at home when she was at work in the local branch – at pre-arranged times when Dad wasn't around – and I would call her and go to the branch to talk to her. All the Samaritans there knew my story, and it was arranged that if I needed to talk and Fran wasn't around, another female Samaritan would talk to me. I couldn't cope with talking to a man, so if a male Samaritan answered I would just say, 'Can I talk to a lady, please.' Dad knew about my calls to the Samaritans, he saw them listed on the phone bill. He didn't mind; if it kept me from talking to anyone else about what was going on, then it suited him just fine. So he said nothing, and I spent many long hours in the middle of the night talking to Fran or one of the other women who did shifts there.

The Samaritans promised me total confidentiality and that allowed me to trust them. Disturbing as they no doubt found my story, they never showed it. They were always there for me and promised me that they wouldn't alert the authorities or tell anyone else without my permission. I knew that I could trust Fran and any other volunteer I spoke to and while they gently encouraged me to get help I never felt out of control with them. During my worst times I spoke to them two or three times a day and the support they gave me during my darkest moments undoubtedly stopped me from killing myself.

As the months went on and my drinking and self-harming got worse, it was my school who called in the authorities. One day, Miss Thomas noticed a huge bruise on my arm. 'What's going on, Sophie?' she asked me. I told her I'd caught my arm in the door. 'It looks like someone's hit you,' she said. She was right: the previous night one of Dad's 'friends' had hit me with a garden cane. Dad had been furious because he'd done it without Dad's permission. That wasn't allowed.

Strangely enough, throughout all this I was still going to the tennis club once a week. I was good, and had been moved into a higher category, which meant a different club night from Dad. He was proud of my achievements and would drive me there and then collect me three hours later.

I don't know why I kept going, perhaps just out of habit. As my self-harm escalated I started to wear tracksuits with long sleeves to cover my injuries, even in the summer. Often I barely played at all, just sat at the side of the court, watching.

One of the players, Hazel, became friends with me. She had children my age and must have noticed that something was wrong. It probably wasn't hard to pick up on the signs. Hazel used to talk to me, to try to find out what was wrong. Sometimes she took me to her house, bringing me back in time for Dad to collect me. I cried a lot and she was upset – she said she couldn't bear to see me like that and begged me to let her do something. I said no, and never told her anything, but I'm sure she pieced it together for herself. She was kind, and became one of the people I dreamed might be my mother.

Things came to a head one day when my friends came to call for me. I hadn't been at school for a while and most of them had given up on me but some of them wanted to know how I was. When I opened the door I more or less collapsed on the path as I was full of drink and paracetamol. One of my friends ran to the school and got Miss Thomas, who came and got me in her car and took me to school where I was taken straight to the headmaster. He launched into me, telling me I was stupid and I would now have to have my stomach pumped.

An ambulance was called and I went to hospital, where I did have to endure a stomach pump. When I went back to school a my few days later the head called a meeting with me, my mum, my dad and Miss Thomas and I was made to apologise for the upset I had caused my family.

Not long afterwards I was called into the head's study and introduced to an education welfare officer. She was a pleasant woman who asked me lots of questions about what was going on. Had I been able to grasp it, this move by the school to alert some outside authority might have offered me a way out. But that wasn't how I saw it at all. I didn't want to be rescued because it never occurred to me that this was a possibility. My whole focus was on staying with Dad.

I believed that the appalling things Dad did to me were the price I had to pay for him loving me. And he had convinced me that he was the only person in the world who did love or care for me. If I didn't have him then I believed I had nothing. So powerfully had he brainwashed me that his hold over me was absolute. Nothing he did would make me betray him.

I had to put anyone who asked me questions off the scent. So I told the education welfare officer the usual story about being upset because my mum had left and hoped she would leave it at that. Much to my distress, she didn't. Instead, she decided some sessions of family therapy might help. She called both my parents and asked them to attend.

In the first meeting Mum broke down and cried for the entire hour. She sobbed about what hell it was not seeing me and how she couldn't cope. I felt angry with her for being so weak. I didn't say anything, but I thought how dare she sit there and cry when she walked out. My anger at that time was all for her, and I was angry with her, not for leaving me to be abused, but for hurting Dad. By this time I had no contact with her, other than these sessions, and I wished I didn't have to see her at all.

That first meeting set the pattern. Each week it was Mum who was the centre of attention as she cried and wrung her hands over how hard she'd tried and how difficult it was being alone and so on. I was furious with her for it, but I sat silent, unable to say anything. And of course it suited Dad fine. While Mum indulged in an orgy of self-pity, no one was asking him, or me, anything and we presented a united front.

After a few sessions the education welfare officer could see that the family therapy wasn't working, so she decided I should have some sessions with a social worker on my own. The woman who was assigned to my case, Jane Gray, was in her mid-fifties, bright and friendly. I liked her, but I wasn't about to tell her anything. We had weekly sessions in which I said almost nothing, apart from how fed-up with my mother I was. If Jane asked me anything about my father, I clammed up.

It was while I was seeing Jane that I became pregnant for

the second time, at fifteen. Once again Dad insisted we tell the story of the 'boyfriend' called Simon who I had met over the CB radio. Dad urged me to have the baby. Our baby. But I couldn't face it and, at ten weeks' pregnant, I drank a whole cup of bleach, followed by a couple of lagers. I wanted to die; I simply couldn't face anything more. I passed out, but Dad found me and got me to hospital, where I was told by the staff that I'd been a 'silly girl'.

Dad was all concern at the hospital, but when I got home a few days later he stormed at me that I'd failed him and needed to learn to cope. 'What's wrong with you?' he raged. 'You could have had that baby.'

Scared that I had failed him again, I cut myself over and over again, hating myself, and sobbing that I was sorry.

When I saw Jane again, a week or two later, she asked me who this boyfriend was. She wanted details about him, and of course that was where my story collapsed, I couldn't provide them.

Eventually she said, 'Sophie, I know what's going on, but you need to tell us. I know your father is abusing you, but I can't help you unless you admit it.'

I was shocked that she knew what was going on, and when I heard the word 'abuse' I felt panic. If she had worked it out then I was afraid that I had failed Dad. He had primed me well. 'These people aren't your friends,' he would say of her and the other social workers. 'Be careful what you say, Sophie. They will take you away from me, split us up, and you'll never see me again. Is that what you want?'

If only it had been what I wanted then things would have been simple. But it wasn't. Being taken away from Dad and never seeing him again, was my greatest fear. I was so terrified of it that, although I longed to tell Jane the truth, I didn't dare. She was kind and supportive, and by this time I was seeing her three times a week and she was phoning me on the days when I didn't see her. But I still couldn't admit to her the full truth.

So I arrived drunk and went into the toilets at the Social Services offices and cut myself before our sessions, but I didn't talk. I could see how frustrated Jane was. Then one day she said to me, 'Sophie, all you have to do is say the word "yes". If you can get that one word out, then it will be enough. Is your father abusing you?'

It was agony to get it out, but eventually, my eyes on the floor, I whispered the word 'yes' in a barely audible voice. 'Well done, Sophie,' Jane said. 'You've done the right thing. Now we can stop what is happening to you.'

I was so afraid. What had I done? What would happen to me? And to Dad? Although it had been a relief to admit what was happening, I was terrified of the consequences.

Within days the wheels had been set in motion. Jane rang me to say the police had been informed and wanted to interview me. 'I'll be with you,' she told me. 'Don't worry, I'll be with you all the way.'

My parents were both informed. Mum was, predictably, tearful and upset. She sobbed over the phone to me – what had she done, she was so sorry, she wished she could turn the clock back. But I didn't care what she felt. It was Dad's reaction that worried me. He was livid. He knew I had said something and he laid into me. 'You've destroyed everything we have together,' he ranted. 'You've lost both your parents now. Is that what you want?

He shouted at me for several days. I was distraught. I sobbed that I was sorry, that I would undo all the damage and say it wasn't true. 'You'd better,' he snarled at me. 'If it isn't already too late.'

All three of us were interviewed by the police on the same day. At the last minute Jane rang me. 'Sophie, I'm so sorry, my boss won't let me go with you, they say you've got to go alone so that no one can put words into your mouth. I feel terrible about it. But you can do it. Be strong, Sophie, and tell them the truth.'

I felt betrayed. She had promised to be there with me and now she was telling me I had to go alone. Numb with terror I got the bus to the police station. I was a complete mess, so petrified I would bump into Dad there that I couldn't think about anything else.

At the station I was led up several flights of stairs, into a room where a man in civilian clothes sat behind a desk. In the corner of the room sat a uniformed woman police officer.

'Now, come on,' the man said. 'What have you been saying about your father? I've interviewed him today and he seems a decent chap. These allegations you are making could ruin him. Think hard, because you can stop this whole thing now.'

Dad had, no doubt, given his usual polished performance; the concerned father, doing his best for his wayward daughter. He could be so convincing that it was impossible to doubt him.

And under the pressure of the hostile interrogation, alone and terrified, I crumbled. If Jane had been there with me I might have been able to manage telling the truth. As it was I said I had to go, ran out and down the stairs and took off up the street.

The woman officer followed me. 'Stop, Sophie, please come

back, we have to question you that way, it's the rules, but we do believe you.'

Nothing on earth would have made me go back. I got on a bus and, afraid to go home in case my parents were there, went to my nan's. She had coped with the whole thing by pretending it wasn't happening, she was too old and it was all too much for her. I hoped I might find a little safety and comfort with her. But when I got there she looked shocked to see me.

'You can't come in,' she whispered as I stood on the doorstep, 'your mum and dad are here.'

My heart sank. I turned around and went home to wait for Dad. When he arrived I told him I'd said nothing. He looked pleased. 'Good girl, you've done the right thing,' he said. 'We can get through this together.'

I knew what that meant. Dad knew he had won and he was very pleased with himself. He could do what he wanted with me and no one could stop him.

As for my mother, I have no idea whether she believed me or not. She was with Dad after the police interrogation, not me, which might indicate that she believed him. Or perhaps she just buried her head in the sand because the idea that it might be true was too much for her, then she would have to face up to her own part in it.

Whatever she thought, Mum never told me. She went home after leaving Nan's and I never even saw her. Nor did I see her for many months afterwards.

Jane was devastated. She felt she had let me down, and I felt she had too, even though it was her boss who had ordered her not to come with me. She was a lovely woman and I could see how genuinely sorry she was. But I had put all my trust in her and taken a huge risk and it had backfired on me so badly that I vowed I would never trust anyone again.

She was desperately worried about me in the weeks afterwards. She knew how at risk I was from Dad and she wanted to find a way to get me out of his clutches. So she began to explore the possibility of having me committed to hospital for my own safety, and she contacted my mother for her support. Of course I didn't know about it until I was told that I was going to a psychiatric unit for a while.

That was how, soon after my sixteenth birthday, I came to be in the psychiatric hospital. Or the nuthouse, as I preferred to call it.

Throughout all of this the Samaritans remained constant, giving me their support and a place to go where I could feel truly safe. And even after I went into the hospital Fran continued to ring me, to see how I was doing. That was why, when I was on the streets in London, it was the Samaritans I called. I wanted Fran. She would help me work out what to do next.

10

Homecoming

I opened my eyes to find a woman squatting beside me holding a cup of tea. She explained that Pam was on her way in to see me. When Pam arrived half an hour later she told me she had spoken to Fran, who wanted to talk to me. Pam sat on the floor beside me and held my hand as I dialled the number of my local Samaritans.

Fran picked up the phone. 'Hello, Sophie. What's happened?' I started to cry. It was so reassuring to hear a familiar voice.

'Oh Fran, I'm sorry, I don't know what I've done,' I stammered.

'Don't worry. At least you're safe now. Will you let me come and get you, Sophie?'

'You'll take me back to that madhouse won't you?'

'Yes,' she replied, 'I will take you back to the hospital, if you'll let me. You can't survive on the streets. You'll end up dead, you know that.'

If anyone else had said that to me, I'd have rejected it immediately. But Fran and I had the sort of understanding that meant that she could tell me the bottom line. I didn't always like to hear it, but I knew that what she said would be the truth.

'I'm sorry, Fran. I've let you down badly,' I admitted.

'You've let yourself down, Sophie. Look how far you've come since I first got to know you. Please don't throw it all away. Don't give up now.'

I was silent, too upset to reply. I knew that what Fran was saying was right, but the thought of going back to the hospital scared me. Every option scared me, except one.

'Fran, I'd be fine if I could live with . . .'

'Oh Sophie,' Fran broke in, 'you know I can't take you home with me, as much as I'd like to.'

She sounded upset. I hadn't wanted to upset her, but I couldn't help wishing that I could go and live with her. She was the one person I trusted and who made me feel safe.

She arranged to meet me outside Peter Jones Department store on Sloane Square in an hour's time. As soon as I put the phone down I regretted agreeing to it, but I wasn't going to let Fran down.

I thanked Pam for her help; without her God knows what might have happened. She hugged me goodbye and even though it hurt my stomach and arms when she held me, I was grateful for her warmth.

I walked to Sloane Square and I sat on the ground outside the department-store window. As I was sitting there waiting I noticed a tatty biro lying nearby. I picked it up and rolled it between my fingers. Then I saw a newspaper poking out of a litter bin. I grabbed the paper and used the pen to write a poem about Fran and her kindness towards me, scribbling on the margins of the newspaper. I hadn't meant to involve her in all this, but once again she was coming to help me.

While I was still writing Fran appeared. She knelt down

on the pavement and put her arm around me. 'What are you up to?'

'I was thinking of you, actually,' I replied. 'Here you are, this is for you.' I handed her the crumpled newspaper with my words scrawled round the outside.

'Thank you,' she said, 'I'll read it later.'

Fran explained that she had brought a colleague with her to drive the car. She introduced me to Joan and they took me to the car, which was parked nearby.

Fran sat in the back with me and held my hand throughout the journey. She kept reassuring me that I was doing the right thing. But my stomach was churning with nerves and I wondered what sort of reception I was going to get back on the ward.

'Do you want me to come in with you and face the doctor, Sophie?' Fran asked.

I did, of course. But I knew that it was something that I would have to do on my own. When I had told Dr Harvey of my involvement with the Samaritans he had been less than enthusiastic. As far as he was concerned, my focus should be totally on the medical staff at the hospital, and I should not be involved with what he called 'a group of little old ladies who probably have nothing better to do'. He was so wrong about that, I wished he could meet Fran and find out just how much the Samaritans had done for me. But now wasn't the time. I was sure he wouldn't be happy with me for running away and I was just going to have to face him.

I explained all this to Fran, who said, 'That's fine, but remember we're here if you need us.'

We'd reached the hospital by this time and I looked up at its imposing walls. This was it – there was no turning back.

I thanked Joan for bringing me back and Fran held me close as we said goodbye. I felt choked and wanted to get away before she saw that I was upset.

'I'll phone you later to see that you're OK,' she called, watching to make sure I went in and didn't bolt again. The thought had crossed my mind. Outside the unit, on the second floor, I rang the bell. Dawn opened the door.

'Sophie! Oh, thank God you're back, I've been so worried.' She threw her arms around me and gave me a big hug.

Much to my surprise, I received a similar reaction from patients and staff alike. In a strange and unexpected way it felt like a homecoming. I felt a little overwhelmed and very touched.

Something was different, though. All the familiar faces were there; except Katie's.

A few minutes later Amy appeared. 'Hi Sophie,' she said, 'Dr Harvey would like to see you straight away.'

I followed her along the corridor. 'Where's Katie?' I asked her.

'She's gone, Sophie. I'll explain later,' she said, opening the door to Dr Harvey's office and indicating that I should go in.

I was terrified of his reaction but he was far more sympathetic than I had imagined he would be. He asked me what I had been doing and then asked me why I had felt the need to run away.

'It was the thought of family therapy,' I explained.

I told him about the family sessions Social Services had organised in the months before I was sent to the hospital. They always started with a slanging match between my parents and ended up with lots of shouting and, in my mother's case, tears. Most of the shouting was directed towards me and I felt that they all thought everything was my fault. It was during one of these family sessions that my mother told me, as she had in the past, that she wished she had never adopted me and that she could take me back.

'I'm sorry,' Dr Harvey said. 'I didn't know about these earlier sessions. There is no need for us to go ahead with further family therapy if you don't feel it will be helpful.'

He smiled, and that gave me the courage to ask the question that most worried me. 'Where's Katie, Doctor?'

'She is back in north Wales.'

Dr Harvey must have seen the shock on my face. He went on, 'When patients do what you two did, it doesn't just affect you, it affects all the patients here. Some of them became very distressed and others were angry that you were throwing away your chance to be helped. Some people have waited a year for a place in this hospital; some have seen their friends die while waiting to be admitted. Then they see you two youngsters coming in as emergency cases, jumping to the front of the queue, and then appearing to throw it all away.'

I looked down at the floor. I had never realised that others might feel angry, or that anyone might be waiting to come into a place like this. I felt ashamed.

Dr Harvey continued. 'I spoke to Katie on her return and she decided that she needed some space to decide whether she wants to be here or not, so she has gone back to north Wales for a week.

'I'd like you to also think, Sophie. I want you to decide whether you want this help or not. If you would also like some time, I will save your bed for you for one week.'

I was silent. I could see he was right; I had to come back

out of choice if I was ever to get better. I couldn't be there because my mother or Jane or even Fran wanted me to. It had to come from me.

So I agreed to go away and think it over for a week. If I didn't come back after that time that was it: my bed would go.

I told Dr Harvey that I would arrange to stay with a friend in west London and much to my surprise he agreed and allowed me to leave the hospital with an allowance for my train ticket and a few belongings in a bag.

As soon as I got back on to the street I felt scared and vulnerable. I had no friend in west London, but I knew Dr Harvey wouldn't have agreed to let me go home. And that was what I wanted. Despite all that had happened in the past, I missed Dad.

It was late afternoon. If I hurried, I would get home before Dad got back from work. I wanted to surprise him. I still had a key, so I could let myself in and prepare a meal for him.

As I sat on the bus I thought about Fran and what her reaction to all this would be. I knew she would be concerned and worried if she ever found out. I had never lied to her before, but this was only for a week and hopefully she would never know.

The street where I lived was a wide tree-lined avenue in a quiet residential area in south London. I got off the bus and hurried up the road towards my house. I could see that the driveway was empty, so I knew Dad wasn't home from work yet.

I hadn't seen or heard from Dad in the two weeks I had been away, as no visits or letters from family and friends were allowed during that initial period in the unit.

My admission to the hospital hadn't appeared to worry Dad – either for himself or for me. He'd seen it simply as an unnecessary hurdle we had to get through before we carried on our life together. I don't think he was afraid of being caught – after the police investigation was dropped he seemed to feel completely untouchable.

As I pushed the door open, my border collie Molly came bounding towards me. I threw myself down on the floor next to her as she jumped on top of me and raced around me excitedly.

I looked around. The house felt familiar and strangely reassuring. I went up to my room and lay down on the bed. I was tired. I had so many memories of this room. Some were good: Christmas mornings opening my presents, and nights when my friends came to stay.

Then there was the other side of my life, the confusing and frightening side. The many times when I had cried myself to sleep, others when I thought I wouldn't survive the night. I didn't want to think about that any more. I got up and went downstairs.

I knew it would please Dad if I did some housework. He liked me looking after him. I put some washing into the machine and began to prepare a meal. I was busily working my way through a pile of ironing when I heard the key turn in the front door.

'Sophie,' he exclaimed. 'My God, what are you doing here?' He hesitated a moment then put his arms around me and held me tightly.

I started to cry. 'Don't you want me here, Dad?'

'Of course I want you here. But who knows you're here? No one must know.'

'No one knows, I'm not that silly!' I said.

Dad laughed. 'That's good. Good girl.'

I told him what had happened over the last few days. Dad nodded and seemed concerned. When I explained about Dalip he became annoyed. 'Bastard,' he said. 'What did he do to you?'

'Nothing, he was very kind.'

I felt reassured. If Dad was concerned about me being with Dalip then maybe he had really changed. This was how a father should react, wasn't it?

I felt a wave of happiness sweep over me. Dad had changed and that meant I could stay with him. Maybe everything really would work out.

11

In Harm's Way

'Sophie, what the hell are you doing there?' It was Fran and she sounded alarmed.

'Fran. How did you know I'd be here?'

'I rang the hospital last night to see how you were and they said you were staying with a friend.'

'How do you know I'm not? I could just be visiting here.'

'It's me you're speaking to now, Sophie, not someone in the hospital. I know you too well. I knew you'd be back there. I didn't ring last night because I knew that *he'd* be there.'

'I take it *he* is my father?' I replied. I didn't like the way she referred to him and I wanted her to know that I was annoyed. I wished I had never answered the phone.

'I'm sorry, Sophie, I know he means a lot to you, I just find it difficult to refer to him in any other way. Anyway, how are you?

'I'm fine. Last night went really well. We had a meal together and we talked a lot and he seems different now.'

'In what way different? Did he say he was sorry for all he's done?'

'Well, no, not exactly, but I could tell he was.'

I heard Fran sigh and felt annoyed. Why wouldn't she give Dad another chance? I was beginning to wish I'd never told her anything. Then I thought of something that would make her change her mind.

'You'll never guess what, Fran. I told my dad about me and that man Dalip, and he got really angry and protective. That's a good sign isn't it?'

Fran sighed again. 'Sophie, when will you understand what he's doing?'

'What's that supposed to mean?' I replied defensively.

'Tell me to shut up if you want, and I'm probably speaking way out of line again, but I'll say it anyway, just in case it finally sinks in. The only reason your dad was annoyed was because he wasn't part of it himself. He can't bear the thought of you having sex with anyone without him being there, organising it, like some sort of business.'

Tears began streaming down my face. I didn't want to hear.

'Stop,' I shouted. 'Just stop Fran, please.'

'Oh Sophie, love, I'm sorry. I didn't want to upset you. I just want to make you see what he's really doing. Did he touch you last night?

'No, he didn't.'

'Are you sure – you're not protecting him again are you?'

'No, honestly, everything is OK.'

There was a pause. 'I wrote a poem in bed last night. Can I read it to you?' I said.

'Yes, please,' Fran said. 'I'd like to hear it.

'OK, here goes . . .'

In my mind, I see a beach,
With miles of golden sand,
I see a group of children there,
All standing hand in hand.

The children smile, and wave at me,
And call me to their side,
And in my thoughts, I walk to them,
Though I'm scared and want to hide.

I know that I belong with them,
I feel we're all the same,
'Cos though the sun has tanned our skins,
Beneath lies guilt and blame.

They tell me that they've waited,
Just waited there for me,
And now that I am with them,
We must walk into the sea.

The sea is now much fiercer,
The waves engulf my head,
And hand in hand, we're drowning,
And joining all the dead.

Now, it feels so peaceful,
At the bottom of the sea,
For now the hurt's been washed away,
My mind has been set free.

'That's it,' I said, as I finished reading.

Fran remained silent.

'Fran? That's *it*! Have I put you to sleep?'

'No, sorry love, I'm here. It's just very sad, and there's you telling me that you're OK.'

She arranged to ring me the following morning and said I was to ring the Samaritans in between, if necessary, and that they would get hold of her for me.

Although I knew that as a Samaritan she would never betray a confidence, I still made her promise that she wouldn't contact the hospital and tell them where I was.

After I had talked to her, I went back to bed. I felt desperately tired – the past few days were finally beginning to catch up with me.

I thought back to the previous night. I hadn't lied to Fran. Dad really had seemed different. I was pleased that he wasn't angry with me, and had seemed genuinely pleased to see me.

I slept soundly for most of the day. At about three in the afternoon I got up and took Molly for a walk. I felt happy. Everything was going well; I wouldn't need the hospital after all.

Like clockwork, at six, I heard Dad's key in the door. I had made him a meal and we spent the evening talking and laughing. He seemed sorry that I had ended up in hospital and told me I would never need to go back there again. I felt sure he loved me and things had changed.

It was around nine o'clock, when the doorbell rang. We were watching TV and Dad went to answer. I could hear a familiar voice.

The door opened and Dad came back. I knew the man

following behind him, it was my schoolfriend Karen's father, Dave.

'Hi Sophie. You're out of the looney bin then?' he sniggered.

I didn't like him and I wished he would shut up.

'How's Karen?' I asked.

'Fine, she's doing really well with her studies and she's got a boyfriend. She keeps meaning to get in touch with you.'

I didn't want to be in the room any longer, pretending to be polite. I hated Dave. He had hurt and abused me in the past and he was the last person I wanted to see.

I stood up. 'Goodnight, Dad, I'm off to bed.'

'OK, love.' He stopped me as I walked past and kissed me on the cheek.

Alarm bells should have gone off in my head at this point, but they didn't. Even though Dad had clearly invited Dave round – a man who, at Dad's invitation, had assaulted and raped me in the past – I honestly believed that Dad had changed and that they would leave me alone. I was in denial, I simply couldn't face the possibility that perhaps Dad hadn't changed at all. So I made my way up to bed and for the next few hours I drifted in and out of sleep, vaguely aware of talk and laughter from downstairs. I was awoken with a start by voices outside my bedroom door. I looked at my bedside clock and saw that it was now three in the morning. I sat bolt upright in bed and strained to hear what they were saying.

'Is it OK?' Dave was saying.

'Yes, of course it is,' Dad replied. 'She'll be fine. You go on in there and I'll join you in a minute.'

My heart seemed to collapse into the pit of my stomach with horror as I heard my father's words. The handle on my bedroom door began to turn, and I buried my head underneath my quilt, shaking with fear.

As I always had, I blamed myself. If terrible things were going to happen to me again, then it must be my fault. The questions buzzed round and round in my head. Why am I so bad? Why me? What have I done to deserve this?'

There were no answers.

Hot tears ran down my cheeks as Dave crossed my bedroom and ripped the duvet from around me.

The next morning I stayed in bed until Dad had left for work, then I dialled the local Samaritans. I had to let Fran know.

'Samaritans, can I help you?'

'Message for Fran, please,' I stammered.

'OK, my name's Jan, what's yours?'

'It's Sophie. Can you tell Fran that she was right? She'll understand.'

I replaced the receiver before she had a chance to reply. I was so distressed that I could barely get the words out. But I wanted Fran to know that she had been right about my father.

I was in a terrible state. Dad and Dave's assault on me in the night had been bloody and brutal and now the pain I felt inside was too overwhelming to ignore any more. I hated myself and I felt a powerful urge to punish myself. I deserved the worst I could do.

In a frenzy of self-destruction brought on by grief, pain, loss and betrayal, I started on my arms. I found a new blade in the bathroom and began to tear deep parallel lines into my skin. I watched the blood running out, but I couldn't feel a thing.

I went downstairs and got a bottle of brandy from my father's drinks cabinet. I took it to my bedroom, where I put on the saddest songs in my record collection, as loud as I could.

As I played the songs over and over again I swigged the brandy and the tears poured down my face. The events of the night before kept going over and over in my head like a film until the room begin to spin and I felt sick.

I lit a cigarette. I had no intention of smoking it. I pushed it as hard as I could into my hand and watched the skin burn. Then, when the cigarette was out, I re-lit it and did it again and again and again, until I couldn't see any skin left on the back of my hand that wasn't burned. But still I felt no relief.

Oblivious to the pain, I was sobbing hysterically. Nothing was going to relieve the anguish I felt, except death.

I went back to the razor blades and began slashing at myself again. I was still swigging the brandy and the room was spinning violently. The cuts were no longer deep; the blade was starting to feel too blunt.

I rushed into the bathroom to search for new blades, pulling assorted packets of tablets, plasters and bandages on to the floor in my desperation. As I realised there were no more blades the panic rose inside me. My heart was thumping inside my chest. I looked under the sink where the cleaning products were kept. I used to hide blades in there, stuck to the inside of the door, but there were none. Then I saw the answer, a way out of the pain and hurt, a way to end it all.

I grabbed the bottle of bleach and took it back to the bedroom. When I took the lid off and sniffed it the contents made my eyes sting. I remembered drinking it before when I had lost the baby – it had nearly killed me then, so maybe it would work this time. I poured some into the half-full bottle of brandy and began to swig it.

As the potent mixture hit my stomach I felt an excruciating burning sensation. My mouth went numb and then began to feel as if it was on fire.

The second mouthful wasn't as bad, and the third was almost easy. I was almost through the bottle when the phone began to ring. I knew it would be Dad, checking to see if I was alright.

'Must get to the phone . . . let him know I'm OK. Don't want him to worry,' I mumbled as I stumbled from my room across the landing to where the phone was.

I grabbed the phone and opened my mouth but no words came out. My mouth was on fire and I felt very sick.

'Sophie?' It was Fran. 'Sophie? Are you there? Are you OK?'

Her voice was urgent, worried. I wanted to reassure her that I was fine. I tried to speak.

'Ummmm,' My throat was burning and it felt as if there were loose pieces of skin in my throat.

'Oh God, what have you done? Sophie? Try to answer me. Have you taken anything?'

'Ye, ye . . .' I couldn't get the words out. A wave of panic swept over me.

'Sophie, let me get an ambulance to you, please.' I could hear the panic in Fran's voice. 'You have to give me permission to call one for you. Come on, just say yes, please, Sophie.' She was shouting now. 'Come on, love, say something, try to stay awake, please let me help you, we know where you live, we can have an ambulance with you in minutes, please Sophie.'

'Ye,' It was all I could manage. But it was enough.

'Right, I'm calling one now.' I could hear the relief in her voice. 'Sophie, I want you to get to the front door and open it. When you've done that, try to get back to the phone and I'll talk to you until it arrives – OK?'

I put the phone down on the shelf and began to crawl downstairs. I began vomiting. I looked down and saw it was full of blood. I was being so sick I couldn't stop.

I made it to the front door, opened it and fell out into the front garden. There seemed to be blood everywhere. Then everything went black.

I opened my eyes. There were bright lights. Everything was blurry. I could hear beeping noises. As my eyes adjusted, I saw that I was lying on a hospital trolley. I closed my eyes.

'I think she's come round now,' I heard a voice say.

I opened my eyes again to see a nurse standing by my bedside. 'Hello, Sophie,' she said.

I couldn't speak. My throat felt as if it had been cut to pieces with my razor blade.

'So what's all this about then, Sophie. Have you had a row with your boyfriend or something?' the nurse asked.

As if I'd do this over a boyfriend, I thought, and shut my eyes again.

The next time that I opened them, Fran was sitting beside me. She smiled and squeezed my hand.

'Hello, Sophie,' she said gently, 'I know you can't speak yet, but I'm here for you now.'

A tear ran down my cheek and Fran dabbed at it with a tissue. I tried to smile but I couldn't. I was so glad she was there.

'The doctors say you've been very lucky. You've had your stomach lined with charcoal to neutralise the bleach. God,

Sophie, I'm so sorry you felt that bad again. She paused. 'They're keeping you in for a few days, so I'll visit again if you'd like me to.'

I nodded.

'I think the nurses are trying to contact your father. Do you want me to tell them where he works?' she asked.

I shook my head. I wanted to keep him away for as long as possible. I knew he would give me a hard time.

Fran leaned over the bed and kissed me on the cheek. 'I'll come and see you tomorrow,' she said.

As she left I heard a voice outside the room. 'Josie, can you go and sit in there with that suicidal one. Best not leave her on her own, I suppose, just in case.' The nurse sounded cold and hard and clearly thought of me as some kind of delinquent.

The door opened and a young nurse came in and sat down next to me, smiling nervously.

I closed my eyes. It would be easier for her if she thought I was sleeping. I didn't want to be any more of a problem. I'd caused enough trouble already.

12

The Reunion

A few days later, Jane, my social worker, visited me. She was very angry that I had been released from the psychiatric hospital without her knowledge and rang the hospital to tell them exactly what she thought of them and how they had failed in their duty of care.

Jane wanted to discuss my options with me, and there weren't many. I could go back to the nuthouse, go into some sort of care or go to live with my mother, who hadn't even been to visit me in hospital. I chose the nuthouse, because to me the other options were worse, and a day or two later I was transferred there by ambulance.

It was terribly hard going back there. I was terrified that if I was there for a long time I would lose my dad. And on top of that I knew Dr Harvey would be angry with me and I was afraid the other patients would hate me for running away. Approval was desperately important to me and I couldn't bear the thought of anyone being angry or disapproving towards me. I wanted to please everyone, which is why I played the 'good girl' so much of the time.

This time, when I entered the hospital, I realised that there were no other alternatives open to me. I had to stick it out and make it work if I was to survive. The dream that I had clung to, of my father changing, being sorry about what he had done and looking after me, had been destroyed. My innermost soul felt broken and I was overwhelmed by sadness. I still loved him desperately, but I knew now that he wasn't going to change and I actually needed the nuthouse. How else was I going to learn to cope with life and to look after myself? And I knew, somewhere deep inside, that this is what I needed to do.

I had a meeting with Dr Harvey in which I apologised for lying to him about where I was staying and told him that I wanted to be well. I wanted to make the treatment work.

He was patient and kind but firm. He listened to my apology and then calmly went over the rules and regulations I would have to stick to if I wanted to continue my treatment there. He said I was not to leave the unit at all for the next six months. After six months I could go out accompanied by a nurse. Sex was totally prohibited; I was to attend a group meeting every day as well as art and writing therapy classes. I was also to have an hour-long class with a teacher every day. Most of the rules didn't seem too bad, though the thought of being stuck in the ward for six months freaked me out a little. But at least it was safe in hospital. I agreed to all the rules.

As I walked along the corridor, after leaving Dr Harvey's office, I heard someone running behind me.

'Sophie! Hello, babe.' The accent was unmistakeable.

My heart leaped as I threw my arms around Katie and we held each other close.

'When did you get back?' I asked.

'Yesterday. I couldn't believe it when Dawn told me you'd

been in casualty, full of bleach. Why did you do that, you idiot?'

'I'll tell you later. How about you?'

'I had a few days in the nuthouse in north Wales. They're complete psychopaths in there. I knew I'd never sort my head out there. I saw my grandmother, though, one of the nurses took me to see her.'

'How was she?' I could see the tears well up in Katie's eyes

'Pretty sick. It was good to see her though.'

Katie and I went into what was known as the 'music room', because it had a battered old record player in it. We had sat in this room before, listening to music and looking out of the window at the open fields beyond it, for hours on end.

The room was empty. I sat in my normal place on the window ledge while Katie went over to the record player and put on our favourite song, 'Broken Man' by Paul Young. Katie joined me on the ledge and we sat staring out, listening to the words.

If you fear the hurt is but a kiss away,
Close your eyes, and take it.
And if you feel, that pain can tear you in two,
Go ahead, and bear it.

When the record finished Katie said, 'go on then, tell me what happened'. I told her about my days on the streets after she left, coming back to the hospital, being released for a week and going home. When I got to the part about Dad and Dave, I became choked up.

'Dave came into the bedroom, and stood by the side of the bed. I tried to pretend to be asleep, but it didn't work. He knew that I was awake.'

My voice was shaky, but Katie urged me on.

'He pulled back the covers and got into the bed with me. I could smell the drink on him and his clothes were dirty and musty. He pulled my nightdress up and I felt his hands all over my body. I told him to leave, but he just laughed at me. I tried to get out of the bed, but I was trapped between the wall and his body. Then I felt his fingers ramming up inside me and an electrifying pain shot through my body.'

'And where was your dad when he was doing all this?' she asked.

'Oh, he was there.' I paused.

Katie sighed heavily. 'Go on, Sophie,' she said, 'you'll feel better if you can tell someone.'

'Dave got out of the bed and started to undress. Dad stood watching. When Dave was naked, Dad told him to get in the bed again. He climbed on top of me this time and began to force himself inside me. A burning pain swept through me and I felt as though I was going to be sick.'

'Oh Sophie,' Katie said, taking my hand.

'It felt like a lifetime before I felt Dave finish. He was panting and gasping heavily all over my face. I turned my head away to avoid his breath, and saw that my dad was leaving the room. He came back holding something and as he got closer I could see it was a wine bottle.' I broke off, close to tears. 'Maybe I've said too much, Katie, this is too difficult.'

'Sophie, you must tell someone; if you don't it will just eat away at you.'

I stopped to get myself back together again.

'Dad gave the bottle to Dave, who rammed it inside me. The pain was terrible, but I couldn't scream, I felt numb, my senses felt destroyed. I think that there's only so much pain you can take before your body just shuts off – you know what it's like to feel like that, don't you?'

Katie nodded and squeezed my hand. There were tears in her eyes.

'I managed to look over to my father who had undressed and was starting to masturbate. I could see that he was getting really excited. Then I felt something inside me that was so sharp. God, I can't describe how sharp it felt, and how much it hurt, yet Dave didn't seem to be applying any force any more.'

I started to cry.

'Let's take a break,' Katie said. 'I'm going to the loo, do you want to get us a drink?'

I nodded and wiped my eyes as I headed for the kitchen. I was back a few minutes later with two steaming mugs of tea. I put the record back on and then sat back on the ledge, hugging my knees tightly and sipping the tea as I waited for Katie.

When she came back her eyes looked puffy and swollen.

'Look, let's leave this, Katie. Let's talk about something else.'

'No, Sophie, you must talk about what that creature who calls himself a father has done to you,' she said.

'Don't call him a creature!' I shouted. 'It wasn't him, it was Dave. We were getting on fine until he turned up.'

'OK, whatever,' she replied. 'I'm sorry.'

I took a deep breath. 'I saw that Dave had a knife in his hand and I knew that he must have put it inside me. It felt like it was still inside. I felt like I wanted to be sick, when I saw the knife and the blood on it, but I knew that I couldn't, it would make my dad more excited if I was sick.'

I stopped, remembering the many times that Dad had enjoyed seeing me bleeding and vomiting with pain after a knife assault.

Katie got up from the window ledge and played the record again. We sat in silence for a few moments.

Eventually Katie spoke. 'And then what?' she said.

'Well, that was it, really.'

'Are you sure?' asked Katie. 'Your dad didn't touch you then?'

'Well, yes, but he didn't hurt me like Dave did. My dad just made love to me.'

'Made love to you? Is that what you think? Is that what it felt like?' Katie looked incredulous.

'Well, yes, I think so,' I replied. 'But I don't really know because there's only been the men who hurt me or used me and my dad. And he does love me, you know.'

'I used to think that my dad loved me,' Katie said. 'But he didn't love me at all, he just used me for sex. That's cruel and wrong and it's what your dad is doing to you. He doesn't care if you live or die.'

'Shut up!' I screamed. 'You don't know that, you don't know my dad, just shut up!'

'Stop kidding yourself, Sophie,' Katie said quietly. 'Just wake up to yourself.'

I couldn't stand any more of this. I screamed at her again. 'Shut up! Shut up! You don't understand. I'm sorry if it was like that for you, but my dad is different, OK?' I began to cry.

Katie was silent. A moment later the door opened and Dawn looked in.

'Are you two OK in here?' she asked.

'Fine,' Katie and I replied in unison.

Dawn left and we sat in silence again.

After a couple of minutes, I stood up and walked to the door. 'I'm tired. I'm going to get an early night.'

Katie nodded and I left the room.

I knew she was right. What she'd said about my dad was the truth. But I didn't want to hear it.

I wasn't ready.

13

Not Alone

'So why did you have to rape her, James?' Mary said angrily.

James was silent.

'Well, go on, tell us. Did it make you feel like a man?'

At this point Helen, the social worker, interrupted. 'Mary, I know you're upset, but try to calm down. It's taken a lot of courage for James to share this with the group today. We should all try to support him.'

It was our daily therapy meeting with all the other patients under Dr Harvey's care. After several weeks in the unit, I barely noticed the microphone and the one-way mirror that had so intimidated me when I first arrived.

Today's was our toughest meeting of the week. On Wednesdays each of us had to talk about what had happened to us that led to our being in the hospital.

James hadn't been in the unit long and until now he hadn't talked about why he was there. On this particular Wednesday he told us, in a hesitant manner, about the rape, and that afterwards he had felt remorse for what he did and had tried to kill himself, rather dramatically, by setting light to a building while he was still inside it. He had been rescued and, after confessing to the police, was now facing trial for both rape and arson. At his preliminary court appearance it had been decided to commit him to the hospital for psychiatric reports while he was awaiting trial.

I listened in horror as he spoke. I couldn't believe that James could have hidden such a secret from us. A wave of nausea swept through me as I thought back to the times when he had hugged me in what I had thought to be an affectionate way. Now, as I tried to take in what he had done, it all seemed very different. I couldn't believe that the staff had put me, Anna and Simone into the men's ward, with a rapist only a few beds away from us. I had liked James and I admired his courage in speaking up, but I still couldn't imagine sleeping properly again while he was around.

The next patient in the circle was telling his story. Paul explained that he had also been referred to the hospital for psychiatric reports pending a trial. He had worked for the Royal Mail in the sorting office, and had one day taken a parcel home with him. He didn't know why he had done it, although he explained that he was feeling very depressed at the time. When he got home and opened the parcel he found that it contained over five thousand pounds. He had immediately panicked and taken the parcel back to work, confessing what he had done to his supervisor, who called the police. He was dismissed from his job and prosecuted.

'Nutter,' Katie said. 'No wonder you're in here, why did you take the money back?'

A few patients laughed. There was an awful irony in the situation – his honesty had backfired on him as he'd lost his job and his freedom through telling the truth. But Paul said he didn't regret owning up, and was glad he hadn't kept the money as he couldn't have lived with himself if he'd done that.

'Nutter,' Katie repeated.

'That's not very helpful, Katie,' Amy said gently. 'I think you should say sorry to Paul.'

'I'm sorry that you're a nutter,' Katie said.

The group sat in silence until, at Amy's prompting, the next person began to tell their story. As the stories went on I realised what suffering each of us had endured, and that no matter how different each story was, we all shared similar feelings of desperation and self-hatred.

Even James, whose crime was so repugnant, had talked about feelings that seemed so similar to mine.

At regular intervals the phone on the table rang and Helen, Dawn or Amy answered and would then direct the group in certain ways, based on feedback from the professionals behind the mirror.

Tough as the Wednesday meetings were they created a very powerful bond between all of us. Opening up about what we'd been through was extremely hard and at first I just couldn't do it. But over the weeks, as I listened to others describe what had happened to them, I found the courage to begin talking about what I'd been through.

Several of the younger women, including Mary and Gina and Katie, had similar stories to mine. All had been violently sexually abused by their fathers, grandfathers or brothers and, as upsetting as the stories were, I gained comfort from the fact that I wasn't alone, as I had once believed.

Sometimes I could hardly believe that here I was, talking about what my father had done, to a roomful of people, all of whom nodded in mutual understanding and support. I still wasn't able to blame my dad, or to hate him, that was another step I didn't know if I'd be able to take. But talking about what had happened was a start.

At no point had the hospital staff suggested reporting my dad, or any of the other abusers discussed in our meetings, to the police. Their focus was on the patients and what was best for us, and they had no interest in the abusers. I'm sure they knew that any suggestion of prosecution would have set me – and any of the other patients – back, as it would have been a terrible ordeal. As it was, knowing they weren't interested in Dad helped me to open up, as I didn't feel that I would be hurting him by talking about what had happened.

As we listened to one another and shared our most private secrets and feelings, the trust and friendship between us grew. I began to feel a sense of safety and friendship in the unit that was stronger than anything I had ever experienced outside. Much to my surprise, I even began to feel sorry for James, as I saw what genuine remorse he felt and how hard he found it to live with himself.

In the world we lived in, inside that small hospital unit, few of the usual social rules and boundaries applied. We were all struggling to find a way to come to terms with our pasts and to be able to rejoin the world outside. We all wanted jobs, homes and families – one day. But inside the unit all we had was one another and, no matter what any of us had done, we came to care for and understand one another.

14

Feeling the Pain

'Come on, Sophie. You're not even dressed yet and Miss Smith is waiting for you.'

I sighed heavily as I pulled back the sheets and dragged myself from my comfortable bed. 'I can't be bothered to get dressed today,' I told Dawn. I didn't tell her that four letters had arrived for me today. Four letters, when one was a rarity! I had already opened the one from my social worker, Jane Gray, but I was saving the rest for later.

'Put your dressing gown on for now then, but hurry. Your lessons are important.'

I smiled. It seemed funny that Dawn was getting so worked up over a few lessons when I had missed so much schooling over the past two years. How could an hour a day with a teacher in the hospital make any difference? But Dawn insisted, so I put on my dressing gown and followed her to the sparsely decorated side room, where Katie and Miss Smith, a rather timid-looking woman, were waiting. Katie had missed so much school that even though, at 19, she was past school age, she still had to attend leasons.

'Sorry I'm late,' I said as I sat down. I smiled at Katie as I spoke.

'That's alright, Sophie,' replied Miss Smith. 'It's Geography today, but before we start – have either of you got any questions relating to yesterday's French lesson?'

'Was it French yesterday?' Katie asked. 'I thought it was Geography yesterday.'

'It was French – do you remember we did a role play?' Miss Smith, who was all enthusiasm, hadn't a clue that Katie was winding her up. It was early November and we'd been coming to these lessons for several months now. We both thought they were a waste of time.

'I thought the role play was last week, are you sure?' Katie asked.

I stifled a giggle while kicking Katie's shins under the table. She let out a mock yelp of pain as we watched Miss Smith dive into her large satchel and start producing textbooks and notes. My late arrival meant the lesson was already late starting and if we stalled for just a bit longer then time would be up and Dawn would be back to collect us. Much to our amusement Miss Smith was very easily confused.

'Look,' she was saying. 'Here are yesterday's notes. It was definitely French – I showed you the map of France, remember?'

'Oh yes, you're right, *merci*,' Katie replied in her broad Liverpool accent.

'So, any questions?' Miss Smith continued.

'Yes,' I said, 'what does purdah mean?'

Miss Smith looked taken aback and began to rummage in her bag. 'Er, right, it's a Hindu custom I think. Hold on a minute – let me nip to the car and get my dictionary and I can give you the proper definition.' She rushed out of the door. Katie and I were left looking at one another.

'Nice one, Sophie,' Katie said drily. 'By the time she gets through all the locked doors and back in again the lesson will be nearly over.'

'I actually want to know what it means,' I said indignantly. 'I had a letter from my social worker and at the end she said "I'll see you when you're out of purdah."'

After nine minutes and thirty-two seconds, Miss Smith returned and excitedly leafed through the dictionary.

'Sorry for the delay, girls – here we are: purdah. It describes the Hindu custom of keeping women in seclusion; in modern days, the veil that Muslim women wear illustrates this. Why do you ask, Sophie?'

'Oh, no reason,' I said. I didn't want to tell her about the letter that Jane Gray had sent me. But I understood now, what she had meant. I was in a kind of seclusion, shut away from the world.

Miss Smith was off on another tangent. 'Can either of you show me on the map the country with the highest Muslim population?'

Katie and I sighed loudly.

After another ten minutes our lesson was over and Dawn came to collect us. 'I hope you haven't been giving Miss Smith a hard time.'

Katie and I shook our heads, all innocence. 'Course not.'

'See you tomorrow, girls,' Miss Smith smiled.

We raced out of the room. I told Katie I'd get dressed and meet her in the TV room.

Back in my cubicle I decided to read the other three letters that had arrived today. I pulled them out of my bedside locker where I'd stashed them, and sat down on my bed to open them.

The first was from Pam, the Samaritan who helped me in London, wishing me well and saying I could call her when she was next on duty.

The second was from my old school friend Karen: Dave's daughter. It was nice of her to write, but she went on about boyfriend problems and it just made me feel we were in completely different worlds. 'Why are you in there, anyway?' she wrote. If only she knew.

I put the letter aside and turned to the last one.

Dear Sophie

By the time that you read this letter, I will be out of the country. I honestly can't live with myself anymore, and with what I have done. I feel that the only way that I can help you now is to be out of your life for a few months, in order to give you a chance to get over everything. I have sold the house and am going on a trip around the world – I don't know when I'll be back, but it won't be for a few months. I have spoken with your mother and I have given her some money from the house sale for you. If you are out of hospital before I return, then she will give you the money – it's not much – but it will be enough to tide you over for a few months.

I'm sorry just to walk out like this and leave you, but it's for the best. I need some time away to get my head together. I don't feel that my life is worth living anymore and to get away is the only way that I can cope, and come to terms with life. You'll be pleased to know that Molly is staying on a friend's farm in Kent. She will be in her element there. Your mum has the address if you want to go and see her.

Anyway, that's all I can say. Please remember that I love you very much. Try to stick the treatment out and you'll be OK.

I love you,

All my love,

Dad

The tears were streaming down my face. I wanted to shout and scream, yet my throat felt blocked; no words came and I gasped for breath. A wave of panic was sweeping over me. I couldn't comprehend life without my father around. He must have known that. His leaving like this would destroy me more than anything else that had happened. I couldn't live without him. And my home, my things, my dog: everything had gone. An ear-piercing scream rang out through the ward. I knew it was coming from me, but I had no control over it or over what happened next.

I awoke in a small white room, devoid of any windows or furniture and with padded walls. I was totally disorientated and couldn't think where I was. A strong fluorescent light shone down on me. I looked down at myself. I was dressed in a paper nightdress.

I tried to remember what had happened, but the last thing that I remembered was reading the letter from my father. I tried to work out what had happened but my head was spinning and it hurt to think. I closed my eyes.

I must have fallen asleep again. I was woken by the sound of the door opening. It was Amy.

'How are you feeling now?' she asked tentatively.

'What's happened? Where am I?' I said drowsily.

'Don't you remember yesterday, Sophie?' I shook my head.

She sat down next to me on the floor and put her arm around my shoulder. She told me I had totally lost control and begun a violent attack on myself. By the time the nurses had been alerted, I was sitting on the kitchen floor stabbing my stomach with a tin opener. Amy explained that when Raj had come into the kitchen to calm me down, I had hurled crockery at him and screamed hysterically. It had taken four nurses to contain me and Dr Harvey took the decision to inject a sedative and put me in the padded room, for my own safety.

I looked at Amy in total disbelief. I couldn't remember anything. It scared me to think that I could be that out of control and not remember a thing. 'Sorry,' I said. 'I'm really sorry.'

'Don't be. We were all very worried for you. I take it the letter from your dad was the reason?'

My eyes began to fill with tears as the sense of loss hit me again. My life felt empty – there was no point going on.

Amy squeezed my shoulder reassuringly and stood up. She offered me her hand to help me up from the floor. 'Let's get you out of here and back on the ward,' she said.

As I stood up a sharp pain reminded me of my cut stomach. I followed Amy out of the room and back into the corridor.

'Go and get dressed, Sophie, and then come to the community meeting. We'll speak about the letter from your dad afterwards, OK?'

I nodded, and made my way – feeling stiff and sore – to my bed.

Anna was sitting up in bed writing in her diary. 'Are you OK, Sophie? You scared the life out of me yesterday.'

'Sorry. Yes, I'm fine now, thanks,' I said, although I felt a long way from fine.

'If you ever want to talk, I'm here, you know,' Anna smiled.

She asked me to push her wheelchair to the community meeting. Some of the anorexics were too weak to walk. Anna could have managed but even that tiny amount of exercise was forbidden, in the effort to get her to gain the maximum amount of weight.

I barely had the strength to push her wheelchair, but I didn't like to say no, so I helped her into it and pushed her along the corridor to the large ladies' ward, where chairs were set up in a huge circle.

All the patients and staff had to attend the daily community meeting. There were about sixty people in attendance, but a lot of them might as well not have been there at all. They just stared out of the window throughout the meeting, never speaking or acknowledging anything that was said.

The meeting was usually chaired by a patient. The staff picked someone who was near the end of their stay in hospital, and well along the road to functioning normally again. It was seen as a real responsibility to be given this job, and while some patients didn't care, others took it very seriously and the power went straight to their heads.

Today's chairman, Robert, was one of these. He was a university graduate who'd had a nervous breakdown. He was training to be in retail management and obviously felt that the community meeting was the ideal forum to try out his supervisory skills.

He raised his eyebrows as Anna and I arrived. I tried to avoid eye contact with him as we found a seat within the large circle of chairs. 'Sophie,' he said in a loud voice as I sat down. 'Would you like to share with the rest of us why you and Anna are late this morning?'

'Not really,' I said. I didn't feel like going into the whole padded-room story. And in any case most people already knew.

'Piss off, Robert,' Katie said. She turned to me and winked.

Robert looked taken aback. 'Right,' he continued in his most officious manner. 'Let's get on with the meeting.' He cast a disdainful look in my direction as he spoke. 'Last night, somebody killed all the goldfish in the tank in the day room. Would anybody like to confess?'

Silence.

'They were killed in a particularly brutal way. Somebody cut them up,' Robert continued.

'Stop, please, don't say any more. I don't want to hear.' It was an elderly patient named Annie who was becoming very distressed. Annie had senile dementia and very rarely said anything to anyone. She smelled of stale urine and Katie and I always avoided seats that she had sat in – if Katie felt particularly mischievous she would steer visitors and guests into Annie's chair and we would sit back and watch.

'Nurse, please take me out of here, away from these murderers,' Annie continued shakily.

A nurse helped Annie from her seat and out of the meeting. The stench of stale urine wafted past us as she was led away.

'Bloody hell,' a patient called Pat said. 'That's the most she's ever said, isn't it!' Laughter rippled around the room.

Annie had just had a course of ECT – electroconvulsive therapy – which involved passing electric currents through her brain. She was always a little more lucid for a couple of days afterwards, but this time she'd excelled herself.

'At least the goldfish massacre got her talking,' Pat said.

'Is that a confession, Pat?' Robert asked.

'Oh, shut up, Robert,' Pat shouted. 'Of course it's not.' Pat had a violent temper and had begun to lose it.

'OK, let's move on,' a nurse called Diane, said quickly.

The next item on the agenda was Christmas, which was now only six weeks away. We were asked to suggest how we might celebrate. Most people said that they'd like to go home, but Amy said we'd each be told nearer the time whether we could leave or not.

Patients were now getting restless. A few simply stood up and walked out of the room and one man started talking to himself. Robert clearly sensed that he was beginning to lose control.

'Right then,' he said. 'I think that's it for today. If you know anything about the fish, or want to confess, then please see a member of staff. Has anyone got any questions?'

'Yes, I have,' answered a middle-aged patient called Tina. Everyone turned to look at her. Tina was very timid and had never said a word before in a meeting.

'Go on, Tina,' coaxed Robert gently. 'What would you like to ask?'

'Mary,' she said, 'did you knit those woolly socks your-self?'

Everyone fell about laughing as Tina looked around, totally bemused.

After the meeting, I was taken aside by Amy, who gently encouraged me to talk about how I felt about Dad's letter.

I began to cry as I tried to explain to her how shocked and bereft I felt.

'So he's still managing to hurt you, even when you're in hospital, is he?' Amy asked.

'Yes,' I answered. 'But I understand why he's done it. He's

gone away because he loves me. It's because he cares – I know that.'

Amy didn't say anything.

'You don't believe me, do you?' I said defensively.

'It's not for me to say,' Amy replied. 'How are you going to cope with him being away?'

'I don't know. It won't change how I feel about him,' I answered.

'Well, that's what we have to work together to resolve. I will try to help you in the best way that I can. Come and speak to me, or another member of staff, whenever you feel bad or upset. We can work through your feelings before things get out of control.'

I nodded.

'Remember, Sophie, that I do care about you. We all do.' Amy smiled as I got up to leave the room.

I smiled at her reassurance but didn't really believe her. How could anyone really care about me?

I went off to find Katie. We understood each other more than any nurse could ever understand – at least that's how it felt.

I found her sitting on her bed, writing in her diary. Like me she did a lot of writing. It was a safe way of releasing feelings, although it didn't give the same sense of relief that cutting ourselves did.

I plonked myself down on the bed beside her. Katie looked up and grinned at me.

'Hello, babe,' she said. 'Good to see you back out of seclusion. How are you?'

'Still a bit tearful and a bit drowsy, but OK. How are you?' I asked.

'Yeah, I'm alright.' Katie held my hand. 'So, what do you think the chances are of us being let out of here for Christmas then?' she said.

'I'd say there's absolutely no chance. We'll have to tell Father Christmas that we've moved.'

'I won't bother,' Katie replied. 'He could never find where I lived before!' She was laughing, but I could see the hurt in her eyes and I felt so sorry.

At least I used to have a good time at Christmas. It always put my problems in perspective when I heard her speak of her family and how she had been treated.

'Don't worry, Katie,' I said. 'This year will be your best Christmas ever – I'll make sure it is.'

Katie smiled. 'Do you want to get some sleep?' she said.

She tucked her diary under her pillow, drew back the covers, got into bed and then gestured for me to get in with her.

I got in and Katie pulled the covers up tightly around us. Katie slipped her hand around my waist and while it made me flinch because of my cuts, the warmth of her body made up for the pain. There was warmth and security in being with her and it felt like the most natural thing in the world to fall asleep in each other's arms.

15

'Tis the Season

It was during the last couple of weeks before Christmas that everything seemed to go really crazy in the hospital.

It began with Stephen, a young Afro-Caribbean boy who suffered from chronic manic depression. Stephen rarely spoke in the meetings, and was usually heavily sedated. He had a penetrating stare, which Katie and I found very unnerving, and he used to get up in the early hours of the morning and pace up and down the ward relentlessly until the night staff put him back to bed.

We first realised that something was wrong when an emergency meeting was called first thing on a Monday morning. All the patients sat around in a large circle, mostly half asleep, waiting for someone to speak.

We knew it must be serious when Dr Harvey came in. He sat down and waited until we were all paying attention.

'There's no easy way of saying this,' he said. 'Stephen went home this weekend on home leave, as he has done several times before. He was due back this morning, but we have just received some terrible news. He threw himself under a train on his way back to the hospital and I'm afraid he died.'

No one spoke or reacted until after the meeting was over

and the staff had left. Some of the patients drifted back to their beds looking totally unaffected by the news. But the rest of us sat mesmerised. I replayed Dr Harvey's words in my mind, again and again.

Eventually we began to talk. No one really knew Stephen well, but we all felt a tremendous sense of sadness and horror as we thought of the pain he must have been in to have done that to himself. We felt we'd all let him down as we'd never got close to him or tried to help him.

Our sadness for Stephen was followed by a sense of horror and panic as we realised that we weren't as safe under the hospital's care as we had believed. The experts had deemed him fit to go home, so Katie and I concluded that maybe they weren't such experts after all. If they couldn't see a suicide looming, then who could? We decided that we should be there for each other so that this would never happen again. But unfortunately, a kind of madness seemed to have been triggered by Stephen's death and it was only days until the next incident.

Maureen was a patient who was causing concern, as she often threatened to commit suicide. The staff decided that she needed twenty-four-hour supervision and a nurse was assigned to go everywhere with her at all times.

Maureen put this to the test a couple of days later, when most of the patients were sitting in the day room watching television. We heard a loud scream and the next moment the door flew open and Maureen ran, still screaming, through the day room, with a charge nurse called Jim clinging on to her arm. She was about five foot ten and heavily built, while Jim was no more than five foot and weighed about eight stone, so the odds were stacked against him.

Maureen lunged towards the window. We watched helplessly as Jim, still hanging on, was dragged after her. Just at the moment when Maureen threw herself out the window, Jim let go, and collapsed on the floor in a heap. Staff and patients ran to the window and looked down on to the gravel below where Maureen's body lay sprawled out and apparently lifeless.

Amazingly Maureen survived, although she broke her arms and legs and cracked her ribs. She was transferred to a general hospital on the other side of London for treatment.

The next incident involved a patient called Luke. By now it was only a couple of days until Christmas and Katie and I were sitting in our usual place in the music room listening to the radio. Luke, a schizophrenic who wasn't one of Dr Harvey's patients, was sitting in the room with us. Although neither of us knew anything about him, he seemed friendly and we didn't mind his company, until suddenly Luke began to get agitated with the radio. He seemed to be taking all the disc jockey's jibes and jokes personally and he got up from his seat and began pacing up and down. At first, Katie and I thought it quite amusing and laughed. But this just made him worse and he began shouting at the radio and at us as well. The DJ made a comment about Christmas shopping and how people who got into debt every year just to buy presents were stupid. It seemed to be the final straw for Luke, who began to scream at the radio.

'Stupid, I'm not stupid. You are! Why don't you shut up?'

'Calm down,' said Katie. 'It's only a radio, don't get so worked up.'

Luke jumped up from his seat, and charged across the room. He picked up the entire stereo and hurled it across the room. It smashed into pieces as it hit the wall.

Katie, seeing the damage he had caused, threw herself at Luke, who lost his balance and fell to the ground as she began to punch him and scratch at his face.

'You bastard,' she screamed. 'You've ruined it for everyone now.'

I tried to pull her away, but I couldn't get her off him. She had lost control, and Luke seemed to be at the receiving end of all the anger that she had built up inside. He was a big, strong man and he could have killed her if he'd fought back, but luckily for Katie he just lay there and took it.

In the end it took six nurses to rescue Luke. Katie was sedated and thrown into the padded seclusion room, while he was treated for shock, as well as the cuts and bruises all over his body.

So much for the season of goodwill. The next day was Christmas Eve and I sat in the music room on my own, listening to a radio that a nurse had donated. Half the patients had gone home and the ones who were left either seemed to be heavily sedated or totally mad.

Tears dripped down my cheeks. I felt so sad and alone. My best friend was still sedated and in seclusion and I felt no one else in the world cared about me. It was only the bolted down plastic white tree in the day room that reminded me it was Christmas at all.

16

Losing Katie

On Christmas Day Katie was eventually allowed out of seclusion at about four in the afternoon. She was still feeling very drowsy, so we sat in the music room listening to the radio – for a couple of hours. We were feeling really depressed and sorry for ourselves, as neither of us had received a phone call from anyone to wish us Happy Christmas. It wasn't as if either of us was expecting a call, but it still felt miserable. My promise to Katie about making it her best Christmas ever had definitely been broken.

The nurses had tried to get us into the Christmas spirit but we couldn't summon any enthusiasm. We could hear shouting coming from the adjoining room where the staff were trying to organise party games – not an easy job, as a room full of psychiatric cases wasn't the best forum for a game of 'Whodunit'. There was always the possibility that one of them might take the game too far and actually kill someone.

So that was it; our Christmas Day was over at seven o'clock when we went to bed together. By this time it was quite normal for us to sleep in the same bed and we spent more nights together than we did apart. Early on it had been brought to Dr Harvey's attention and he had called us in and re-emphasised the rule about sex being totally prohibited – even between people of the same sex.

Katie and I had found this hysterically funny and had explained to him that sex was the furthest thing from our minds. We just liked the closeness and warmth of sleeping with each other, and we were doing no more than cuddling.

Thankfully we were allowed to continue sharing a bed. I still felt suicidal and depressed most days and I still struggled daily with wanting to self-harm. The bond I had with Katie was often all that kept me going. She gave me support, warmth and affection, and her wicked scouse humour made me laugh even when all I wanted to do was cry.

The days between Christmas and New Year seemed to go on for ever. All the meetings and groups had been cancelled, so there really was nothing to get up for and we spent most of our days in bed, so bored that we had even started to miss daft Miss Smith, the teacher.

The only excitement we had was when one afternoon Katie took me to an area that was normally out of bounds for patients. Someone had forgotten to lock the door to what turned out to be a huge laundry room. Katie pointed to a large silver hatch, opened it and beckoned. I peered inside, but couldn't see a thing.

'I have a plan,' Katie said. 'I've been looking out of the window in our music room and I can see this goes into a large container outside. It must be a laundry chute.'

'Don't tell me you're thinking . . .' I said.

'Yes, come on, let's go down, it'll be like a rollercoaster ride.' Katie started to push me towards the chute.

I took a step back. 'Are you sure? How about if you're wrong and we hit a pile of cement. It will kill us.'

'Easier than taking an overdose,' Katie said reassuringly.

She started to climb in, head first.

'Hold my feet,' she said. 'Lower me down, and then get in behind me. We can go together.'

I held Katie's feet and eased her into the dark hole, then put my head and shoulders in after her.

'OK, are you ready?' I said. 'Once my feet leave the floor there's no turning back.'

'Let's do it,' Katie yelled from the depths below me.

'One, two, three,' I said, as I lifted my legs off the floor.

We both screamed, as our bodies hurtled through the darkness at what felt like a hundred miles an hour. It was terrifying and in my head I said goodbye to the world as we were thrown from side to side in the metal tunnel, before we landed.

I opened my eyes. I knew I must still be alive as my legs hurt. Looking around I saw that I was on a giant bed of dirty pillowcases and towels in a large white skip with a plastic cover over the top. But there was no sign of Katie.

Suddenly a head popped up from under a pile of bedding.

'Hiya, babes,' she said brightly. 'God, this stuff smells.'

I started laughing hysterically. Katie joined in too and soon we were crying with laughter.

After we'd calmed down I looked up at the cover. 'I wonder how much oxygen we have?'

Katie managed to stand up. She reached up and punched a hole in the plastic cover. 'Plenty now,' she said as she collapsed back into the bedding, laughing.

We managed to climb to the top of the container and, by tearing at the plastic, make a big enough hole to crawl through. From the top of the container we jumped down on to the ground.

'Where are we?' I asked

'Um, let me see, I think we're at the back of the hospital kitchens,' Katie said.

'Katie,' I said. 'I hate to mention it, but what do we do now? We're locked out of a secure unit.'

We both started laughing again, so loudly that a hospital porter came out of a side door to see what the noise was.

'What are you doing here?' he said angrily. 'Go home.'

'We are home,' Katie said. 'We're from the unit upstairs. Could you let us back in?'

'Don't be stupid,' the porter said. 'Go home or I'll call security.'

We ran round to the front of the hospital, where we paused for breath. I looked at my watch. It was nearly five thirty and visiting time was due to start.

'We'll have to pretend we're visitors,' I said. 'Come on.'

We walked in and retraced the route I had taken with my mother six months earlier. This time we held hands as we ran along the corridor, enjoying a rare sense of euphoria. When we came to the flight of stairs that led up to the unit, we joined the queue of people waiting on the stairs. A couple of regular visitors did double takes as they saw us. I kept my head down until I heard the sound of the door being unlocked and the file of people moved forward.

As we reached the top of the stairs we saw Raj standing at the door. We'd almost made it through when Theresa, one of the other patients, spotted us.

'Ooh, look at you two,' she said. Raj did.

'You two – nurses' office – *now*,' he shouted.

We ran along the corridor to the nurses' office, still

laughing. It was worth the telling off we'd be given – we'd had a real laugh.

A couple of days later it was New Year's Eve. We'd gone to bed, but we got up at five to midnight to see the new year in. We both felt hopeful that 1986 might bring us some happiness and a chance to make something of our lives.

It was a strange feeling to be linking arms with the other patients and staff as we sang 'Auld Lang Syne'. There was an invisible link of sadness and hope that held us together. I made a wish to myself that this would be a new start for all of us.

On New Year's Day the ward slowly began to fill up again. Most of the patients who were returning after a break looked dreadful. I was puzzled; I thought they'd come back looking rested and happy, but it seemed that a lot of them had gone back to their old habits over Christmas, abusing drink, drugs or food. The privilege of going home had put their treatment back weeks.

Before the end of the morning we were called to another emergency community meeting in which we were told that one of the patients, a man called Ian, had hanged himself on New Year's Eve, leaving a note for his parents to say that he couldn't face another year.

There was an uneasy silence around the unit as we left the meeting and went into our separate therapy groups. Ian hadn't been under Dr Harvey, so no one in our group knew him very well. But we still felt guilty that we hadn't been able to reach out and help him. It made us realise, once again, that we all walked a tightrope between life and death. It seemed no more than chance that Ian had slipped off and not one of the rest of us.

The events of the past few weeks involving Stephen, Maureen and now Ian were lodged in all of our minds. We realised that the security that was around us in the hospital didn't mean much if there was no peace in your self.

After the grim Christmas period I hoped January would be better. But it wasn't. I watched in horror as Katie slowly deteriorated. I could see it happening before my eyes, yet I couldn't reach her. No one could. The anger that she felt, which had erupted in her attack on Luke, became more and more evident. It was as though, now that the pressure valve inside her had been released, she couldn't shut it down again. Whereas before she had turned the anger she felt against herself, by cutting her arms, now she was violently attacking anyone who provoked her.

I seemed to be the only person that she hadn't attacked and Amy asked me to try to get through to her when she was calmer. I did try, but it made no difference. Katie had become uncontrollably bitter, especially towards men.

One night, towards the end of January, I went to bed, leaving Katie alone in the music room, as no amount of persuasion would get her to come with me.

At about one thirty in the morning I was woken up by the sound of screaming outside the hospital. I jumped from my bed, and rushed to the window to look out. I saw someone standing in the middle of the main road, wearing only a night-dress and screaming obscenities at the top of her voice. Cars were swerving violently to avoid her.

I knew immediately who it was. 'It's Katie,' I shouted, 'Oh God, let me get to her.'

By now there was a large group of patients and several nurses all trying to see what was going on. I pushed my way through the group and began to run down the corridor. A couple of nurses ran after me and held me back, while Simon, the night charge nurse, dashed outside with several security staff.

Unable to go out to her, I went back to the window. By this stage a motorist had stopped to avoid knocking her down, and Katie had begun kicking his car. When the driver got out of the car to see what was going on, she began a violent attack on him, punching, kicking and scratching at his face.

Katie was dragged back inside by Simon and the security guards and put into seclusion, while Dr Harvey and the police were called. In the end no charges were brought against her, but Dr Harvey decided that she needed to be somewhere with better security for her own safety. The next morning she was put into an ambulance and sent back to the hospital in north Wales. We never had the chance to say goodbye.

I felt devastated. I kept thinking that if only I hadn't left her alone in the music room then it might never have happened. I felt I had let her down and hoped that she would one day forgive me. Katie had been the one person I was closest to and trusted most and I didn't know if I could face being in the unit without her. It felt as though the bottom had fallen out of my world and I began to sink into a deep depression.

The staff and patients did their best to comfort and support me, but life just wasn't the same without Katie. I missed her humour, her warmth and her fighting spirit. I had never loved anyone as much as I loved her – except perhaps my dad – and I felt bereft.

My mood wasn't helped by a visit to a gynaecologist a few

weeks after Katie left. I'd always had painful periods, but they were getting worse and I had mentioned it to Amy, hoping that she could give me some stronger painkillers. She had reported it to Dr Harvey, who had recommended that I be taken to Queen Charlotte's Hospital for a specialist examination.

The day of my appointment was the first time I'd been out of the hospital in well over six months. Helen drove me there and we travelled in silence as I tried to take in the enormity of the world around me – people and cars and noise. I watched it all flash by and felt pleased that I was no longer living in it. I was in a cocoon in the hospital and the outside world suddenly seemed large and dangerous.

I was relieved that the gynaecologist was a woman. I had been terrified that it might be a man and I didn't know whether I could face that. After examining me she said, 'There is some internal damage. We'll need to do some further tests, of course, before I can confirm the extent of it and make some recommendations about how we can help you with your periods.'

'Can I have a hysterectomy?' I asked. I hadn't planned to say it, but I felt I wanted to be rid of the part of me that caused such a lot of pain every month and which was such a fundamental part of being a woman. After all, I hadn't had a lot of joy from being a woman.

The doctor looked taken aback.

'I would never recommend such an operation on someone as young as you,' she answered. 'Don't you want children?'

'Could I have them now, even if I did?' I replied.

'I don't know. You have considerable damage inside, but it's too early to say without the tests. Let me put it another way: would you want children if you could have them?'

'No,' I replied. The idea frightened me. I would be so afraid of getting it wrong and I felt that by having lost two babies I had already somehow failed as a parent.

The doctor prescribed some painkillers and said she'd refer me for tests and Helen and I returned to the hospital.

I did have further tests a few weeks later, and they revealed that a considerable amount of scar tissue was a contributing factor to my painful periods and would also have an impact on how successful any future pregnancy was. I was told to think about the hysterectomy and come back in a few years if I still wanted it, as it was too big a step for such a young girl.

When Helen and I got back to the hospital I went straight to bed. The dark cloud of depression had still not lifted and I felt that all I wanted to do was sleep for ever. Nothing seemed worth bothering with now that Katie had gone.

I slept for several hours and was awoken by a hand on my shoulder. I opened my eyes expecting to see Dawn or Amy but it was another patient, Dina, who was standing next to me smiling.

'Are you getting up again today?' she asked.

I didn't answer.

'I know I'm not Katie,' she went on, 'but I do want to be your friend.'

I was surprised, and sat up in bed. She leaned over and hugged me – it felt strange but somehow comforting.

'OK, I'll get up,' I answered. I didn't really want to, but I didn't like to be rude to her.

We went into the music room and I sat on the window ledge in my normal place. I hadn't sat there much since Katie had left as it didn't seem right without her. Dina sat in the armchair, we put some music on and, bit by bit, began talking.

Dina was twenty-five years old, mixed race and attractive. I hadn't had much to do with her up to now, as she spent a lot of time on her own, reading. She explained that she'd had a nervous breakdown a couple of months earlier. Like me, she'd been adopted and she had recently met her natural mother for the first time. She said it had been a dreadful experience, as her mother had rejected her once again. I listened with horror as she recounted the story, and told her how sorry I was.

Dina changed the subject. 'So, Sophie,' she began, 'how long have you known that you're gay?'

I laughed nervously, startled by her words, although I tried to appear unperturbed.

'You are gay, aren't you?' Dina continued.

'What makes you say that?' I replied cautiously.

'Oh,' Dina said. 'I just assumed that you and Katie were an item, in the same way that Mary and Gina are, and I am with my girlfriend Roz. I'm sorry if I've jumped to the wrong conclusion.'

'Oh no, don't apologise. You just took me by surprise, that's all. I didn't realise that you and Roz were together.'

Dina smiled. 'We've been together for just over a year now. She's been very good to me, she visits me every day, but sometimes I think that it's only my depression that's kept us together.'

Roz was a striking-looking woman in her forties whom I had seen a number of times. Dina explained that she was afraid Roz would end the relationship once she had recovered. She was so scared of losing Roz that this actually stopped her from getting better.

I felt sad as I listened to her. I'd heard this fear before from others who talked in the group about feeling that their partners were just waiting for them to be strong enough to be able to face the relationship ending. It scared them so much that they clung on to their depression and mental illness for fear of losing the one person that they felt loved them. I used to think that at least I was alone, so that was one problem I didn't have.

Dina and I chatted for over two hours. We talked about adoption, depression, suicidal thoughts, self-harm and our distrust of men. But we also talked about simpler things, like what books we had read. That felt good. It had been easy to forget, sometimes, that there was more to life than counselling and group therapy. Everyday conversation was a rare thing in the unit, where conversation so often centred on the grim side of our lives.

Katie and I had often talked openly about self-harm and then realised that visitors were overhearing and beginning to look uncomfortable. It was only at that point we remembered slicing at yourself with a razor blade wasn't normal conversation in the 'real' world. Katie being Katie played up to it, saying the most outrageous things. We would time how long it took the visitor to move away from us.

Dina and I talked until Dawn came to say it was dinner time. We had begun to form a friendship. Not one that could replace what I felt for Katie, and I knew I was no substitute for Roz. However, it was good to have an ally in the hospital that I felt I could start to trust again.

I never did answer Dina's original question about how long I had known that I was gay, because I was confused. Did hating men mean you ended up loving women? Was my closeness to Katie something more than friendship? There were too many questions buzzing around in my head, and I didn't know the answers.

17

Nothing to Lose

Dear Sophie,
Hiya babes!

Well life isn't much fun in 'ere. I miss you so much, really I do. They say that if I behave myself for a while then I can come back. I do want to come back because it is the only place where I know I can be helped. You're in the best place, babes.

How is Dawn? I did write to her but she hasn't replied yet. If only I could see her and tell her how much I care and tell you the same. If I didn't love you so much, I wouldn't mind about not coming back, or not wanting to get better.

Not much has happened since I last wrote. One of the patients got a video in last night called *Nightmare On Elm Street* – what a mistake. Quite a few patients were really disturbed by it. We only have three seclusion cells here, and nine people needed seclusion! Well, that was a night to remember. I didn't get any sleep whatsoever, and I had 200mg of chlorpromazine (are you still on that?).

This morning at the breakfast table this lad (who stabbed his brother) threatened to hit me, so I lost my temper (after he threw a punch) and I picked up a knife, and nearly put it in the bastard's back! I got jumped on by seven staff – I still don't know where they came from. It's the first outburst I've had since I've been here – not bad eh?

I've had some bad news. My mum's had a nervous breakdown again and she's in a psycho hospital in York. She wants me to live with her after we both get out, but I know it won't work. What do you do? Anyway, that's enough of my worries. You have enough of your own without me adding to them.

I'll close for now. Write soon. Keep your head up high and keep smiling. Life can only get better! Who am I kidding?

I'm always thinking about you,

Love you always,

Your big sister Katie, xxx

I read the letter several times. It was so good to hear from Katie. I could see she was trying to put a brave face on what had happened, and that she wanted to come back. I just hoped that she could be strong enough to keep her temper under wraps. There was no way that Dr Harvey would let her back until she calmed down.

It had been a difficult few weeks since she left. Although we wrote to each other every day it wasn't the same and I felt lost without her. Around this time, I also received a couple of postcards from my father. It hurt to hear what a wonderful time he was having. So much for sorting his head out. There was no mention of that or anything that he felt, only the good times he was enjoying.

The combination of Katie's absence and Dad's cards left me so low that the nurses had to force me to get out of bed every day. I didn't want to talk anymore. Katie had talked far more than I had and it hadn't got her very far.

Talking about what had happened didn't make the pain and the hurt that I felt go away. In fact, it just made me feel worse because it brought painful memories and feelings to the surface, and I had no idea how to deal with them. All I wanted to do was sleep all day and all night. Dr Harvey increased my medication in order to alleviate the depression, but the cloud didn't lift from over me.

I wished that I could wake up one morning and find the painful memories of what my dad and his friends had done wiped from my mind – but they were always there. I relived what had happened again and again and it hurt just as much every time. It was like having the same nightmare over and over.

I wrote a poem, which I read to Dawn.

> My world is spinning round and round,
> I'm feeling so confused,
> For after all that's happened,
> My heart's still feeling bruised.
>
> And when I think about the past,
> And look at what I've gained,
> I wonder if it's worth the fight,
> My hurt has still remained.
>
> I want my wounds to heal again,
> I want to be alright,
> But by myself, I just can't bear,
> To stand alone and fight.

> I wish someone could stand with me,
> And help me to survive,
> So, if my fire of hope runs down,
> They'll keep the flames alive.

'Is this all to do with Katie going?' Dawn asked.

'Not all of it. Katie leaving just made it worse,' I answered.

'Let's talk about it,' she replied, taking my hand and leading me along the corridor and into the room where we had our group meetings. She gestured for me to sit down, drew a chair up close to me and took my hand.

'Come on, my love,' she said. 'I think we need to talk.'

I nodded.

'Let's start with your dad. Do you want to talk about what happened?'

I didn't answer. I couldn't see the point of going over it again. Dawn seemed to understand.

'We don't need to talk about what he did to you, unless you want to, that is?'

I shook my head.

'Let's talk about how you actually feel, and how he made you feel. From what you said in the poem it sounds like you feel very alone. How long have you felt like that?'

'For years and years now I can't remember when it started,' I replied.

'Do you not feel that anyone cares for you?' she asked.

I paused for a moment.

'My dad cares for me and I think Fran does. Fran is my friend at the Samaritans.'

Dawn nodded. 'Anyone else? How about your mum?'

'Which one?' I asked.

'Either,' Dawn said.

'Well, one doesn't care what happens to me and the other doesn't know me. We haven't even met.'

'Why do you think your adopted mum doesn't care?'

'For a start, she left me without even telling me. How far back do you want me to go?' I asked.

'As far as you want,' Dawn answered.

'She didn't just let me down, she let my dad down too. She was never a proper wife to him. It's no wonder that he had to look elsewhere,' I said hotly.

'Elsewhere being you, I suppose?' Dawn said.

'Well, yes,' I replied. 'I ended up taking her place. I was left doing the cooking, washing, cleaning, shopping . . .'

'Having sex?' Dawn interrupted.

'Yes,' I answered, 'you know that.'

'You seem to think that you were just performing the duties of a wife. Do you think that husbands would normally inflict the type of pain that he put you through on their wives?' Dawn asked.

'I don't know,' I replied.

Dawn was silent for a moment.

'Do you think that most fathers do what he did with their daughters?'

'No,' I answered.

'So what's made him different from other fathers?'

'What's made me different, you mean,' I laughed as I spoke, because I was nervous.

'How do you mean?' Dawn continued.

'Well, it's more to do with me that it happened, it has to be. Remember, it wasn't just him, it was his friends as well.'

'So? What does that mean?'

'It means that it's me and not my dad. It's something that I obviously do, it's a signal that I give out, without knowing it, that people can read.'

'Did your dad tell you that?' Dawn asked.

'I can't remember who told me,' I said. 'But it's true. Look at what happened when I ran away from here with Katie.'

Dawn nodded. 'Go on,' she said.

'Well, a complete stranger approached me, at the station, for sex. There were hundreds of people there and he approached me. It's not the first time it's happened either. I've lost count of how many strangers I've had sex with now. So it's got to be something about me, hasn't it?'

Dawn was silent for a moment before she spoke.

'It's not anything that you do, Sophie. You just have no respect for your body anymore. You seem to think that the only way you can get love and attention is if you have sex with someone.'

'It's the only thing I'm good for,' I replied.

'No it's not, you have a lot to give. People do love and care for you, for who you are, and not for what they can get from you – you have to realise that.'

I smiled at Dawn. She was trying hard to convince me but I couldn't believe what she was saying, even though I'd have liked to.

'So, on to your natural mother. Do you feel you want to meet her yet?' she asked.

I shook my head. 'No, not while I'm like this.'

Dawn nodded. 'How do you feel towards her?'

'I think about her a lot. I wrote her a poem.'

'Why don't you send it to her?'

'I'd better not,' I answered. 'Maybe I'll show her one day.'

Dawn nodded. 'I think it might be a good idea for you to meet her now. Why don't you write to her and see if she'd like to meet?'

'What if she rejects me?' I asked.

'If she does at least you'll have our support to get through it. And perhaps she won't reject you. She might want to get to know you.'

I laughed at what I considered Dawn's naiveté. 'Listen,' I said, 'she's already rejected me once before, remember? When I was a baby. If she could do it then, she can do it now. Anyway,' I continued, 'mothers are like that, in my experience. When the going gets tough, they're gone.'

Dawn smiled. 'Oh well,' she said. 'It's got to be worth a try. After all, you've got nothing to lose. If it works out then you'll be pleasantly surprised, won't you? And if it doesn't then it's only what you've expected.'

I shrugged my shoulders. 'Maybe. I'll think about it,' I replied.

The seed had been planted. Dawn was right, I thought, I didn't have anything to lose. Maybe I would test the water and send a letter to my birth mother suggesting we should meet. She would probably prove to be unreliable or uninterested, but it was worth a try.

18

Going Back to the Start

I had first traced my birth mother just before I came into the hospital. It had been my social worker, Jane, who suggested it and once I decided to go ahead it had only taken a day to find her, by looking through the records at Somerset House.

I found my birth certificate first, and saw that my real name was Anna, which felt strange. Her name was on the certificate: Juliet Hudson, but the section for the father's name was left blank. Next I found her marriage certificate, and then a birth certificate for her son – my little half-brother. From there it hadn't taken long to find her number in the phone book.

It hadn't been hard to make the call to her, because I fully expected her to tell me to get lost. A man had answered and I asked to speak to Juliet. She picked up the receiver a few seconds later and I said, 'You won't know who this is.' She replied, 'I think I do know,' and went on to say how much she had hoped I would get in touch.

We had a short conversation – neither of us really knew what to say. I told her I was a complete mess and she said she was so sorry, and that she had thought she was doing the right thing by giving me up. 'Your parents have been good to you, haven't they?' she asked. I didn't know what to say.

I told her I would contact her again and then put the phone down and thought, 'Shit, that wasn't supposed to happen.' I felt in shock, and wasn't sure what to do next. I had been ready for a rejection, but not for a mother who might want to know me.

Soon after that I had come into the hospital. Dr Harvey had been told about her, and had asked me whether I'd like to see her, but I'd told him I didn't feel ready. He'd asked me to work through my feelings about her with Dawn and Amy, and to consider seeing her.

Now I felt I could cope with the idea, if she wanted to see me. But I was very worried that I might have the same experience as Dina. What if, despite her interest over the phone, she didn't really want me in her life at all?

Dawn and Amy spent a lot of time, in our daily therapy meetings, exploring the different reactions that I might get and trying to prepare me for a possible rejection. They wanted to make sure that I was strong enough to cope with any outcome. I went through the motions and said the right things, but deep inside my feelings of self-worth were still so low that I didn't care if I was rejected.

Eventually, soon after my seventeenth birthday, it was decided that I was ready, and I phoned my mother again and asked if we could meet. She said yes immediately and arranged for me to meet her outside Charing Cross station at lunchtime on the following day. I was to spend a couple of hours with her in central London and then she agreed to bring me back to the hospital.

I called her on the patients' pay-phone and a queue formed behind me as she got me to write down the registration number and description of the car that she was driving.

She said nothing about me being in the hospital, but I felt very nervous. Would she be disappointed in me? I expected that she would.

In the writing therapy class that day I read out another poem.

> The blade will tear my flesh apart,
> The blood will flow away.
> The wound is deep – I feel no pain,
> My heart fills with dismay.
> And later, when the blood runs dry,
> The scars I'll need to see,
> They'll stay as a reminder,
> Of the badness within me.
>
> And as I rip the flesh apart,
> My thoughts spin round and round.
> Still, my badness lies within,
> My heart begins to pound.
> I see my blood trickling down –
> Trickling down my arm,
> Before, I felt so hurt and sad,
> Now, I'm scared yet calm.
>
> But then, I start to feel so hurt,
> Though there's still no physical pain,
> The hurt is still inside my head,
> So I cut my arm again.

This was the one meeting that I actually enjoyed – one where I could write and not have to speak very much. This time my poem had prompted a discussion about self-harm.

'I cut myself when I feel like that too,' Mary said. 'It's such a release, isn't it? When you see that blood and you feel the pain?'

'I don't even feel the pain after the first cut,' I answered. 'That's why it gets so hard to stop once I've started, because I want to feel pain. I know it's all that I deserve.'

Everyone in the room had hurt themselves in some way. It was the one thing we all had in common.

'Do you feel like hurting yourself at the moment, Sophie?' Amy asked.

'It's always in the back of my mind,' I replied. 'Sometimes the feeling is stronger than others, but it's always there.'

'You haven't answered the question. Do you feel like hurting yourself now?' Amy said.

I nodded and felt tears welling up in my eyes.

'In that case, do you think it's wise to go and see your natural mother for the first time tomorrow, while you're feeling so vulnerable?' Amy continued.

'There will never be a right time. The sooner I get it over with the better.' I looked up as I spoke. My fellow patients seemed to be nodding in agreement with me.

After the meeting I decided that it would be better if I could try and sleep until the morning to stop the thoughts and worries in my head. But when I eventually got to sleep I had nightmares so Dawn agreed to give me a tablet to sedate me until morning.

I awoke the next day with my heart full of excitement and trepidation. Dawn insisted that I should have breakfast before

I left, but I could only pick at it, I was far too nervous to eat.

I kept telling myself that today the final piece in the jigsaw of my life would be fitted into place. I would at last find the answers that I had been looking for. In my heart, I longed for my mother to welcome me into her life and into a normal family. I saw her as a kind of perfect fairy godmother, who would make everything alright again. I'm sure the abandonment I suffered from my adoptive mother fuelled this fantasy of a mother who would truly want me and love me – a fantasy no real woman could live up to.

After what seemed like the longest morning of my life, during which I paced the corridor so many times that Anna had gratefully received twelve cups of tea from me, the time came to leave. Dawn drove me to Charing Cross and then tried to find somewhere to park so that she could wait with me.

'Don't wait, Dawn,' I said, in a brightly confident manner. 'I'll be fine. It will be hard to get a parking space anywhere today. I promise I'll be OK waiting on my own.'

Dawn, who probably wasn't fooled by my false buoyancy, seemed reluctant to leave me but as it really was impossible to park she agreed to drop me off.

'Promise you'll ring me if there are any problems, so that I can come and get you straight away,' she said. 'I don't want you going walkabout on your own round here.'

I smiled. 'Don't worry, I'll call you if I need to, I promise.'

'OK then, kid, you'd better get going then. You don't want to be late. Good luck.' I got out of the car and Dawn waved as she drove off.

I walked to the front of the station where my mother had

said to wait and stood there, clutching a small bunch of white freesias Dawn had bought for me to give her. There was only five minutes to go. I felt sick, and the noise of the traffic was making my head spin. The streets I had once been so used to now felt like a scary place to be.

Moments later a white car screeched to a halt in front of me. Before I had time to check the registration number, the woman in the driver's seat wound down her window and yelled, 'Quick, jump in. I can't stop here.' I ran around to the passenger side and scrambled into the car. We sped off and I looked over at the driver. As soon as I saw her face I knew that she was my mother. It felt as though I was looking at a mirror image of myself.

There was no big emotional greeting, like you see in films, where people are running across a station concourse with their arms outstretched. I had somehow imagined it would be that way even though I knew she was picking me up in a car, and I felt a twinge of disappointment.

Meanwhile, Juliet was talking non-stop. Being in the hospital had made me comfortable with silences and her chatter felt like constant buzzing. I tried to tune in to her words.

'Where do you want to go?' she was saying.

'Somewhere quiet where we can talk,' I answered.

'I know . . . there's a place on the South Bank overlooking the river. Will that be alright?'

'Yes, fine,' I answered politely.

She had a very well-spoken accent. I had been aware of it on the phone and was now doing my best to try and drop my south London drawl.

'I wonder if I'd have such a well-spoken accent as you if I'd stayed with you,' I said. I started to laugh nervously as I had been thinking these words to myself and couldn't believe I had actually said them.

She smiled. 'Well-spoken? Me? Anyway there's nothing wrong with the way that you speak – it's nice.'

She chatted away until we reached the South Bank, where she found a car park. We both got out of the car and it was then, for the first time in seventeen years, that she held me in her arms again. It was a long embrace and when we finally pulled apart I could see that her eyes looked glassy. I still wasn't sure what I was feeling.

It was then that I noticed that she was now holding a small bunch of white freesias.

'Snap!' I said, as I gave her my bunch, which had been squashed during our embrace.

She laughed, and we swapped flowers.

'Come on, I'll get you a coffee.' She headed towards a coffee bar and I began to hurry after her. A few minutes later we had settled at a table overlooking the river.

'You look hot,' she said. 'Why not take your jacket off?'

I froze. Three years of self-harm sat under my jacket. I couldn't risk being rejected this early on.

'I'm fine,' I said.

'I've been so nervous,' she said. 'I couldn't sleep a wink last night. In the end I had to get up as I was driving James mad. Did you sleep OK?'

I nodded. I guessed this wasn't the time to tell her about the medication. I had all kinds of questions I wanted to ask, but I didn't know where to start. I needn't have worried, though. She was happy to talk, and to fill in some of the blanks. She told me that she had married a man called James a couple of years after giving me up for adoption. They lived in Essex and had a son, David, who was ten. It had seemed strange to hear about my half-brother – a half-brother who knew nothing of my existence.

She said that when she first met James she had told him that she had a daughter and he had been surprised to learn that she had given me up. He had assumed that I was still around and was ready to treat me as one of his own.

There was a pause. This was it. I had to ask the only question that really mattered.

'Why did you give me up then?' I blurted.

'I really believed I'd be giving you a better chance in life.' She paused. 'I met your father when I was working in Switzerland. I was a nanny there and he was working as an engineer. He was Italian.'

'What was his name?' I asked.

'Joseph,' she replied. 'He spoke no English and I spoke no Italian. We communicated in French. It wasn't a one-night stand or anything – we had a good relationship and we were in love.'

She stopped to sip her coffee. She looked nervous.

'So what happened? Please tell me. I won't be angry or upset but I need to know.'

She put down the cup. 'Well, when I found out I was pregnant I panicked. I knew that Joseph would want us to marry, and I just wasn't ready for that. So I finished the relationship and came straight back to England. Joseph never knew that I was expecting his baby.'

I was silent as I tried to digest all that she was saying to me.

'I came back to England with the intention of keeping you. I told my brother in confidence, but he told our parents, and all hell broke loose. They didn't want me to keep you. They convinced me that it would ruin my life and yours as well. They said that it would be fairer for you if you had the chance to be brought up by two parents instead of one. I believed they were right. But from the little I know already, I obviously made the wrong decision. I know that sorry won't mean much now – but I am sorry.'

'That's OK,' I said. However, this was tearing me apart and I felt far from OK.

'Was it hard to give birth to a baby and then give it up?' I asked.

'Yes, of course it was, and I didn't give you up straight away. After you were born I couldn't decide, so you ended up being fostered for a while. If my parents had been more supportive then I would have kept you – I have no doubt of that in my mind.'

She looked relieved as she finished speaking. She had answered the questions she had probably been dreading for seventeen years.

'Have you got any photos of David on you?' I asked. I wanted to see what my half-brother looked like.

She produced a photo out of her bag and handed it to me. 'You can keep it if you like,' she said.

This must mean she isn't going to see me again, I thought. I looked at the photo intently. He just looked like any other ten-year-old boy. I began to study the background to see what sort of house it was.

Juliet seemed to sense what I was doing. 'It's a three-bedroom bungalow, nothing grand,' she explained.

I felt embarrassed. 'Oh, I'm sorry, I didn't mean to be nosy. I'm just interested,' I said apologetically. My mind was racing.

This might have been my home. This might have been my life.

'Why a bungalow?' I asked.

'For James's wheelchair,' she answered

'Sorry,' I replied. 'I didn't realise, you never said, not that you had to.' I was beginning to stumble over my words.

'That's alright, I never think of telling people because I don't think of him as any different – it's just a different way of getting about.'

'Yes, of course.' I felt my face flush and I wanted the ground to open and swallow me up.

I began to apologise once more, but she was speaking again. 'I met James when I was visiting a friend of mine in Stoke Mandeville Hospital. James was in there recovering from a broken back after a car crash. He was there for two years and is paralysed from the waist down. After my friend came out of hospital I continued to visit him. James received a large amount of money as compensation for the crash and after this came through he married a nurse on the ward who had been caring for him.'

I sat in silence, afraid to say anything in case it came out wrong.

'Anyway, when the money ran out and it came to the time when James was to leave the hospital, the marriage broke up. The rest is history, really. We fell in love, were married and had David.'

'Wow, what a romantic story.'

She smiled. 'Would you like another coffee?'

'No thanks,' I replied. The combination of caffeine and my medication sometimes made me high. I needed to stay calm if I was going to stop her rejecting me.

'Or something to eat, maybe?' she continued.

'No, thanks, I'm on a diet.'

'So am I – again!' she said.

We both laughed. We were both overweight and it was such a relief to identify with someone who was big like me. My adoptive parents were both very slim.

I wasn't on a diet, but food was a major issue for me and I found it hard to eat in public. Dad had always used food as a weapon and a bribe, first feeding me endless sweets as a child, then telling me I was too fat, then withholding food in return for sexual favours, under the guise of teaching me how to 'manage a budget'. For much of the two years before I went into hospital I had either been hungry or gorged on whatever I was given, not knowing when I would eat again. As a result I felt ashamed of my size and embarrassed about eating in front of anyone else.

'At least you know where you've inherited your size from now,' Juliet joked. 'You can blame me for that too.'

'Did I say that I blamed you for anything then?' I spoke calmly but inside I was in turmoil. It felt like a raw nerve had been exposed. I swallowed hard.

'I wouldn't blame you if you were angry with me,' she replied.

'I don't blame you. I don't blame anyone.' I was saying what I thought she wanted to hear. I couldn't let her see that there was a part of me that felt angry at everyone.

'Are you annoyed that I haven't told David about you?' she asked.

'No, not at all,' I lied. Why would she tell my brother when she wasn't going to see me again?

'I will tell him when the time is right. I'm not ashamed of

you,' she said. 'And I'll tell my parents, too. The important thing is that I can see you and get to know you before I have to share you with everybody else.'

I wished that I could believe her. I wanted to, but I couldn't trust her yet. I couldn't allow myself to be hurt by her.

I knew that she wanted to know what had happened to me and why I had ended up in a psychiatric hospital, yet she was too afraid – or perhaps too sensitive – to ask. The question hung in the air between us all afternoon. I certainly wasn't going to volunteer any information. I didn't want to put her off me completely before she'd had a chance to get to know me, if that's what she really wanted.

I was due back at the hospital. In the car Juliet chattered on and I tuned out for most of it. I felt mentally exhausted and spent the time replaying the moment when I first saw her over and over again. It had been a once-in-a-lifetime experience; one that I knew would always stay with me.

We parted company at the hospital and she promised that we would meet again soon. I wanted to believe her, but the fear that I would be rejected was still there.

As I walked along the corridor of the main hospital on my way back to the unit, I noticed a sign to the hospital chapel. On impulse I went in. It was tiny, just two rows of pews and an altar at the front. There was no one else in there, so I sat down and closed my eyes, taking in the stillness of my surroundings. I replayed the day back in my head and found myself saying 'thank you' for being brought safely home.

I went up to the unit. I knew everyone would want to know what my mother was like, and how I had got on with her and I couldn't wait to tell them how well it had gone. Maybe this would be the beginning of some new-found happiness. Maybe this new mother – my birth mother – would give me what I so badly needed.

19

Letting Go

Inevitably, perhaps, the bubble burst. I had secretly dreamed that my real mother would get me out of hospital and welcome me back into her family. I wanted her to be perfect, and to make everything alright for me, but of course she could never do that.

She did write to me and I wrote back. Her letters were warm and she made it clear she wanted me in her life. But despite our promising start, I found that hard to believe or accept and I refused to let her in or get close to her. I 'tested' her feelings for me by insisting that she tell her son about me immediately, and then felt she had failed me when she wrote to say she was waiting for the right time. I convinced myself that because she was 'posh' and I was in a nuthouse, I wasn't good enough for her.

In reality she couldn't win. Her parents, who had been instrumental in having me adopted, were still alive and she had a young son. So it was understandable that she might want to take her time about telling them that her long-lost daughter had turned up in a psychiatric unit, in a very unbalanced and fragile state. But I didn't want to wait and pushed for positive action and acceptance, as proof that she cared. I think she really did care, but she couldn't fulfil all my expectations.

I remained cool towards her and gave her every opportunity to back off. She asked to visit me, but I said no. Eventually, because she didn't know what I really wanted, she did back off – thus fulfilling my prophecy that I wasn't worth it and was too much for her, and confirming, in my mind, that I had been right to expect rejection.

With hindsight I can see that she was in an impossible situation, but at the time I simply felt that here was one more person letting me down. I felt angry and hurt. And no doubt my feelings for her were further confused by my feelings of betrayal and anger towards my adoptive mother.

Dr Harvey decided I needed more intensive therapy to work through my feelings about her, and put me into one-to-one counselling with one of the nursing sisters. We had an hour together each day and I talked at great length about how I had felt when we met and how I had come back down to earth with a bump afterwards.

Refusing, or unable, to see that my mother did want contact with me, I found it hard to cope with what felt like yet another let-down in my life. Once again I blamed myself for not being good enough and I even managed to self-harm again by finding a sharp edge on my hospital locker and pushing my arm into it as I lay in bed one night. As a result I was reported to Dr Harvey and was put on 24/7 watch, which meant a nurse was with me at all times.

Even that didn't seem intimidating or scary anymore. I had been in hospital for nearly a year now and was used to going to the toilet or having a bath with the door unlocked. Staff would pop in at regular intervals to ensure I was safe, and more often than not another woman patient would be sitting by the side of the bath on a stool, chatting and keeping me company. It was common practice for patients of the same sex to sit and talk while one of them was bathing. Inhibitions about our bodies quickly vanished and it was only when new patients expressed shock at this that I was reminded of how I'd once felt.

Now things were so different. Routines which once seemed loopy or scary were completely normal to me. I felt safe and protected and the unit was my home.

Katie and I still wrote to each other two or three times a week. I still missed her terribly and hoped she might be allowed back. Her letters and those I received from Fran, my Samaritan friend, were my lifelines. In my darkest moments I would take them out and reread them to comfort myself. Fran also called me, at a prearranged time, twice a week. It was the highlight of my week when, as I was sitting in the television room in the evening, someone would shout out that there was a phone call for me. 'For me?' I would always say in a surprised voice, getting out of my chair. I was always touched that Fran was still there for me, loyal, supportive and dependable. She was the closest that I had to what I believed a real mother should be – someone who would love me and accept me for who I was and who would always stand by me. I used to wish that I had met her outside the Samaritans, so that maybe she could have adopted me. I was certain that if she did, my past would be healed and my life would be good again.

Some of the patients spent every night on the phone to friends and family and had visitors on a daily or weekly basis. I never had any visitors. Katie never had any either and we used to shut ourselves away in the music room at visiting times. It didn't hurt too much, when we had each other, but with Katie gone I felt I was the only patient who had no one. It was during this difficult time, as we were finishing one of the group therapy sessions, that Dawn dropped a bombshell.

'I'm going to start a workshop solely for those of you who have been sexually abused, in which I hope you'll feel able to talk about your experiences in more depth.'

There was complete silence, until eventually Gina spoke.

'And you think that will help, do you? Raking up the past? It's never helped us before has it?' she asked, sarcastically.

'This will be different. Up to now you've been in groups with people with all kinds of difficulties. It should be easier to talk if you're with people who have been through similar experiences,' Dawn explained.

'We'll see,' replied Gina.

'The first group will be tomorrow,' Dawn said. 'Please will the following people attend: Gina, Mary, Dina, Sophie, Theresa and Claire.'

We left the room in silence. I felt something close to panic. This sounded like it could be hard for all of us.

The next day the six of us sat in the therapy room with Dawn and Helen. At first no one spoke. Then Theresa began to talk. She was one of the newer patients and seemed quite keen on opening up in the therapy groups.

'I was abused by my next-door neighbour who used to babysit me,' she said. 'He had sex with me over a period of four years.'

Gina and I shuffled uneasily in our chairs as she spoke. Her openness was both refreshing and unnerving.

'When you say sex,' Dawn asked, 'what exactly did he do?'

'Is this absolutely necessary?' I found myself saying. 'I think we know what Theresa means.' I could hear that I sounded like some kind of prude but I had to stop her; if Dawn got details from Theresa she would expect them from the rest of us.

'Maybe we do,' replied Dawn, 'but I want Theresa to tell us what happened.'

I sighed loudly as Theresa began to speak again. 'He had full intercourse with me,' she explained.

We sat in silence as Theresa described her experiences in great detail. She spoke as if she was talking about someone else's life, and her voice never once faltered or broke. I wondered how she had managed to block out all her feelings about it. I decided that either she didn't believe that it had happened to her at all and was in denial, or she was on strong medication. Whatever it was, I wished that I knew her secret.

I hoped Theresa might take up the whole time, but she finished speaking and Dawn moved on to Dina. I was next to her, and my head started spinning as I struggled to think what to say.

'Right, Sophie,' Dawn said a few minutes later. 'Would you like to tell us about what your father did to you?'

'I've said it already, many times now,' I said solemnly.

'I'm sure you haven't shared everything with us,' Dawn replied. 'Try to share with us something that you find really difficult to talk about, something that he or his friends did that you have never shared before. Can you think of anything?'

I was silent, as the feature film of unshared memories started to play in my head.

'We'll move on,' Helen said, 'and come back to you in a moment, Sophie. Right, Mary, what would you like to share with the group today?'

I looked at my watch. If Mary had a lot to say I might still be OK.

'I have a lot of things still in my head about what happened,' Mary said. 'I can cope with the sex part, just about.' Her voice faltered as she spoke. 'It's my dad going out of his way to really hurt me that I can't understand. Why would he want to inflict pain on me? What did I ever do to deserve that?' Mary looked upset and Gina was now holding her hand. The door in my head had been opened.

'I feel like that too, Mary,' I found myself saying. 'I can't understand why my dad did that either.'

'You both know that it wasn't your fault, don't you?' Helen said. 'I know that we've been over this before, but you're still intent on blaming yourselves. Do you think you'll ever stop feeling guilt over what was forced on you?'

'It wasn't forced on me at all,' Mary said. 'I could have said no, I could have screamed at the top of my voice, I could have gone to the police, I could have . . .'

'And why didn't you?' Helen interrupted. 'Was it because you were scared? Was it because you loved your dad too much? Was it because you thought he would stop one day?'

I felt a lump in my throat. I looked around the group and saw that we were all close to tears.

'When it's the only love you have, you'll put up with anything,' I said. The group was silent.

Mary spoke. 'My dad used to beat me after he'd had sex with me. It felt as though I wasn't even good enough for sex. I couldn't even do that right. He used to want to see me cut and bruised and then he'd get excited and have sex with me again.' She began to cry.

'OK Mary, you've done very well. Take a few deep breaths and then I'd like to try something with you,' Dawn said. 'Are you willing to give it a go?'

Mary nodded.

'There must be many things you'd like to say to your dad. Questions that you want to ask?'

Mary nodded again.

Dawn picked up a cushion and put it on to a chair, which she placed directly opposite Mary. 'Right. I want you to imagine that the cushion is your dad sitting in that chair.'

A ripple of nervous laughter went round the group. Dawn sensed our unease. 'I know it seems strange, but after the first few minutes of this you'll see how real it can become.

'Before we start this I want to make clear to you, Mary, that you are perfectly safe. Your father cannot hurt you. We are all here with you.'

'Her father can't hurt her because he is a cushion,' Gina said sarcastically.

There was another ripple of laughter.

'Please, Gina – we need the total support of the group for this to work. Are you ready, Mary? I want you to ask him all the questions that you have in your head.'

Mary began to speak to the cushion.

'Dad, why did you want to hurt me?' she said calmly.

'Go on,' coaxed Dawn.

'Maybe he didn't hear you,' Gina joked.

Mary carried on speaking.

'Dad, why did you have to hurt me so much? Why did you want to make me feel pain? Why did you touch me and not touch any of your other children? Why do you hate me so much?' Her voice had started to shake. I was transfixed. We all were.

'Do you hate your father, Mary?' Helen asked.

Mary nodded.

'Well, tell him how you feel. Now's your chance.'

This time Mary's voice was high and loud as she tried to control her anger.

'Yes, I do hate you, Dad, I hate you for ruining my life, for making me feel worthless and cheap, for making me feel more pain that I should ever feel in my life and for betraying the trust that I had in you. YES I do hate you. I REALLY HATE YOU MORE THAN YOU CAN IMAGINE.'

After screaming those last words she burst into sobs.

The electrifying power that her words had generated swept around the group. We had never seen that kind of anger in Mary before.

Dawn picked up the cushion and gestured towards the chair that the cushion had been on.

'Sit here,' she said. Mary moved over to the chair while Dawn placed the cushion on to Mary's chair.

'Right,' Dawn said. 'The cushion is now Mary and Mary, you are now your father.'

Mary nodded as she wiped the tears from her eyes.

'Right, Dad,' Helen said. 'You've heard what your daughter has to say to you. How do you feel?'

'Empty,' came the reply from Mary.

Suddenly Mary broke down in tears. 'I'm so very sorry at what I've done to you,' she said to the cushion. 'I know it doesn't mean much and I know I don't deserve your forgiveness but I truly am sorry.'

'Tell your daughter why you hate her so much, Dad,' Helen asked.

Mary looked confused. 'Hate her?' she said. 'I don't hate her, I love her – that's why everything went so terribly wrong because I love her too much.'

The role play went on, with Mary and the cushion swapping seats and Mary having a conversation with herself. The conversation that she would never actually have with her father but had always wanted.

As the role play finally ended Mary looked drained and slumped back into her chair.

Watching her had been such a moving experience that many of the group sat and sobbed. I would never have believed that role play using a cushion could evoke so many feelings. After the first few moments of listening to Mary we had forgotten that the cushion was there. It was as if her father was in the room.

Dawn turned to me. 'Right, Sophie, would you like to try the same thing?'

I shook my head.

'You mentioned earlier that your father did things to you that you can't talk about. What did he do?'

I closed my eyes, played the film in my head and found myself answering her.

'He was perverted, he used to like to see me suffer. It would excite him if he made me sick.' I felt the tears well up in my eyes as I spoke.

Dawn placed the cushion on the chair in front of me.

'Here's your dad,' she gestured towards the cushion. 'Tell him how you feel.'

'I love you, Dad.'

'Anything else?' Dawn asked.

'I don't understand, Dad. I don't know why you would want to hurt me so much.' My mouth felt dry.

'What did he do to make you sick?' Dawn said.

I took a deep breath. 'Do you remember, Dad, how my period seemed to make you worse 'cos you said that it made me more of a woman?' The tears were now tumbling down my face.

'Remind him of how bad he used to make you feel,' prompted Dawn.

My voice was becoming shaky. 'Do you remember how you used to take a tampon out of me if I had a period, and force me to hold it in my mouth, while you had sex with me? It used to really excite you, especially if it made me vomit.'

Nausea swept over me. I was afraid I would be sick if I opened my mouth to speak again.

I was suddenly aware of someone else speaking.

'Bastard,' Gina said.

'Don't call him that, Gina, leave him alone.' I glared at Gina. She had attacked my dad and I couldn't allow that to happen.

'Go on, Sophie,' coaxed Dawn. 'Gina – try to stay calm please.'

'You could be so caring,' I continued.

'Oh please!' shouted Gina. 'I can't bear this.'

'Gina, please be quiet or you'll have to leave the room,' Helen said.

Dawn knelt on the floor next to me and squeezed my hand.

'I don't know why you would want me to be sick or want to cut me with a knife or put a broken bottle inside me. I know you liked the blood but you knew the pain was too much for me. You knew I wanted to die. I wonder if you wanted to kill me.' My tears were flowing and I could hear other people crying.

Gina sprang out of her chair and hurled the cushion across the room, before picking it up again, screaming and banging it against the wall. I jumped up and started screaming at her to stop. The phone was ringing and I could hear the key in the door being turned outside.

Dawn and Helen calmed us down. Gina held me tight, sobbing that she was sorry. I felt shaky and very tearful and left the room in a daze. All I wanted was to go to bed.

Dawn gave me the cushion and I lay with it next to me, not touching it but sobbing when I looked at it and realised what it represented – the person who was everything in my life that was good and everything that was bad. My parent, my protector, my best friend – my abuser.

20

Getting There Slowly

Though I would never have believed it in the beginning, the cushion therapy heralded the start of some sort of recovery.

In the following weeks we repeated it many times. In addition I was still having one-to-one counselling every day and group therapy three times a week. I was also still attending the writing and art therapy groups and fitting in my lessons with Miss Smith, who had reported an improved commitment from me since Katie left.

I received my first two visits during this time. The first one was from Fran, who was summoned by Dr Harvey. He wanted to talk to her about how she felt the Samaritans could help me. She told me afterwards that she had told him that Samaritans wanted to work with the hospital and not against them and Dr Harvey seemed happy with her reassurances.

My second visit was more surprising – my adoptive mother turned up for the first time since she had left me in the unit over twelve months earlier. It was an awkward visit. She seemed nervous and wary and although she stayed for about an hour, I could tell that she was itching to leave after five minutes.

There were many things that I wanted to say to her but felt I couldn't. I knew that anything resembling a challenge would upset her, she would cry, become hysterical and I would feel guilty and apologise. It meant that I had never managed to ask her the questions I wanted her to answer, like how much she knew of the abuse and why she had left me with Dad. Instead, we made small talk about the meals in hospital and how her job was. It was tiring and I was glad when she left.

I felt she was almost a stranger to me; I barely knew her, and I hated her. My feelings towards her hadn't changed at all. I felt she was a weak person who had let me down. I was encouraged to work through my feelings about her in the weeks that followed her visit. Dr Harvey wanted to get to the bottom of why I was always trying to be the strong one for both my parents. I had grown up learning to protect each of them, in different ways. All the anger I should have directed at them I turned on myself, and that was the hardest thing to change.

One of the things that helped me most was discovering that there were people who liked me for being the person that I was, people who cared for me with no hidden agenda. I had come to believe that there would always be a catch, but the patients I grew close to in the hospital helped me to change that view. Dr Harvey seemed pleased by my progress and the fact that I was at last able to talk in groups about what my father had done to me. Many cushion therapies followed and while I still apologised for my father and excused him, I was beginning to learn that it really wasn't my fault, and it hadn't been a moment of madness that had made him do it, as I would have liked to believe. Dr Harvey said that they had been cold-blooded and premeditated attacks. So premediated, in fact, that he had been able to involve his friends. It was painful to hear, but I knew it was the truth. Despite all this, I still loved him. And I wasn't alone. Despite all the anger and hatred that some patients felt towards their abusers, for the most part they still loved the person who had hurt them so much. Dr Harvey analysed and theorised, but he couldn't change the way each of us felt.

Katie wrote to say she had decided that she didn't want to come back to the hospital. She had been released from the hospital in north Wales and said that she was strong enough to cope on her own now. However, her letters were sent from a variety of addresses, including the north Wales hospital, where she was readmitted when she found life too much. It was hard to keep track of where she was or what she was doing and I wished that she could come back to the hospital and be with me so that we could take care of each other.

Although I had good friends now, life just wasn't the same without Katie. I often thought back to all the fun we'd had: winding up the teacher, going down the laundry chute and the night we ran away and she took a hairdryer. I loved her and missed her and the days were longer without her.

I used to write and fill her in on the hospital news, and there was one incident in particular that I knew would make her laugh.

A suggestion was put forward in a community meeting by a patient called Steve, who wanted a snooker table. The subject was debated at length over the course of several meetings and the staff eventually agreed that it might serve as a useful recreational activity.

The snooker table was duly installed in the day room. On day one Steve smashed a patient called Barney over the head with a snooker cue. Steve was warned, Barney was stitched and a new cue was ordered. On day two, a patient called Miriam took the pink ball away. Despite a full search it couldn't be found so a new ball was ordered. On day three, a new patient called Jake, who had anger management issues, threw the white ball out the window. Dawn dashed into the room when she heard the sound of breaking glass and asked what had happened. Jake was a keen cricketer and it was reported that the ball was probably in north London by then. Jake was warned and a new ball was ordered. On day four, a patient had a nightmare, got out of bed and ran pell mell through the men's ward and into the day room. He hit the table at full speed, slid over the top of all the balls, potted three reds and landed on the floor with a broken ankle. On day five the table was taken away by the hospital porters and we were issued with a deck of playing cards.

As the months went on it was inevitable that some of my closest friends would be discharged from the hospital, and I found it very unsettling. First Simone went, then Anna, who had finally reached her target weight. Soon after them Gina, Mary and Dina were all sent home. Simone had drawn me a picture and left it on my bed. It was a charcoal drawing of a clown that was crying, with the words 'tears of a clown' written on it. Next to that she had written, 'To my little clown Sophie, love Simone'. I put it on the wall next to my bed and cried myself to sleep at night when I looked at it. It felt as though my home was breaking up again – and this time I was losing a family that was very special.

Most of the patients who had been discharged came back as day patients, arriving at nine and staying until four, but it wasn't the same and they sensed my distress, even though I tried to put on a brave face and crack jokes.

After four the ward buzzed with the noise of new patients who I couldn't be bothered to get to know. I looked on as the friendships between patients grew and the music room, which Katie and I had once believed to be ours, was filled with other people.

I knew that I was approaching the end of my stay in hospital and that it would soon be my turn to be pushed back into the real world. But it was still a shock when Dr Harvey told me that he was going to allow me to have weekend leave.

At first I felt pleased that he considered me well enough to leave for a whole weekend. But then I began to feel afraid and uncertain. Where on earth would I go?

My adoptive mother was out of the question. Although she was living fairly nearby, in south London, I didn't even consider going to stay with her, I was still far too angry and hurt.

My birth mother was out of the question too. We still wrote to one another intermittently, but our relationship had never developed beyond the early stages and I couldn't possibly ask to stay with her.

More than anything else in the world I wanted to stay with Fran, but that was out of the question because of the Samaritans' strict rules about personal contact with clients.

Eventually I wrote to Hazel, the woman I had become friends with at the tennis club. She had always been kind to me – I had her on my list of people who I wished had been my mother (along with Fran, my teacher Miss Thomas, my social worker Jane, and – once I got to the hospital – Dawn). When I first arrived in the hospital, Hazel wrote to me and offered to visit. She wasn't allowed to, but it was good to know she hadn't forgotten me.

That had been a while ago and I realised it might be a surprise for her to get a letter from me out of the blue but I had to start making contact with the outside world, and I couldn't think of anyone else. I waited nervously for her reply, and was ecstatic when she wrote back and invited me to her home for the weekend.

After that I counted down the days on my calendar until the Friday when I was allowed to leave. For once it was me waving to the few lone faces at the window.

Excited and nervous, I got on the train at Clapham Junction. It was an old train with separate small carriages and no adjoining corridor, so the guard had to wait for the train to stop at a station before he could get into the next carriage to check the tickets. Two stops after leaving Clapham Junction the guard got into the carriage where I sat on my own. I showed him my ticket and he sat down in the seat opposite me and started to make conversation. As we approached the next station he smiled and leaned forward. 'Why don't you join me in the guard's van for the rest of the journey?' he asked.

I knew it wasn't a chat that he wanted, but I still nodded in agreement and at the next station, with a sad and heavy sense of inevitability, followed him to the guard's van at the end of the train. After all this time, and all this treatment, I was still instantly identifiable to a predatory man as a girl who might be good for sex. And I was still unable to do anything but dumbly respond. My sense of worthlessness was written all over me, and men like this one could see it, but I didn't think of it in that way. I simply thought I must be truly bad, and being picked out in this way simply confirmed it.

Within moments of pulling out of the station, I was going through the motions of having sex with him. I felt nothing, emotionally or physically – my mind and body had completely switched off.

After the sex he asked me my name. I smiled to myself. Maybe one day I would meet someone who would want to know my name before we had sex.

As I got off the train at the end of my journey he handed me a piece of paper with his phone number on it. I walked towards the ticket barrier and saw Hazel's beaming face. As I hurried through the crowd towards her, I threw the piece of paper he'd given me on to the ground. Hazel hugged me and led me off to her car.

That guard will have to find some other girl, I thought. I've got something better to do.

21

Strangers

The weekend with Hazel was lovely – although inevitably there were difficult moments.

I enjoyed being in a non-institutional environment and doing normal things. We didn't go out – I wasn't used to shopping trips and outings – and I was happy just to spend time with her at home. It was lovely being able to sit and chat; Hazel didn't pry, but made it clear I could talk as much or as little as I wanted. It was a novelty being able to use the bathroom in privacy with the door locked. But at the same time once I had gone to bed it was weird to feel that I couldn't just get up again and wander around, as I had done for years. Hazel's house was still and dark and I felt trapped in my bedroom and slept very little.

Back in group therapy on Monday morning I told them excitedly all about it. Gina, Mary and Dina were still attending the group therapy sessions, as day patients.

'On Saturday night we stayed in watching a film on TV and my friend cooked me a really nice meal,' I said happily.

'That sounds good,' Amy said.

'Oh yes, really riveting,' Gina said sarcastically.

'Well it beats sniffing glue all weekend, which is what you and Mary probably did,' I answered angrily.

Gina grinned back at me, which in turn made me smile.

'So, how was the train journey? Did it seem strange travelling alone on a train after all this time?' Dawn questioned.

I smiled.

'Did you meet anyone?' Mary asked.

'Yes, some bloke – and don't ask me his name because I don't know.'

Mary and Gina began to laugh.

'How much did you get for it?' Mary said.

'Nothing,' I replied.

'God, you're getting cheaper and cheaper, Sophie,' Dina said. 'Don't do it for nothing!'

'Have all of you had sex with strangers?' Helen asked.

We all nodded.

'Right,' said Dawn. 'I think we need to spend some time on this – I want you to share an experience with us and then we'll talk about why you felt you had to do it.'

We looked around at each other anxiously. I didn't mind telling about the men, but I didn't want to talk about why I did it. I wasn't sure I wanted to know, as it felt too painful.

Mary took the plunge first and told a story about a man she'd met at a bus station. He'd taken her to a hotel, had sex with her and started to beat her so violently she was afraid for her life. Luckily her screams had alerted the hotel owner, who banged on the bedroom door and she managed to get out. She had vowed that she would never put herself in that situation again, but had since been picked up by another man in a similar way, and said she didn't know why.

I went next. 'One night when I went to a phone box to

call a friend,' I told the group, 'I was aware of a man waiting to use the phone and it made me feel a bit uneasy. As I left the phone box and held the door open for him, he smiled and thanked me and then asked me if I wanted to go to his party.

'I said yes and he gave me his address. I went home and got changed and ten minutes later I was standing at his front door ringing his doorbell. He seemed surprised – and pleased – to see me.'

'I bet,' said Gina.

I carried on. 'Inside it was very dimly lit and there was a fog of cigarette smoke. There was soft music playing and through the haze I could see a man and woman sitting on a settee, but they got up and said they had to leave. I was surprised as they were the only other people in the room and this was supposed to be a party.'

A ripple of laughter went round the group.

'I asked the man why they were leaving, and he said it was "our party" now, so I knew then that he had just got me there for sex.'

'Don't worry,' Gina said. 'We've all done it.'

I looked around the group to see nods of agreement. Gina, Theresa and Dina went on to share their stories of sex with strangers.

'OK, thanks everyone,' Dawn said. 'Let's talk about feelings now. Who wants to start off by telling us why they slept with a stranger?'

Silence.

Eventually Mary spoke. 'I dunno. I guess I wanted to feel close to someone.'

There was a murmur of agreement from the group.

'I used to do it to punish myself,' Theresa said. 'I wanted to relive what had happened to me with the next-door neighbour 'cos I thought that's all I was good for anyway.'

'How about you, Sophie?' Dawn prompted.

'I wanted to be needed and loved and if someone has sex with you then they must like you and maybe they will then grow to love you,' I replied.

'So did the strangers who had sex with you love you?' Dawn asked.

I shrugged. I knew the answer but I didn't want to say.

'You all need to gain some self-respect,' Dawn said. 'These men don't love you – they just want sex and probably can't believe their luck when you give it so freely. It's not about love for the men who have sex with you and I'm sorry if that's how you see it. We need to build on this in future sessions.'

We dutifully nodded in agreement, although I wasn't sure that I agreed or understood, and the group ended.

'What a load of rubbish,' Gina said after Dawn had left. 'How does she think she's going to give us our self-respect back by just talking about it. I can't ever imagine liking myself again.'

I felt the same way. My feelings of low self-worth went into the very core of my being. That's why I didn't care if I had sex with a stranger. I found it hard to care about what happened to me.

Before we could debate the subject in group again there was a ward round, and Dr Harvey broke the news I had been anticipating – that it would soon be time for me to leave the hospital.

It was ironic, because for the first few months I had longed to get out and dreamed of the day when I would be released.

Yet now it was here I felt so afraid. I didn't want to hear what Dr Harvey was saying.

I didn't feel ready to cope on my own. In many ways I was a different girl to the terrified sixteen-year-old who had arrived. But recovery was such an openended concept, and always consisted of three steps forward and two steps back. Some days I felt stronger and more positive. But on others I felt so low that I didn't care whether I lived or died. I was very affected by the mood of those around me. And it was so easy to slip back to mentally beating myself up, there was a comfort factor in self-harm and suicidal thoughts, while being positive took real effort.

And the hospital had become my home and my security. I didn't want to leave. I felt shaky as I tried to pay attention to what Dr Harvey was saying. 'Although your weekend away went well, Sophie, I don't think you're quite ready to be on your own in the world, do you?'

I shook my head.

'What I suggest is that we get you transferred to a hostel, a halfway house where you will have professional support. The one I have in mind is in Bristol. I've arranged for you to go there tomorrow for two days. Then I'd like you to come back here and we'll see how you got on.'

I left the room with my head spinning at the thought of leaving. I couldn't believe that Dr Harvey was doing this to me when I was beginning to trust him.

The next day I still felt dazed as I made the trip across London to Paddington station where I caught the train to Bristol. I felt scared as I sat on the busy commuter train, surrounded by people in suits. I wondered if they looked at me and saw a messed-up girl, or if I was a woman now. I had no sense of reality or how I might be perceived and it scared me. I had never been to Bristol before and had been told by Dawn to take a taxi from the station to the hostel. I was tempted to keep my taxi money and find a cheaper way to get there, but I was so nervous I felt sick and I knew I hadn't the energy to walk or find a bus.

The taxi pulled up outside a large house. I knocked and the door was opened by a boy of about my age, with a cigarette hanging from his mouth.

'Yeah,' he said.

'I'm Sophie. The hospital sent me.'

He gestured for me to enter the house and ambled away up the corridor. After a few moments a woman appeared, wearing a smart business suit and with immaculate hair and make-up.

'Hello, Sophie, I'm Monica. I manage the hostel although I don't actually live here. In fact, I'm not here very much at all,' she laughed loudly. 'Let me show you to your room.'

She led me along the bare, cold hallway and up two flights of stairs to a large dormitory, containing six beds.

Someone lay in the bed nearest to us, tightly wrapped up in a quilt. 'Come on, Jane,' Monica said. 'You'd better get up sometime today.' There was no reply from the bump under the quilt.

There was a strong smell of burning and fresh paint.

'What's the smell?' I blurted out.

Monica ushered me out of the room, and closed the door behind us. 'Last week Jane got a bit upset and set light to the room in the night.' She must have seen the look of alarm on my face. 'Don't worry, the fire only caused superficial damage and everyone was alright.'

'Oh good,' I said, attempting a smile.

Over the next couple of hours I was introduced to the other residents, many of whom were heavily sedated. I sat in an art therapy class where people threw paint at a canvas to express how they felt. Most of the paint ended up on the floor or on other people. I wondered what that meant.

I was told the residents took it in turns to cook. Today Mark, who had been very depressed, had forgotten to cook. An argument broke out between Mark and another resident who was both angry and hungry. To calm the situation down, a support worker called Grace went out in her car for some fish and chips.

After dinner I sat in the TV room and watched the other residents drinking lager from cans and sniffing glue. The staff were nowhere to be seen. I looked at my watch. It was 6.15 p.m. so I still had just enough time to get back to London. I slipped upstairs to my room, collected my bag and quietly let myself out.

My arrival back at the hospital at ten past midnight was greeted with some surprise. Not that I had left the hostel, because they had eventually noticed I had gone and had alerted the hospital and the police. The surprise was that I had returned straight away and not ended up on the streets, sleeping rough.

Mike, the night charge nurse was euphoric. 'Well done, Sophie, I'm so glad that you've come back straight away, and not hurt yourself. Dr Harvey will be pleased with you.'

My heart sank. This was not the reaction that I had intended. I had hoped that my failure at the hostel would prove that I wasn't ready for the outside world. Instead it was being seen as a great success. I had to do something.

Mike's first mistake was to send me off to bed without searching me. I had bought razor blades in Bristol – just for security, of course. I had expected them to be taken off me, but Mike was so happy with my 'responsible adult behaviour' that he didn't think to check. I went back to my bed and unpacked my bag, slipping the razor blades into my jeans pocket. I picked up my towel and soap bag and walked back along the corridor to where all the night staff chatted and drank coffee.

'Mike,' I said, 'I know it's late but I feel hot and sticky. Can I have a quick bath?'

'Of course you can,' he said. 'Be quick though, it's late.'

'Thanks,' I said, heading along the corridor to the bathroom. 'Don't worry about supervising me, I won't be long.' I called over my shoulder.

That was his second mistake. Any psychiatric patient who asks not to be supervised is up to no good. Everyone knew that, except, it seemed, Mike.

As soon as I got into the bathroom, I began to tear at my skin with the razor blades. I cut my arms and then my legs and then my stomach. I wanted to prove to them that I was unable to cope and at risk. 'You can't release me, please don't release me from here,' I kept repeating as I cut myself over and over again. The pain was excruciating. Not the physical pain, that disappeared after the first cut, but the inner terror I felt. But as I slashed at myself I felt relief and comfort. All I could see was blood. The redness before my eyes became brighter and brighter, the smell of blood stronger and stronger, until the room spun round . . . and then there was nothing.

I awoke the next morning to see Dina sitting on my bed, grinning.

'What are you trying to do? Impersonate an Egyptian mummy?' she said.

I laughed, but it hurt, so I had to stop.

Dina ripped my bedclothes off with a shriek of laughter and when I looked down at myself I saw bandages around my legs and stomach. The night before came back to me; I really had let rip on myself and now I was a painful, bloody mess. But I still felt the sense of relief it had brought me. And if Dr Harvey decided that because of this I wasn't ready to leave, then it would have been worth it, however angry or disappointed in me he might be.

'Come on, get up, it's eleven o'clock and there are still a couple of hours before the ward round when you'll have to face the doc. It's a nice morning. Let's see if we can sit in the grounds outside until we're called.'

I rolled out of bed as this seemed to be the only way to move. Dina helped me to put a baggy tracksuit on. The waistband hurt my stomach so I rolled it down. I started to walk but fell down immediately.

'Hold on,' Dina said. A few moments later she appeared with a wheelchair. I crawled into it and Dina pushed me along to the day room where everyone was having morning coffee.

Dawn saw me and made her way through the throng of patients and smiled at me. 'What a mess you are,' she said as she put her hand gently on my shoulder. 'I don't know – what are we going to do with you?'

As a day patient Dina was allowed into the grounds – with permission. She asked if she could take me outside until the dreaded ward round. Dawn agreed. She said that she figured I had put myself off cutting for a while so I was probably low risk.

Five minutes later Dina and I were sitting in the spring sunshine in the hospital grounds. After about five minutes Theresa joined us. She opened the carrier bag that she had with her and brought out a two-litre bottle of cider and eight cans of lager.

She tossed me a can of lager. 'Drink this before you see the doc. I think you might need it.'

Over the next hour the three of us drank most of the alcohol Theresa had brought. We had a great time – until Dawn came to find me.

'Hello, mate,' Dina shouted as Dawn approached. 'Come an' 'av a beer with us.' Theresa and I started to giggle uncontrollably.

Dawn was angrier than I had ever seen her before. 'Look at the state of you, Sophie. Get in the wheelchair. As for you two – get back on to the ward now.'

She pushed me in silence into the building and up to the room where we had ward rounds. Still without a word she opened the door and pushed me into the centre of the room. My wheelchair came to a halt in front of Dr Harvey.

After what seemed like an eternity he spoke.

'I'm very disappointed in you, Sophie,' he began. 'Yesterday you tried to undo all the progress you have made so far by cutting yourself to pieces. Today you have decided to drink alcohol, which will make you very sick: it doesn't mix with the medication you are on. Do you have anything to say?'

I looked down and tried to keep the tears in as my bottom lip started to tremble.

Dr Harvey carried on. 'It seems to me that the cutting you did was not an expression of your self-hate, as it has been in the past. It was something different yesterday, wasn't it?'

I nodded.

'Do you want to tell me what it was about before you start being sick?' He looked at his watch. 'Judging by the smell of alcohol on you I predict we have about half an hour before you wish you were dead.'

I knew he was angry and it hurt to know I had let him down.

'I cut myself yesterday because I didn't want you to release me,' I said.

Dr Harvey's voice softened.

'I'm glad you are able to admit it. Thank you. Do you remember all those ward rounds where you begged me to let you out of here? Week after week, month after month?'

'I know,' I answered. 'I hated it at first. But now this is the safest place that I've ever been in and I don't want to face the world again. I want to live here for ever. Please don't release me.' I began to sob loudly.

'You're ready, Sophie. You must believe in yourself. The progress you've made has been brilliant.' It was Raj who was speaking.

'I'm not ready,' I shouted. 'Look at all these cuts. Give me a razor and I'll do it again. I feel really, really suicidal.'

Nobody reacted.

'Do you remember what you were like when you came in?' Dawn said softly. 'You were a scared and vulnerable child. You had no self-respect at all and you were intent on destroying yourself twenty-four hours a day. You didn't dare trust anyone, you wouldn't tell us about your past and you were scared of all the staff. You wouldn't let anyone who cared close to you, but you were happy for people who didn't care to hurt you.'

Dawn waited for me to wipe the tears from my eyes and

smiled at me. 'Do you think that the old Sophie would have brought herself back from the hostel in Bristol yesterday? You came back from that hostel because you realised that it was a step backwards for you. A part of you said "this is not for me; I'm better than this", isn't that right?'

I nodded, as I began to understand what she was saying.

'It was a nuthouse, that's why,' I said.

A wave of laughter went round the room.

'And you came back here,' said Dr Harvey. 'You didn't take yourself off to get used and abused on the streets. You've done a good job of cutting yourself – you're scared Sophie, we can all see that, and you wanted us to change our minds. We'll help you in every way we can to face the world again. You've been very strong – and whether you feel it or not, right now, you're nearly there.'

I wanted to sob that this was my home and I had nowhere else to go. But Dr Harvey was bringing the round to an end. He asked me to give some thought to where I might like to go and to come back to him in two weeks.

22

The Big Wide World

Over the next week I resigned myself to leaving the hospital and, while I was scared, there was also a small part of me that believed – no matter how low I felt at times – that I was meant to live and would get through this.

There were too many bad memories in London, so I decided I would make a fresh start somewhere else. I had no idea where, and I was very scared of doing it on my own, but I was determined to manage.

I asked Miss Smith to lend me a map of Britain and I sat on my bed and flicked through it. My eyes finally settled on Basingstoke. I knew nothing about it, but I could see that it wasn't too far from London or from the town where Fran lived.

I got up and found Dawn in the day room.

'Can I go to Basingstoke?'

Dawn looked bemused.

'It's where I want to live. Can you sort out a day trip for me? Tomorrow.' I sounded more sure than I felt.

'Yes, of course,' Dawn said. 'Who do you know in Basingstoke?'

'No one,' I said sadly, as I walked away.

'Sophie,' she called after me. 'We do care, you know. Please don't think that we don't just because it's time for you to go.'

I shrugged and walked along the corridor back to my bed. As far as I was concerned I was being rejected, so the sooner I left the better.

The people I'd been with for the past twenty-one months in the hospital were like my first true and real family, and as far as I was concerned they didn't want me anymore. I was hurt, scared, angry, betrayed and sad. A very small part of me understood Dawn's words but I didn't want to accept it, so I pushed it to the back of my mind and put my survivor armour back on. It would have been nice if I could have skipped out of the hospital, fully aware of why I had to move on, but it was simply too painful for me to be able to do that.

The next day I found myself on a train to Basingstoke. What had seemed like a good idea the day before, now felt completely ridiculous. What was I doing travelling to a town that I didn't know to make a new future?

When the train pulled in I stood on the platform, wondering what to do next. I had no idea, so I drifted towards a coffee shop on the platform. I bought a drink and sat at a table outside. This whole adventure suddenly felt like a big mistake.

As I sipped my coffee I saw a man at the next table reading the local paper. That was it! The local paper would have jobs and flats in it. After the man left the café I grabbed the paper from the table where he'd left it and searched for the job pages. As I scanned all the ads my heart sank – all the ads seemed to be asking for work experience and qualifications that I didn't have. And twenty-one months in hospital? I knew this new start wouldn't be easy but suddenly it felt more difficult than I could ever have imagined.

There wasn't a single job in the paper that I felt I could apply for, so I asked someone for directions to the local job centre. Half an hour later I stood in front of the job boards. They seemed similar to those in the paper, until one leapt out at me. It read: 'Enthusiastic, streetwise person required. Must be discreet, hardworking. Good salary to right person. Sense of humour a must.'

It seemed so different from the rest and I was curious, so I went up to the desk to enquire.

The clerk had no more details, just what was on the card in the window. She picked up the phone and made a call.

'Here's the address,' she said. 'He'll see you in twenty minutes.' Then she looked past me to the next person in the queue.

I took the card and walked away. There was no way I could go for an interview in jeans – was there?

When I got outside I decided I would ask someone for directions and if it was nearby I would go, just for the interview experience. I asked a passing woman and was told the address on the card was just around the corner.

I still wasn't sure what to do. I decided I would walk to the traffic lights and if they were green when I got to the end of the road I would go to the interview.

When I got to the corner the lights changed to green. This was beginning to feel as if it was meant to be. I looked into a shop window and tried to arrange my hair neatly before walking up the street.

I soon found the address on the card. I was still fifteen minutes early. I had nothing to lose as I wouldn't get the job anyway, so I rang the bell and waited. After five minutes I rang the bell again. Obviously the employer had seen me out of the window and was now avoiding me. I was just about to leave when a man appeared beside me with a newspaper in one hand and a cup of coffee in the other. He wore a suit and I guessed he was about twenty-five.

'Hi, are you here for the interview?' he said cheerfully.

'Er, yes,' I answered. 'Are you?'

He laughed. 'I'm the boss. Hold this a sec.' He thrust the cup of coffee into my hand as he put the key in the lock and kicked the bottom of the door, which was jammed. 'Come on in.'

I followed him up a flight of stairs. Paint was flaking off the side of the walls and the building smelt musty and damp.

At the top was a large room with a desk and two chairs at the far end of the room under the only window. There was no carpet and in the middle of the room there was a pile of rubble. I looked up and saw a gaping hole in the ceiling.

'Sorry about the mess,' he said. 'I've just moved in and there are a few teething problems.'

He went over to the table and gestured for me to sit down. I put his coffee on the desk and sat down gingerly in the seat opposite him.

'I'm sorry about the way that I'm dressed,' I said. 'I came here a bit unexpectedly.'

'Don't worry about it,' he said. 'Probably a good idea not to wear your best clothes in here right now.'

I smiled, privately grateful he didn't know that these jeans were my best clothes.

He reached out to shake my hand. 'I'm Mike Jenkins, Managing Director.'

'Sophie Andrews,' I replied nervously.

'Are you from London, Sophie?' he asked. I nodded.

'Great, me too,' he answered.

He seemed very natural and I started to feel a little more at ease.

'So, Sophie, what brings you to Basingstoke?' he asked.

I froze. I wasn't prepared for this question.

'OK, let's try an easier question,' he said. 'Do you have any qualifications?'

My mind went blank again. I had scraped through a few exams at school, but that was it.

'A few,' I mumbled. 'Not many though – I'm sorry.'

'Don't worry,' Mike said kindly. 'I don't have many qualifications either, but I qualified from the university of life. How about you?'

I grinned. Finally there was a question that I could answer.

'Yep, I have a degree in the university of life.'

He smiled. 'I thought I could see a certain spark of that in you. Let me tell you a little about the job. Basically, this is a new company, and this is my empire.' He gestured around the room. 'I used to work for a large company as private detective – tracing people for private clients, finding debtors for finance companies, finding lost relatives, and so on. Then I decided I didn't want to line someone else's pockets anymore, so I'm working for myself. I moved to Basingstoke as I couldn't afford office space in London.'

'Sounds great,' I said. 'I found my natural mother, that's

the closest I've come to detective work.' I was surprised at how easily I blurted this out; hospital had somehow made it easier to share my past.

'That's a good start,' he said. 'Must have been a big step?'

I nodded.

'I'm looking for someone who is, how do I say this, um, streetwise. Basically I don't care what you've done in the past, as long as you aren't a thief. I expect loyalty and confidentiality but I don't ask questions. Our job is to find people – how you do it is up to you. I can teach you a few tricks, but the reason a private detective is successful when Joe Public isn't, is because we bend the rules. Are you OK with that?'

I wanted to jump up and hug him. I could hardly believe he didn't want to know what I had been doing since leaving school. I couldn't believe my luck and tried to contain my excitement as I answered.

'Mr Jenkins, I can guarantee you a hundred per cent loyalty and confidentiality. I would do anything to have this job and for you to give me a chance. I am a hard worker, I'm not a thief. I haven't been in prison but I've had a shit couple of years and I need a break to make a new life.' I stopped speaking and looked at him. Would he give me a chance?

'OK,' he said. 'Let's see how it goes. There's only me and you for now. I don't want to expand too quickly and anyway, I only have two chairs.' He smiled. 'I'll put you on a small basic salary but fifty per cent commission for every person you find. Can you start two weeks from today?'

I nodded.

'Good. I'll see you then.' He stood up and shook my hand.

I walked outside and wanted to scream at the top of my voice that I had a job. It didn't seem like a normal kind of job that you would find in the careers lessons at school, but it didn't matter. Someone wanted me and it didn't seem to be for sex. I couldn't ask for more.

23

Saying My Goodbyes

I made my way to a wooden bench halfway up the street and sat down. My stomach was churning. This was it – my future away from the hospital in the 'real world' had begun. Questions raced around in my head: How would I cope? Would I be able to do the job? And most important of all – where would I live?

I got up from the seat and went to find a newsagent, where I bought a local paper. I stood outside the shop and anxiously scanned the few adverts for house shares. Five minutes later, I was in a phone box arranging to see a room in a shared house. The man gave me directions and told me to come round straight away. It was in walking distance of the town centre and I was soon standing outside a terraced house on a quiet side street.

The man who answered the door was in his mid-thirties, casually dressed and was holding a cat.

'Hi, you must be Sophie. I'm Steve. Come in.'

I stepped into a narrow hallway.

'Do you like cats?' Steve asked.

'Yes, I like all animals,' I replied.

'Great, I have three cats and Nick, who also lives here, is a vet.'

I followed him up a very steep staircase and into a small bedroom. 'The rent's lower because it's so small,' he said apologetically.

I looked around. Compared to my bed-space and locker in the hospital this room was huge. It had a bed, wardrobe, table and chair and there was a window that looked out on to a huge garden.

'Wow, this is great!' I said.

Steve laughed. 'Don't get too carried away. Anyway, the rent covers shared use of the bathroom, dining room, kitchen, and there are two living rooms: one is mine and the other you would share with Nick.'

As we toured the house, which was cluttered with ornaments but clean, Steve told me he was a milkman and had to go to bed early, so it was important to him that the lodgers didn't make a noise at night. I assured him I was very quiet. He asked me what had brought me to Basingstoke and I told him I was moving because I had to leave my accommodation in London and that I had found a good job so needed somewhere to stay. For the second time that day luck seemed to be on my side – he didn't ask for references or any details about my past. All he wanted was a month's rent and a month's deposit.

I tried to look confident as I told him I would send him a cheque to cover both and would like to move in in two weeks' time. I listened as he went through a comprehensive list of house rules, and when I had agreed to be a quiet and cat-loving lodger, we shook hands on the deal.

I said goodbye, hurried down the street, turned the corner and burst into tears as the enormity of what I had done hit me. In just a few hours I had found a job and somewhere to live. And I felt terrified.

As I walked back into the town I saw a chemist and immediately felt a sense of relief. If I could get some razor blades I would feel better. I took a deep breath outside the shop, wiped my tears on my sleeve and rehearsed the story that I would use if I was questioned: I was doing a craft project at college and needed the blades to cut some shapes out of card.

The minute I got outside the shop I opened the packet and pulled out a blade. I felt the sharpness against my fingers and felt reassured that I could cut myself if I needed to. Meanwhile I had to get back to the hospital. A feeling of panic was beginning to erupt inside me.

On the train back I went to the toilet, took the blades out of the packet, put them in my sock and replaced my shoe. I hoped that my good news about the job and the house would distract the staff from searching me. Back at the hospital, I brushed past Dawn and Amy who were waiting for me. I said I needed the toilet but on the way I rushed back to my bed, where I retrieved the blades from my sock and stuck them in my toilet bag – I would find a safer place for them later on.

I went back down the corridor and found Dawn and Amy who were keen to hear my news and were amazed as I told them about my job and house-share.

'Well done, Sophie,' Dawn said. 'I'm just worried it might be a bit too much too soon. You don't sleep very well at night and when you go to work you'll need to get into a night-time sleep routine. How will you cope living with two men, and can you afford it?'

I burst into tears as the enormity of her words hit me and Dawn held my hand, while Amy said she needed to contact Dr Harvey so that he could talk it over with me.

'You told me to leave,' I sobbed, 'and now I've found a

new home and a job and you need to speak to Dr Harvey. What are you doing to my head?'

Dawn put her arms around me. 'Sophie, it's not about not wanting you; you're ready to move on. But if I'm honest, I think Dr Harvey didn't expect you to get a job and a place to live all in one day. He thought you would realise how hard it was and that when you came back we could work out a way for you to go to a hostel.'

Amy came back in. 'Dr Harvey is on his way. While we're waiting, do you mind if we give you a quick search?'

Dawn stood up and led me by the hand to the medical room where I stripped and was searched for blades or any other forbidden item.

'Well done,' Dawn said. 'You even managed to go out and not buy blades.'

I nodded, repressing a stab of guilt at her misplaced faith in me. The blades now hidden in my toilet bag gave me a sense of security I badly needed.

Five minutes later Dr Harvey opened the door, came in and sat opposite me.

'Right, Sophie, what's been happening? Amy says you have a job and a new home?' His voice was kind.

I told him about my day out, and as I did so I realised that there were a few things I'd missed along the way. I had a job but I didn't know the salary, hours of work or what my duties would be. I had a new home but didn't know if my salary would be enough for the rent or if I had enough money to buy food and live. I didn't know if I could live with two men and I didn't know anyone in Basingstoke apart from my new boss and new landlord.

'I think there could be a few loose ends,' Dr Harvey said

gently. 'I wonder if this is a step too far. You've been in hospital a long time – wouldn't it be better to go to a hostel where they can give you emotional support? I know you didn't like Bristol, but there are others.'

'No thanks,' I said.

'Let me contact Basingstoke Social Services so we can find hostel accommodation there for you,' he said.

I shook my head. 'Dr Harvey, this hospital is my home. I would rather make a fresh start than go somewhere that is a lesser version of here. Please can I stay? Just for another six months?' I pleaded.

'Sophie, we've been through this before. You will end up being institutionalised and you don't need to spend the rest of your life in hospital. You are so much stronger and more able to deal with your past. We want to support you now so that you can get out into the world and build a life.'

'Three months then?' I begged.

Dr Harvey smiled and shook his head. 'If you are intent on not going to a hostel then I will need to get Helen to work with you to get some additional support.'

Dawn went to get Helen while I sat and cried. Despite all that Dr Harvey had said, I couldn't help feeling rejected.

When Helen arrived I told her about the letter from my dad and his promise to leave money for me with my mother. She took my mother's phone number and said she would sort out money to tide me over for the first few months, to cover rent, clothes and living.

Dr Harvey spoke again. 'I will need to speak to my colleagues in Basingstoke to get you some support. And we need to think about medication. You'll need to find a GP in Basingstoke but I'm reluctant to write a prescription for your antidepressants. It concerns me that if you felt suicidal you might take an overdose. What do you think?'

'If I want to take an overdose, I'll buy paracetamol,' I answered. 'They're more likely to kill me than the antidepressants anyway.'

Dr Harvey smiled. 'I'm glad you've learned something while you've been here.'

He got up to go. 'Well done, by the way, for finding the job and the place to live. Maybe you should give my eldest son some advice on how to do it.' He laughed loudly and I grinned back; this was the first time he had ever let me see a glimpse of his own life. It felt special.

The next two weeks were an emotional roller coaster. My mood swung between deep sorrow at leaving my 'family' in the hospital, euphoria at the thought of a fresh start at life, anger at the rejection I felt and panic as the reality of coping alone began to sink in. Needless to say, during one of the down periods I used the blades that I had hidden. The hospital staff dressed my wounds and took the blades from me but didn't otherwise react or, much to my disappointment, tell me that I had to stay longer. Helen had sorted out all the money matters with my mother. My rent had been paid by cheque and I had £1000 deposited in my bank account for my new start. Helen had wanted me to go with her to buy clothes for work but I felt I couldn't face it and had given her my sizes and left it to her to sort out. Once bought, my new clothes sat in bags by the side of my bed. I couldn't even face looking at them because it would mean having to face the reality of what I had done.

I had written to Katie with the news of my new home and she had written back, warning me that life outside hospital

was hard. She was still flitting between the north Wales psychiatric hospital and her flat in Colwyn Bay. She said she still
self-harmed and that she sniffed glue every day. I felt sad, and
hoped that this wasn't going to be the path that my own life
would take, though I feared that it might be.

Dr Harvey had arranged for me to see a psychiatrist once
a week in Basingstoke, and for a local social worker to be
assigned to me. He contacted Jane Gray to let her know, and
she immediately phoned to wish me luck. I remembered the
letter that she had sent me months earlier when she had said
she would see me when I got out of purdah. Well, this was
it, my final night in purdah was a couple of days away, and
then I would be free. The trouble was, I didn't want to be.

My last full day in the hospital was a Saturday. At the end
of our last group session I read another poem I had written,
in which I talked about how scary life was, and my fear that
I might lose control and die. Afterwards, the room fell silent.

Gina said, 'Are you going to be OK? You won't kill yourself
when you get out, will you?'

'I don't know,' I said. 'I hope not.'

'Me too,' Gina said. 'It would be a shame if you gave up
now, but it's hard in the outside world. I only manage because
I come here as a day patient.'

After the group session I went back to bed. I felt emotionally
drained. The other patients were planning a leaving party for
me in the evening; Amy had baked a cake and brought it in
and I knew I'd have to make an effort. But I just wanted to
close my eyes and wake up in Basingstoke – the last two weeks
had been hard, but the next twenty-four hours were going to
be much harder.

I was woken a few hours later by Dina, gently shaking my

shoulder and telling me it was time for my party. I sighed as I pulled the covers back and slid out of bed. I brushed my hair, cleaned my teeth and tried to look enthusiastic as I walked towards the day room. I could hear the sound of a guitar and riotous laughter and shrieking. I walked in to a rousing chorus of 'Congratulations'.

The entire unit was there – staff, as well as patients. I was deeply touched and as I looked round at them I thought about all the tears, the anger and the pain we had shared over the past twenty-two months.

Many of the patients who had left the hospital had come: Mary, Gina, Anna, Simone, James, Paul, Theresa and Dina. The one person who was missing was Katie.

Dina came over and put her arm around my shoulder. 'Enjoy your last night, Sophie. Everyone loves you and wants to say goodbye.' The word love brought tears to my eyes. These people were my family and tomorrow I would lose them.

The staff had given me unconditional care, but the patients who had become friends had given me much, much more. They had shown me that I wasn't alone with the pain that I felt, that even the most horrific things in life are not insurmountable.

I began to open the pile of cards. There was a large one, signed by most of the staff and Amy, Dawn, Helen and Miss Smith had written me separate cards. They all said how much they cared and as I read them I cried.

When the cake was finished and the music finally stopped, the day patients went home and the resident patients went to bed. As I had so many times before, I sat on the floor in the corridor talking to the night staff. Even though I was tired, I didn't want to waste a minute of my last few hours.

The morning dawned and I packed my bags: the holdall I had arrived with plus two NHS plastic bags full of poetry, letters, drawings and memories.

Helen was driving me to my new home. She took my belongings to her car and said she would wait outside. I sobbed uncontrollably as I said goodbye to my special nurses Dawn and Amy, who both had tears in their eyes. I cried again as I said goodbye to each patient; we wished each other well and promised to keep in touch, but I knew we wouldn't. This was a phase in our lives that we would need to move on from. I wasn't going to be a day patient, so I needed to start fresh and wipe the slate clean.

The last person I had to see was Dr Harvey, who had come in especially to see me. He ushered me into the music room and asked me to sit down.

'Well, Sophie,' he said, 'you're off now into the big wide world.'

'Yes,' I replied. 'Thanks for all you've done for me. I really didn't think that this place could help me at first. But it has; it's kept me alive. I prayed for the first six months that you would let me out, then I prayed for the last year or so that you would keep me in.'

Dr Harvey laughed. 'I wasn't sure if I would be able to help you when you were first admitted. You were so intent on destroying yourself that I thought it might be too late to save you. In fact, there were a few moments when I thought we had lost you – when you ran away, and then went to stay with your father and swallowed half a bottle of bleach. But you came back, and since then I've seen a real change in you. You've done really well.'

'I just hope I can cope now,' I said.

'You can do it,' Dr Harvey said. 'I don't say this to all the patients under my care, but you're a fighter. I see a spirit in you which means you have a chance to rebuild your life. In the nicest possible way I want you to know that I never want to see you again.'

We both stood up and Dr Harvey shook my hand, then smiled and squeezed my shoulder gently before he left. I decided to have a few moments to myself in the music room, where I had spent so many hours with Katie. I hoped we would both survive. I walked around the room. I felt I was leaving part of her there and as I left I whispered 'goodbye'.

I walked along the corridor, saying my goodbyes to the anorexic patients in their cubicles, and went out through the unit's heavy metal door. I made one last stop at the hospital chapel, where I sat in a pew at the front.

'I don't know if there's a God, or if there is anything out there at all,' I said softly. 'But if there is, please help me: I'm scared.'

Then I walked out of the hospital. I couldn't look back at the world I was leaving behind, so I wiped away my tears and went towards Helen, who was waiting beside her car. This was to be the beginning of my new life and I had to make it work.

24

First Steps

We travelled in silence. I felt too upset to talk and Helen understood and didn't make small-talk. After an hour we arrived at the house in Basingstoke and I saw that Fran was waiting for me outside, as arranged. I felt hugely relieved that she had been given permission to come.

Helen handed me a long list of contact numbers and explained I should not struggle on alone, and to use any help that was available if I felt down. Then she hugged me and left. Fran held my hand and told me not to worry and we rang the bell.

Steve came to the door and offered to help me with my bags. I was suddenly aware of the plastic bags with 'NHS' emblazoned on the side. I passed him the holdall.

'Is this all you've got?' he asked, 'or is there more in the car?'

I shook my head.

'This must be your mother,' he said, as he reached out to shake Fran's hand.

'Pleased to meet you,' Fran said, taking his hand. She hadn't corrected him and I felt a glow inside.

Fran helped me to settle into my room. It was bright and

airy and still felt huge compared to the space I had in the hospital. Fran hung up my new clothes in the wardrobe.

'Wow, this is nice,' she said. 'You'll look really smart tomorrow.'

I tried to smile. I didn't want to even think about the next day.

'Do you have any food?' she asked.

I shook my head.

Fran took me to the local shop, where I bought a few essentials, and then to a pub for a meal. I was quiet. All I could think about was that soon I would be alone.

'I know you must be scared,' she said.

I told her I was, and that I felt like cutting myself.

Fran had learned enough about self-harm by now to know that stopping me was more dangerous than allowing me to do it. The most important thing was that I cut myself safely; prevention just led to my feelings becoming out of control. In the past I had taken an overdose when I hadn't been able to get to my blades.

'Do you have any blades?' she asked. I told her I did.

'Do you have a bandage? Antiseptic?'

'No – but I'll get some if I need to,' I said.

'Listen, Sophie – I can't stop you self-harming, but will you try to ring the Samaritans before you do, and at least tell someone how you feel?'

I nodded. I thought I would be able to do that.

We finished our meal and I clung on to Fran and sobbed in her arms as she said goodbye to me. I wished that she could be my mum and take me home, but her role as a Samaritan didn't extend to that.

'Take care,' she said. 'Good luck at work tomorrow. I'll

go into the Samaritans and give you a ring tomorrow night to see how it went.'

I gulped a 'thank you' through my tears.

As Fran drove away I opened the door to my new home and went upstairs to bed. I lay on the bed and sobbed into my pillow. She had been gone for five minutes and already I wanted to tear myself to shreds.

I carried on crying all evening. Worried that I would be heard, I had a bath so that the noise of the running water would drown out my tears. But back in my bedroom I still couldn't stop my sobs.

When my bedroom door suddenly opened, I froze, a panic deep inside me reawakened. Then I saw the culprit was one of Steve's cats. I patted the bed and it came over and jumped up, then sat on top of me purring loudly. I thought of my dog Molly, and realised how much I had missed the unconditional comfort of animals. The cat seemed happy and stroking it calmed my tears. But eventually it meowed to be let out of the room and I was back on my own again. As the evening dragged on, I heard the movements in the house fade away and realised Steve and Nick must now be in bed.

Fran had asked me to call the Samaritans if I felt like self-harming. I had thought of nothing else all evening. At 1 a.m., unable to sleep, I got up from my bed and got dressed. I picked up my keys and my purse and quietly slipped out of the house. There was a payphone in the hall but it wasn't private enough, so I walked up the street to look for a phonebox. In my early teens I had spent many nights leaving the house and ringing the Samaritans from a phonebox. Some nights, after my dad had sex with me, I just needed to get away and talk to someone who could help to calm me down.

Sometimes the person on the other end would ask me if I was safe being on the streets at night, and I would find this funny, as I was a hundred per cent safer on the streets than I was in my bed at home. After five minutes I saw a red phone box on the other side of the street. When I got inside I dialled the number.

'Samaritans, can I help you?' It was a woman's voice, and the words were comfortingly familiar.

'I hope so, I feel really bad. I want to cut myself,' I said.

'Well, let's talk about why you feel that bad. My name's Denise, what's yours?'

'Sophie,' I said, and started to cry. I felt like such a failure – my first night out of hospital and here I was in a phone box calling the Samaritans because I wanted to self-harm. I felt as if all the months in hospital had been in vain.

Denise phoned me back and I talked to her for forty-five minutes. She prompted me to talk about how I felt when I cut myself – the initial euphoria, the release, the calm afterwards – and as I talked, the urge to actually cut myself began to slowly diminish.

After the call ended I went back to the house and straight to bed. I couldn't sleep, but at least I was resting. And I was surviving my first night on my own.

I finally fell asleep at 7 a.m. and I had to get up half an hour later. I put on my new suit and avoided looking at myself in the mirror. I didn't like seeing myself at the best of times and I could only imagine how ridiculous I would look in a suit.

I was so nervous – it felt like the first day at a new school. My stomach was churning and I had cramps. But I forced down a bit of breakfast and then walked to work.

Mike had cleared the office of rubble and put in some new carpet and desks and chairs. I sat at my desk and he explained the tricks of the trade. He was funny and friendly and I started to find my feet and understand what I needed to do.

I worked very hard that first week, determined to do my best, but I found it very tiring. I was used to sleeping during the day and staying up all night, and I was finding it difficult to change that. I felt insecure and on edge, jumping at the slightest noise. The cats kept coming into my room and while they were a comfort, the opening of the door scared me. Eventually I wedged a chair under the door handle in order to feel safer.

When I did manage to sleep, nightmares haunted me. But the worst times were the evenings. By this time I had been introduced to Nick, but I felt very alone, as he would often be in the shared living room with his friends, and I felt embarrassed about joining them. I would get home from work at five thirty and spend the rest of the evening in my room. I felt very low and by Thursday I was nearly asleep on the desk at work. Mike threw a ball of paper at me.

'Wakey wakey,' he said. 'You won't earn any money like that.'

'God, I'm sorry,' I spluttered, turning scarlet. I picked up the phone and got on with my work.

I had already asked him about my basic salary and worked out that unless I turned into Sherlock Holmes in my first month, I wouldn't be making enough money to pay the rent and have enough to live on. This worried me, as I didn't want to start dipping into the money in my bank unless it was an absolute emergency. I needed to do well at my job in order to survive, and falling asleep at my desk wasn't the best beginning.

I was relieved when Friday came round. I was looking forward to a weekend of sleeping. At lunchtime Mike got up from his desk and put his jacket on. I thought he must be going out for lunch but he took my jacket from the new coat-stand, threw it over to me and started jangling the office keys.

'It's Friday,' he said. 'We've had a good week and you seem to be picking up the job. Let's go and celebrate.'

'Can I just make one more call? I think I am on to this one, I know where he is.'

Mike laughed.

'Well, you've certainly got perseverance – maybe I should call you Percy. You've impressed me this week; you've kept on trying and you've solved cases some people might have given up on. But leave it for today; your case will still be there on Monday.'

I followed him from the office to the pub over the road. I was still on antidepressants and I hadn't had a drink since the day in the hospital when Theresa had given me cider and lager. I hoped one quick drink wouldn't hurt.

Mike helped me off with my jacket. 'What do you want to drink, Perce?' he said.

'Erm, half of cider please,' I replied.

'Pint of cider for Percy please, Jim, and I'll have a pint of lager. Percy – this is Jim the landlord of this fine establishment. Jim – this is Percy, my new office manager.'

'Office manager?' I said laughing. 'There's only you and me there!'

'Ssssh,' said Mike, 'don't tell anyone.'

Jim held out his hand. 'Pleased to meet you Percy – interesting name.'

'I've only had it for the last five minutes,' I joked.

Mike beamed with pride.

I had only planned to stay for a quick drink, but I couldn't seem to find the right moment to leave and after the fifth drink, I abandoned the plan. Mike and I sat laughing and joking for the rest of the afternoon and evening. He told me a lot about his life and his upbringing, which had been hard; his move to Basingstoke was to get away from bad memories in London. He had been married for just over a year, although as the evening went on he began to imagine that his wife may have left him – so at seven he phoned to tell her he might be late home.

I was tempted to tell him about my past but stopped myself. Nice as he was, he was my boss, and it might not seem as interesting on Monday morning to remember that your 'office manager' had been in a nuthouse.

At ten we fell out of the pub and hugged each other goodbye several times before staggering in opposite directions up the street.

My first week at work was over and I loved my job!

The next morning, I loved my job a bit less. I had gone home and fallen asleep immediately – the deepest sleep I'd had for a long time – but at about 4 a.m. I started to be sick. I was sick for four hours and felt as if my head had been hit with a mallet. I remembered Dr Harvey telling me, when I drank alcohol in the hospital garden, that my antidepressants mixed with alcohol would make me wish I was dead. I hadn't felt too bad that time, but this time I had drunk far more and his words came horribly true. The cider and medication cocktail was so potent I was ill all weekend. Something would have to go – so I put my medication in a box and decided I wouldn't take it again.

I also decided that I wouldn't need a social worker or a psychiatrist and I threw the list of contact numbers Helen had given me in the bin. I didn't feel this was a risky thing to do, it was a reaction to feeling I had been rejected. If they didn't want me, then I wasn't going to follow up their suggestions: I would do it my way.

Week two of my new job followed the same pattern as the first. I enjoyed work, the evenings were long and depressing and the nights were full of memories that I couldn't erase. On Friday, Mike took me to the pub at one o'clock and we drank until ten. I was sick again at the weekend but not quite so badly. I reckoned the medication was gradually leaving my system.

In one week I managed to trace twenty-seven people for our major client, a finance company. Mike was brimming with pride and reminded me how much commission this would mean. He started to spend more time out of the office as he said he needed to look for more clients now that we were up and running, and he put the advert back in the job centre and said we needed to expand. I was pleased that he was happy with me, but now he was out a lot, I was on my own nearly twenty-four hours a day. I didn't like my own company and the impact of coming off the antidepressants was starting to kick in.

On the Thursday night on my way home from work, I stopped at the off-licence and bought cider and cigarettes. I had never really smoked, but I couldn't stand the way that I felt when I was on my own in the house every evening and I thought a drink and a cigarette might help me to relax.

I went back to the house, had a shower and got changed and then, as Nick wasn't in, I went into the lounge to watch

television. I settled on the sofa with a can of cider and cigarette, followed by another and another. It was after nine and
I was half asleep when Nick came into the room. 'Mind if I
join you?' he said.

I sat up on the settee so that he had room to sit down.
This was the first time that we'd both been in our shared
living room and I was glad that I'd been drinking as it made
me feel more relaxed.

'I'll get a beer,' Nick said, and he left the room and came
back with some crisps and eight cans of lager.

Nick was in his late forties, well built, with a bushy beard
and thick wavy hair. I thought he would look more at home
on a farm than in a city veterinary practice. I wondered why
a professional of his age didn't have his own home, but I
didn't know him well enough to ask. I kept the conversation
safe and asked him about his job. He seemed to have plenty
of tales to tell and didn't ask about me, so I started to relax.
Perhaps if more nights were like this, I wouldn't get so
depressed.

After a couple of hours I told Nick I was going to bed.
He asked me to stay a little longer, so I agreed to have just
one more drink. We finished our drinks and Nick edged
towards me, putting his arm round my shoulder. I felt his
hands start to rub my breasts and froze, but he didn't notice,
and began to kiss me.

'Don't kiss me, please,' I said.

Nick ignored me and started to pull at the button on my
jeans. I knew that it would be easier to get it over with than
to make a scene trying to stop him, so I moved from the settee
and lay on the floor. Nick jumped up and started to strip off.
I pulled off my jeans and he threw himself down on the floor

beside me and started to pull at my top. I lifted my arms up and let him pull it over my head. He tried to kiss me, but I turned my face away.

'If you want sex just get on with it,' I said.

Nick looked taken aback but carried on. As I felt his penis inside me I started to block it out of my mind. I was good at that, I'd had many years of practice with my dad and his friends.

Nick was panting and gasping on top of me and I counted down the minutes until eventually it was over.

'Is there anything you'd like me to do for you?' he asked.

'Get off me, Nick, and go to bed, that's all,' I answered.

He got up and grabbed his clothes. 'Are you OK?' he said. 'Do you want to come and lie in bed with me? I could hold you.'

'I'm fine, thanks Nick. I'll go to my own bed. See you tomorrow night.'

He left and I got up and started to get dressed. I turned the television off, took my empty cans back to the kitchen and washed up my glass and ashtray. Then I gave the cats some milk and made my way to bed.

In my room I undressed again and got into bed. But every time I shut my eyes, I saw Nick having sex with me. I sat up in bed and put the light on. This was ridiculous – he hadn't raped me, so why was I feeling so upset? I felt sticky and dirty, that was the problem, I decided. I wanted to have a bath but was scared to get up in case I woke Steve. I used to have baths in the middle of the night in hospital but I didn't feel I could do that here. I lay in bed watching the clock and all the time my anxiety worsened. I heard a creak on the landing and shot bolt upright in bed. The living room floor was one thing, but I didn't want him in my bed, because I would never be able to erase it. There was silence again; the noise must have been one of the cats. I flopped back down again in bed and started to cry. I didn't want to leave my room in case he was waiting outside. I couldn't get to the toilet or the bathroom. I felt like a prisoner and I felt dirty, I could smell him on me, taste his breath and hear his voice.

My head started spinning, but now it wasn't Nick's voice that I could hear, it was my dad's. I felt as if my dad had just had sex with me. I felt sick and I felt trapped. Why had I let Nick have sex with me? Why had I let my dad have sex with me? Why had I let his friends have sex with me?

I hated myself; all I seemed to be good for was sex. I wanted to scream, but I couldn't. I jumped out of bed and grabbed my blades. My head started buzzing at the thought of the relief that the cutting would bring. I had no antiseptic or bandages, but I couldn't wait. I needed to do this. I needed to feel pain and punish myself for what had just happened.

I unwrapped a fresh blade from the pack and then laid a towel out on the floor and placed my left arm over it. I counted to three and pushed the blade in, dragging it down the full length of my arm. The blood started to bubble out. It looked good as it dripped on to the clean towel. I challenged myself to cut fifty vertical lines down my arm. One, two, three; the lines started off straight, but as the blood flowed I couldn't see where I had cut before. I counted to fifty – now I would cut fifty horizontal lines across the same area. I knew this would hurt more as I would be cutting over fresh cuts and I felt pleased that I was feeling the pain.

By the time I had finished blood was pouring out of the top of my arm, but I felt such a release. My head had stopped spinning and I felt so calm. I bound my arm up tightly with the towel and curled up on the floor with the quilt wrapped round me. I rested my head on my arm and felt the blood running through the towel and on to my face. Now I would get some sleep.

25

High Expectations

I was woken up by the sound of the front door closing. I looked at the clock – it was 8 a.m., and it must have been Nick leaving for work. I tried to lift my arm and winced. The towel was drenched with blood and the carpet underneath was discoloured. I looked in the mirror on the dressing table. My face was stained with blood where my arm had rested on it. I tried to put on my dressing gown, but my arm was too swollen to fit into the sleeve.

I put on some tracksuit bottoms and a baggy T-shirt and went into the bathroom. I started to unravel the towel. My arm was twice its normal size and the cuts were starting to bleed again. I needed bandages and disinfectant.

I made my way to a chemist, then home again to dress my wounds, before going in to work a couple of hours late. I apologised to Mike, who said I looked rough and should go home. I couldn't contemplate the thought of being at the house alone, so I told him I would be fine, and stayed. My arm was throbbing and I was exhausted, so I was pleased when Mike eventually went out to meet a client – at least I could just get on with my work and I wouldn't have to pretend that I was feeling alright. Although the cutting had brought me a kind of relief, there was a sadness deep inside me that just wouldn't go away.

It was Friday, so after lunch Mike came back to the office and invited me to the pub. I didn't want to go, but the thought of being in my room on my own felt worse.

After a couple of drinks Mike asked me what was wrong. I said that I got a bit depressed in the house on my own, and that I wasn't looking forward to the weekend ahead.

'Jim,' Mike called to the landlord. 'Do you have any jobs going in the evening. Percy could do with the extra money.'

'Actually,' Jim answered, 'I need someone else on Tuesday, Thursday and Saturday nights. Would that be any good?'

I was taken aback at this sudden turn of events, but pleased. 'I haven't worked in a bar before,' I said.

Jim didn't seem worried. 'We can train you. It's more important that you get on with people, and you seem to be able to do that. We'll start you tomorrow night and see how you get on . . . 7 p.m. OK?'

'Great,' I replied. 'Thanks.'

Mike ordered two more drinks and carried them over.

'Thanks,' I said.

'I don't like to think of you being sad – it might be a good way of making friends,' he replied.

I felt overwhelmed. Three weeks in and I had another new job. It all felt very exciting, but scary too.

We stayed in the pub until closing time, staggered out and hugged before we went our separate ways. I realised that I had begun to really like Mike, and even to trust him and feel safe with him. Could it be true that I knew a man who liked me and didn't want sex from me? I knew I couldn't let my guard down too much in case I was wrong, but so far it felt good.

The next night I started my job in the pub and despite feeling terrified, I was amazed by how much I enjoyed it. Remembering the long orders was hard; every time I had totalled the order up in my head and a customer spoke to me, I forgot the figure. Serving drinks, talking, smiling and adding up all at the same time wasn't as easy as it looked.

I quickly realised that if I smiled and laughed with the customers they would ignore the fact that I had poured a pint with more head on it than lager. It was fun, I wasn't alone, and there were plenty of people to talk to.

After the pub closed Jim told me that it was usual for the staff to stay behind for a lock-in. The doors were locked and Jim's wife Anne appeared from the flat upstairs. Jim, Anne and I, along with the other two staff members, Cara and Nicky, sat on the bar stools and drank well into the early hours of the morning. By 3 a.m. I was convinced that Cara and Nicky were my best friends and that Jim and Anne were my ideal parents. At four I told Jim how much I had enjoyed my first night at work and staggered into the night.

On Sunday morning I woke with a terrible hangover. I went to the bathroom and unwound the bandages from my arm. It was still swollen and throbbing and started to bleed again. I knew I'd have to be careful to ensure it didn't get infected.

Sunday was a depressing, lonely day. Steve was at home and he threw open all the windows and played loud music. Nick was in our shared lounge drinking beer with his friends and playing computer games on the television.

I had bumped into him downstairs and he asked me how I felt about the other night. I said it was OK, and he was pleasant and said it had been nice. But I didn't want to spend time with him or be around him. Instead I sat in my room and wrote. I wrote about how I felt, I wrote to Fran and I wrote to Jane Gray. I went downstairs to get a hot drink and bumped into Steve.

'Hi, Sophie,' he said. 'Did you get your phone messages?' I shook my head.

'I thought not,' he said, gesturing towards a wipe-clean white board on the wall next to the telephone. 'You might need a board of your own soon.'

'God, I'm sorry,' I answered. 'I didn't realise we had a board.'

'Well, now you know. Anyway, see you later, I'm off out.'

I looked up at the board and saw my name underlined at the top and at least a dozen messages listed underneath. There had been calls from Fran, Jane, Basingstoke Social Services, Dr Harvey, Amy, Katie – I'd had no idea everyone was calling me.

I tore off a slip of paper from a pad by the phone and started to make notes of my calls. It was nice that Dr Harvey and Amy had rung from the hospital, and it was nice to see that my old social worker Jane had called, and Katie – I had sent her my address and number – it would be great to talk to her.

Then I saw the next message, and all the others went out of my head. Had I read this right, my dad had rung! I couldn't believe it, the number was a London one – could this be true? My dad was back.

The phone rang and I snatched the receiver. 'Dad!' I said, excitedly.

'No, Sophie, it's me.' It was Fran's voice. I broke down and sobbed when I heard it. The familiarity of her voice always made me feel less alone.

'What on earth's happened?' Fran said. 'I'll need to get permission, but then I'm coming over. I'll see you in an hour, if that's OK.'

I went back to my room to wait for Fran. I felt a huge amount of emotion: excitement and fear. Despite what my dad had done, I still missed him. He was back now, and maybe he would have changed and everything would be alright. I so wanted it to be true that I made myself believe it.

When Fran arrived she sat on my bed with a cup of coffee perched on her knee, while I sat on the floor.

'I've been getting really worried,' she said. 'I've rung you several times and you haven't rung back. What's been happening?'

I told her about the past three weeks at work, sleeping with Nick, cutting my arm, Friday nights in the pub with Mike, my new job in the pub, and now today's news about my dad ringing.

'God, Sophie, what a time you've been having,' she said. 'Do you need stitches in your arm?'

'It's OK, I think,' I replied.

'So – let's talk about your dad. Are you going to ring him?'

'Yes of course! It will be wonderful to speak to him again, although I am a bit nervous; he won't be very happy if he thinks I've told people in the hospital about us,' I said.

Fran was silent for a few moments. 'If you must ring him,' she said, 'can you do it while I'm here, so at least I can pick up the pieces.'

'Fran, don't say that, please. He will be OK with me now, I know he will.' I was trying hard to reassure her, and perhaps to reassure myself at the same time.

We went for a walk in the park and Fran pointed out that

my dad might still want to hurt me and that I should start to look after myself and protect myself from him. I listened to her words and knew they were true, but didn't want to believe them. I told her he would be different now and that this would be a new future and a new start. I so desperately wanted to believe that Dad would have changed and would be a proper dad to me now, even though this was hopelessly unlikely.

I knew Fran felt uncomfortable, but she accepted what I said and didn't judge. She told me to ring the Samaritans if I needed to and to try to call before I cut myself.

We went back to the house and she hugged me goodbye. I held on for as long as I could and after she had driven off I went back into the house. I was thrilled that Katie had rung – I would call her back later. But first I wanted to talk to Dad. I wrote his phone number down, before collecting my purse and going back out again. When I reached the phone box I stared at the number for a few seconds. It had been more than eighteen months since I last saw him, the night I ended up in hospital after drinking bleach. I tried to shut the thought out of my mind.

I dialled the number.

'Dad!' I shouted. 'It's me! When did you get back?'

'Hello, love,' he said. 'I got back last weekend. It's so nice to hear your voice. I've missed you.'

'I've missed you too,' I said. 'How did you know where I was?'

'I rang your mother and she said that you were out of hospital and had moved to Basingstoke. God knows why you went there! Have you got a boyfriend or something?'

'No, of course not.'

'That's good then,' he laughed. 'I thought you'd ditched your old dad.'

'No, Dad.'

'Well, we have lots to catch up on. I'm staying with a friend, so I can't speak now. When can I see you? How about Wednesday?'

'Yes, Wednesday is fine,' I was pleased I didn't have a shift in the pub that night, otherwise I would have had to swap.

'Alright, love,' Dad said. 'I have your address from your mum, so I'll pick you up at about seven. I have a new car. I think you'll like it.'

I replaced the receiver. My head was brimming with excitement. I wanted to tell the world that my dad was back, but I didn't know who to tell. I couldn't think of anyone who would be pleased for me.

I didn't want to go back to the house, so I decided to walk into town and go to the pub for a drink. Jim was surprised to see me but said that it was busy and I could work an extra shift if I wanted. I jumped at the chance.

I told Jim that I was excited because my dad had returned from an overseas trip. He said it was good to see me looking so happy. I felt more confident and chatty than usual, and the more I chatted the more the customers drank.

Jim was pleased and said he was glad I had dropped by. He wondered if I would like to work on a Sunday on a permanent basis. I jumped at the chance – it would mean I wouldn't be on my own on the longest day of the week.

As the evening passed, I started to speak to a man called Clive who was on his own at the end of the bar. He was in his early twenties and had a kind face and a good sense of humour. He told me he was from Dublin and was working on a building site. He was sharing a house with a group of other labourers. He didn't like weekends, as lots of his friends lived near enough to go back home and he was always left on his own. I told him I felt the same and that was one of the reasons I worked in a pub now. He laughed when I joked and I began to relax in his company. But it was still a shock when he asked me for a date. I wasn't used to being asked out; men usually just wanted sex from me, and this felt quite alien, so I stumbled and spluttered over my words.

I had told Dad I hadn't got a boyfriend and didn't want to have to lie if he asked me again, so I said no to Clive, but it felt good to have been asked.

On Monday evening Fran rang me and I told her I was seeing Dad on Wednesday. She was silent. I rang my old social worker Jane and told her the news about Dad. She told me not to go on my own and that she could arrange for a social worker from Basingstoke to go with me. I said no, and felt disappointed that neither of them wanted to give Dad another chance – I was prepared to, so why wouldn't they? I refused to consider that perhaps they were the ones who were right, and that, in my loneliness and longing for the loving connection with Dad I had as a small girl, I was blindly ignoring the fact that there was no reason on earth why he would have changed.

26

Nothing Changes

On Wednesday I bought some new clothes in my lunch hour and had my hair cut on my way home from work. I wanted to look my best and wanted Dad to see that I was well. I stood in front of the mirror and wondered how I might have changed in the last couple of years.

A car horn sounded and I raced outside. Dad was leaning against the gate and I flew into his arms.

'Hello, love,' he said. 'You've put on some weight haven't you?'

I nodded, embarrassed.

Dad was deeply tanned and looked well.

'Wow, look at the car,' I said, as he stepped aside to reveal a silver Porsche parked by the kerb.

'I said you'd like it,' he replied.

I jumped in the car beside him. He grinned at me and leaned over me to help with my seatbelt. It didn't feel right but I tried to dismiss my unease.

'So,' he said, 'tell me about what happened to you in that nuthouse, apart from putting on weight.'

'Nothing much, Dad. Tell me about your trip.'

Soon we were heading out of Basingstoke on the motorway.

Dad drove fast and dangerously and kept looking across at me to check my reaction to his manoeuvres. I grinned back and listened as he talked about his round the world adventures. He had visited every continent, so he had a lot of stories to tell.

After half an hour we came off the motorway and started heading down country lanes, the Porsche screeched round the winding roads until we came to a stop outside a country pub.

'Come on,' he said. 'I'm starving.'

Inside, Dad ushered me to a table in the far corner. Without asking me what I'd like to drink he went to the bar. When he got back he placed a glass of coke in front of me.

'No alcohol for you, young lady,' he said. 'Are you still drinking?'

I shook my head. 'Not really, Dad.'

His words had stung me. My drinking as a child had either been with him, when he encouraged me, or in the night after we'd had sex. He had always said I could help myself to drink if it made it easier, and it had numbed some of the pain, so I'd ended up having a drink before going to school. I hadn't thought of myself as having a drink problem before, and in fact when I went into the hospital, where alcohol was banned, I hadn't missed it.

He passed me a menu.

'Don't know why I'm giving you this,' he laughed. 'You look like you've eaten already.'

I put the menu down. His words stung again. I remembered as a child how he had bought me sweets and crisps as a reward for good behaviour each week. On Sunday afternoons I had waited expectantly as he went to the shops and brought back a bag of treats. Food as a reward system had been part of my life. I knew by the amount of sweets he gave me how pleased he was with me.

Then, after Mum left, he'd started to ration my food, telling me that if I was good with his friends I could have some of his. Never certain of whether I would have anything to eat or not, I learned to eat when I was given food, and not necessarily when I was hungry.

He interrupted my thoughts with another question.

'Are you still smoking?'

'No Dad, I'm not.' I hoped he couldn't see that I had lied. I remembered the times when I would put a cigarette out on myself, and how he would do it too. He would leave matches and cigarettes in my room.

'And no boyfriend either?' he asked.

I knew this was the important question. In the past he had been angry if he thought I had slept with someone else. I reminded myself that I wasn't at home with him anymore and it would be OK to have a boyfriend now, wouldn't it? Or had I known that he would get angry if I said yes. Wasn't that why I had turned Clive down?

'No, Dad – no time for a boyfriend.'

Dad smiled, content with my answers.

The waitress came over and Dad ordered steak for himself and fish for me. It didn't seem worth making a fuss and saying that I would have preferred to choose my own meal.

I told him about my work at the detective agency and my new job in the pub and he seemed genuinely pleased that I was working and earning my own money. I asked him about my dog Molly, and he told me she was still on a farm with a friend but that he would take me to see her one weekend.

This was the dad I loved and wanted more than anything else in the world. The caring dad, the loving dad. I wished it could always be this way. I tried to hold on to the memory.

The meals arrived. I wanted to eat it but I felt sick and my stomach was knotted, so I was only able to pick at mine. Dad was so angry at the waste that he ate it himself.

As we got up to leave my sleeve slipped back, exposing the bandage.

'God, you're not still cutting are you, after all those months in hospital?' he said sharply.

I nodded and my eyes filled with tears.

'What a waste of everyone's time you being there then,' he laughed. 'At least the medical insurance paid out for your stay so something good came out of it. Come on, let's get you back to your house full of men.'

He stood up and I followed him back to the car. My mind was in overdrive. I remembered that when I was in hospital I had been asked to sign some insurance forms. I hadn't known what they were, but now I realised that Dad had the family insured against long-term hospitalisation and had made money from my time inside. My heart sank.

We sped off into the night. Dad put the stereo on and I realised how much I had missed music. We started to sing along to the songs and I felt happy to be with him. He was a good person deep inside and I knew that he cared. He had always told me he cared.

The car was slowing down and a couple of minutes later Dad parked in a lay-by on a quiet country road. He turned off the lights, but kept the music on. I didn't look at him. I knew what was going to happen. My heart was pounding. Oh God, surely not. He was different now, he had to be, he knew what I had been through, he knew how much he had hurt me. He had said when he went abroad that he was going to sort himself out, hadn't he? I sat in the darkness, as the music played on, paralysed by fear and grief.

Eventually he spoke. 'This is a great car, but we're never going to be able to have sex in it. I should have borrowed someone else's car but I wanted you to see the Porsche,' he said remorsefully.

'Yes, it's a great car.' Oh God no. Please no.

'I wonder if we could find anywhere on the other side of the bushes. Hold on,' he said. He got out of the car and disappeared. I sat, transfixed, unable to move or think.

'There might be somewhere in there. Not very private though,' he said as he got back into the car.

'Dad, do we have to do this?' I managed to say.

'You are pleased to see me, aren't you?' he said.

'Of course I am. I just don't feel like sex, that's all.'

'Are you sleeping with the men in that house, 'cos if you are I'll . . .'

'No, Dad. I'm not sleeping with anyone. I promise.'

'I love you, Sophie.'

'I know, and I love you too.'

I heard him unzip his trousers.

'Show me that you love me. Show me how much you have missed me.'

Like a robot I reached out and started rubbing his penis to make him hard. He groaned and I felt the tears running down my face, as he reached over, took my head and pushed it down into his crotch.

My mind went into shutdown as I went through the motions. I couldn't think about how having his penis in my mouth made me feel. If I started to, I would be sick, and that would make him angry, or worse – even more excited.

He finally let out a gasp, his body shuddered and I knew it was over.

'I've missed you,' he said. 'And I do love you, despite what people might have told you in that nuthouse.'

I tried to clear my mouth and face of the taste and smell of semen. He held me close to him and I cried into his chest for about ten minutes. He stroked my hair and rocked me gently. Then he zipped up his trousers, started the car and drove me back to the house.

27

The Mist Clears

Ten days later Fran and I were sitting in the shared living room. Nick was out and Steve was in bed with a bad back, so I had the house to myself for once.

'I find it really hard, Sophie. I can't understand why you still love your father, especially after what happened when you saw him last week,' Fran said.

'There is a caring person underneath all the mixed-up stuff,' I said. 'I just need him to understand that I have to move on now and can't have sex with him again.'

Fran was silent.

I always felt sad when our conversations ended this way. I knew that Fran didn't approve but that she wasn't going to say that. She said that the Samaritans were there for me whatever I did and irrespective of anyone's personal views.

I was still clinging to my belief that Dad cared, and was misguided, not evil. But although I held everything together at work, at night I cried myself to sleep. The only person who truly knew that I was on the edge was Fran. Just having her there made me feel safer and less alone.

Dad had been ringing me at least once a day, trying to

arrange to see me. I made excuses and stopped returning his calls, even though it tore me apart inside. Every night when I came home from work I turned the corner at the end of the road and looked to see if he was there. I missed him and wanted to see him more than anything else in the world, but I knew I had to hold on and be strong. If I didn't break free now, then he would take me back to the dark, terrifying place. I had been through so much to escape. If I had sex with him again it would destroy me, because I would end up killing myself.

I often felt suicidal, but I had to try and hang on. I had clawed my way, one agonising step at a time, towards a fresh chance in life and, broken though I felt, there was enough spirit left in me to feel that I wasn't going to let Dad destroy it.

I went through the motions of going to work and when I allowed myself to, I found that I enjoyed my jobs. I had grown into my office manager role, training three new members of staff, and Mike was pleased with me. He gave me a pay rise and increased my commission. I no longer needed the pub job to pay my rent and live but I kept it as I still preferred to be out of the house at night. I didn't tend to socialise with the new people in the office because I took my job as office manager very seriously, and didn't want to compromise that in any way.

Nick had made passes at me several times since we'd had sex, but although we had a few groping sessions I had refused to have sex with him again and he eventually gave up. However, sadly my refusal was not as a result of my increased self-esteem so much as the fact that I knew I simply couldn't stand any more bad memories associated with the house where I was living.

I wasn't really interested in having a relationship, but Clive persisted in asking me out for a date and eventually I said yes. He met me from work on a Monday evening and took me for an Indian meal. We laughed and chatted and I felt easy in his company. At the end of the evening he walked me home and when we got to the house I asked him if he wanted to sleep with me. He looked taken aback and said he would do at some point but not after a first date. I couldn't believe that he was rejecting me and he couldn't believe that I was asking him to sleep with me. But we started going out once or twice a week, on nights when I wasn't working. Eventually he said he would like to have sex. I didn't want us to sleep together in my room so I told him that I didn't feel it was private with Steve and Nick around.

Clive shared a room at the top of a house with five other men, so we had sex in a single bed with other men sleeping in beds next to us. Afterwards I got up and went home. I wanted to be in my own bed and I knew Clive felt uncomfortable. He was a nice man who treated me well, but he didn't seem to want sex very often, which in my mind meant that he didn't care for me. So after a few more dates I ended it. Clive seemed heartbroken but I couldn't understand why; I didn't think it had been very serious for either of us. I told him I would like us to stay as friends but he never came to the pub again.

Meanwhile, Dr Harvey called me a few times but I didn't return his calls because I felt that I had failed and let him down. Although I had a home and two jobs I was managing successfully, I was still struggling with depression and the urge to self-harm and I felt that emotionally I had made no progress at all.

Looking back I can see that this wasn't true at all. It took a lot of courage to keep going to work and trying to make a life for myself, and the depression and continuing urge to self-harm were only to be expected, given how recently I had left hospital. I wasn't failing, I was saying no to my dad for the first time in my life, and I resisted the urge to self-harm more often than I gave in. But it was a lonely, hard and desperate struggle and from where I was it was hard to see any success in it. So I ignored Dr Harvey's calls, along with those from Basingstoke Social Services. The only people I spoke to who knew about my past were Fran and Katie. I had begun calling her every week, but the calls were often distressing. Katie was sniffing glue and taking drugs and sometimes she wouldn't know who I was. At other times we would talk for ages on the phone about the good times we'd shared in the hospital. But it was clear that Katie was struggling even more than I was and I felt sad. Sometimes I wished I could just turn the clock back and we could be in the hospital together again.

It was around this time that my birth mother, Juliet, who was still in touch occasionally, wrote to say that she had told my brother, David, about me. She said he had been pleased to learn that he was not an only child, and would love to meet me. I was glad that she had finally told him, but I was also nervous about meeting him, wondering if he would have expectations I couldn't fulfil.

I caught the train and Juliet and David met me at the station. David, who was then thirteen, treated me like a big sister who had simply been away. He asked for help with his homework, chatted and was so at ease that it didn't seem to be a big deal for him at all.

I was quite the opposite, very tense and on edge, despite the fact that Juliet and her husband were pleasant and friendly. I kept looking around their home and wondering what I would be like if I had grown up there, with them.

In the afternoon I watched David play tennis and it felt odd, and nice, that I had loved tennis at his age.

By the time I left I was a little more relaxed. It had been a nice day, but it was hard for me to feel connected to these people whom I barely knew. I told them little of my life, but before getting the train back to Basingstoke I promised to come again.

At around this time, Mike advised me that one of our clients, Paul Hobson, would be coming up from Devon to meet us. As office manager, he wanted me to be there to help persuade Paul to give us more business. I sat in the meeting feeling totally out of my depth as Paul and Mike discussed percentages and rates and volume of work ratios. But when Mike handed over to me and asked me to predict a percentage success rate I surprised myself by answering confidently. Paul was impressed, a deal was signed and Mike whisked us to the pub for a celebratory drink. He booked a restaurant and persuaded Paul to stay overnight.

By seven we were all in a merry state when Jim called Mike over and said his wife had rung and there was a family crisis. Mike called me over to the bar and explained he would have to leave. He gave me a thick wad of notes and told me to entertain Paul. A few hours earlier I would have been horrified at the thought of an evening with a client, but the drink had relaxed me and I assured Mike that I would take care of Paul.

I took him to the restaurant, where we chatted over a meal until the restaurant owner made polite noises for us to leave. We went back to the bar in the hotel where Paul was staying and after a few more drinks Paul invited me back to his room.

This was the moment when I should have said no and left. But despite the fact that I was there in a business role and had done a good job in our meeting, Paul clearly spotted the vulnerable girl behind the confident young woman facade. And the moment he asked me back to his room I slid back into my old habits; I was still the worthless girl men just used for sex.

Dutifully I went back to Paul's room with him. It was only when I crawled out of his bed to go home in the early hours, that I realised I wasn't just sleeping with another nameless man again – this was our client, and I would probably lose my job.

I ran home, got into bed and pulled the duvet over my head. I didn't want it to be morning, but the alarm seemed to sound as soon as my head hit the pillow and I knew I would have to face the music.

When I walked into the office Mike was alone. I pushed the door open and waited to be sacked.

'Morning, Percy,' he said.

I looked at him and he smiled. Clearly he didn't know.

'Sounds like you had quite a night! You've just missed Paul – he said to say bye.'

I said thank you to God in my head: Paul hadn't told Mike. I was saved.

'One thing though,' Mike said. 'When I said "entertain" the client I didn't mean sleep with him.'

My heart sank, but Mike was laughing.

'Anyway, whatever you did he seemed very bright and chirpy this morning, so good work, Percy.'

Hugely relieved, I settled down at my desk. I wasn't proud of what I'd done, in fact I felt awful about it. But I was lucky to have Mike as my boss. He didn't ask questions about my past, he didn't judge and he seemed to care about me.

While work was manageable and sometimes even fun, my depression hit me as soon as I walked through the door in the evening. I tried to get extra shifts at the pub, because at least after a night in the pub I would be drunk and that made it easier to sleep.

But the pressure was building. The strain of putting on a brave face to the world was enormous. Only Fran and the Samaritans knew I was at risk of going over the edge, but even they couldn't seem to reach me. I felt like Jekyll and Hyde and the cracks were beginning to show.

Every time I walked into the house the board by the phone was full of messages from Dad. He was getting angry and I knew that the longer it went on the more chance there was of him coming to the house. Memories of what he did to me were haunting me every time I closed my eyes. I wasn't sleeping and I couldn't be bothered to eat.

It was a Friday night when the bubble burst. I had been at work until lunchtime and spent the normal Friday afternoon and evening in the pub with Mike. But despite putting on a chirpy front, I had felt all day that a cloud was engulfing me. I stopped at the off-licence on the way back to the house and bought a bottle of gin.

When I got back I saw that Dad had rung three times. Steve was in bed and Nick was out so I sat on the floor by the phone, poured myself a large gin and bitter lemon and got my address book out. I needed to hear some familiar voices. The first person I rang was Katie, but it was Friday night and she was so out of it she didn't know who I was. I tried Dina, but her girlfriend Roz answered and explained that Dina had left her. Two months after leaving hospital, Dina had got it in her head that Roz would finish with her now that she was better and, despite Roz's reassurances, Dina had walked out and disappeared. I felt sad for Roz, who had stood by Dina through thick and thin. She asked for my number and said that she would like to stay in touch with me and see how I was doing.

The third call I made was to Gina. She seemed pleased to hear from me but said that she had split up with Mary and that she was self-harming every day.

When I put down the phone I wondered what it was all about. We had all been in hospital and here we all were feeling so bad that we wanted to self-harm or die. Life didn't seem worth it. The fight wasn't worth fighting.

I felt sad, alone and vulnerable. I picked up the phone and called Dad. He was angry that I had ignored him, angry that I had made excuses, angry that I had rejected him, angry that I was drinking and angry when I started to cry. When he had finished being angry he hung up.

I went to my room. I couldn't cope with what was in my head anymore. I couldn't cope with my dad being in my head every time I closed my eyes. I felt that all my efforts to survive had been in vain. I wanted to sleep and not wake up.

I poured another drink and took a packet of paracetamol out of my bedside drawer. I took two tablets and washed them down with gin. Then I took another two, and another two. I sat on the floor and cried. I had no music in my room so I started to sing to myself. I carried on swallowing tablets until I'd finished the packet of twenty-four, gagging as I struggled to swallow them and tasted their chalkiness.

I needed more, so I stumbled down the stairs and out of the front door. I wandered down the street, crying uncontrollably. I realised now that most shops would be closed. I slumped down on a wall next to a bus stop and felt my eyes start to close. All I needed was a little nap and I would be fine.

'Are you OK?'

I jumped up, startled. There was a middle-aged woman standing in front of me. She had a kind face.

'Ye . . . ye . . . yes,'

'You don't look it, let me get you home. Do you live with your parents?'

The word 'parents' hit me hard.

'No.'

At that moment a wave of nausea swept over me and I started to feel very sick. A white tablet appeared back in my mouth and I discreetly tried to spit it out. The woman noticed it on the ground.

'Oh my God,' she said. 'Have you taken tablets too?'

I nodded.

She sat down next to me and put her arm round my shoulders.

'Do you really want to die?' she asked.

'I don't think I do want to die, but I really don't want to live, if that makes sense. I feel like I'm in a void, somewhere between living and dying. My head feels like it's going to explode. I can't put an act on anymore.' I started to cry.

'You wait here,' she said gently. 'Let's get you to hospital.'

Five minutes later the woman had disappeared into the night and I was in an ambulance going to hospital.

I lay on a trolley and explained that I had taken about twenty tablets with gin and that it had been a big mistake because I was drunk. The nurses nodded in an uninterested fashion as they made me swallow a tube and washed out my stomach.

The doctor who came to see me said he thought I had got to the hospital in time and there would be no lasting damage. He wanted me to stay in overnight and have blood tests in the morning. The duty psychiatrist would also want to see me.

I was transferred to a ward, where a nurse put my clothes into the locker by my bed. When she disappeared from her station at the top of the ward, I pulled off the blue paper nightie I was wearing, got dressed and left the hospital. I wasn't about to get sucked back into psychiatric treatment: I could manage on my own.

Something changed for me that night. Explaining to the woman in the street how I felt had helped me to see what I was doing. The overdose had been a way to try to block things out. Living was hard, but I finally realised that I didn't really want to die. However tough it might be to move forward, and build myself a life, I wanted to live.

I let myself back into the house and went to bed. Something had lifted in my mind and I realised just how much I had moved on. Maybe, after all, there was a chance I might make it.

28

Falling in Love

The next day I slept until lunchtime and woke feeling very groggy. I went downstairs to get a coffee and was met by Steve, holding the phone out to me. It was Fran, so I waited for Steve to disappear into the kitchen before I started to tell her what had happened the night before.

Fran listened patiently and then asked me why I hadn't called the Samaritans. I tried to explain that it hadn't been a suicide attempt. I hadn't wanted to live but that didn't mean I wanted to die.

She said she understood and that she would ring me on Monday to see how I was feeling.

A few minutes later the phone rang again.

'Hi Sophie, it's Roz. I know we only spoke last night, but I've been thinking. I know you were friends with Dina and not me but I do care about you and I hope we can still be friends even though Dina's not here anymore.'

'Of course,' I said.

Roz invited me to go up to her flat in London for a meal that evening. I told her I had to work, but that I had Friday nights off. I thought about the night before. I could hardly describe having a stomach pump as the best ending to a Friday night, but Roz didn't know that.

I arranged to go the following Friday and forgot all about it until the following Friday afternoon when Mike came back to the office to take me to the pub.

'Oh, sorry Mike,' I said. 'I won't be able to come, I'm meeting a friend in London.'

'That's OK,' he replied. 'If you have a hot date then I wouldn't want to get in your way; it might be a good move to see my wife tonight for a change.'

'It's not a date,' I laughed, 'it's a woman.'

We went to the pub for lunch and then I went home, got changed and made my way back to the station. It felt weird when the train pulled into Paddington – I hadn't been there since the day I had come out of hospital several weeks earlier.

At seven o'clock I stood outside a large house and rang the buzzer that said 'Roz and Dina'. Roz buzzed the door open and I walked up the dark stairway to the attic.

Roz was a striking-looking woman. She was in her forties, slim and tall with short, dark hair. She had a boyish figure but had a smile that lit up her whole face. She looked like a woman but there was a confidence in her bearing that I associated more with a man.

I handed her a bottle of wine and bunch of flowers that I had bought at the station. She gestured for me to follow her into the flat. I was met with the smell of cooking. It felt unfamiliar – Steve and Nick rarely cooked and I barely ever ate in the house.

'It's only lasagne,' Roz said. 'I thought I'd make something easy so that we have time to talk. Let me take your jacket.'

'I'll keep it on,' I said, pulling it closely around myself. I didn't want her to see the bandage on my arm.

'It's OK if you've cut yourself. Remember I'm used to it after living with Dina,' Roz said. 'But keep it on if you'd like.'

She ushered me along a narrow hallway to a small room with a kitchen in the corner of it. There was a brightly coloured two-seater sofa and a television and stereo, but not much room for anything else. The lighting was soft and the room felt warm and friendly.

'Nice flat,' I said. 'Have you lived here long?' I felt awkward now that I was here, and wasn't sure what to say.

'It's more of a bedsit really. There's this room, a bathroom and bedroom and that's it. Just as well Dina didn't have much stuff,' she said drily.

We sat down and began talking, but the only thing we seemed to have in common was Dina, and Roz was understandably still hurt and reluctant to talk too much about her ex.

But when the conversation ran dry she started to ask me about me. I wasn't good at talking about myself, but Roz was patient and seemed to understand and gradually I began to tell her about what had happened since I left hospital.

In return Roz told me that she drove a London bus as her day job but was also a self-employed driving instructor, working part-time in the evenings to help pay the bills.

We balanced our meals on our knees and listened to music. I felt relaxed in her company and the conversation seemed to flow.

I suddenly noticed the clock on the stereo. I had half an hour to get the last train to Basingstoke. Roz tried to call me a taxi, but they were all busy.

'You're never going to make it back,' Roz said. 'Why don't you stay here? I'll sleep on the sofa and you can have the bed.'

'Are you sure? I don't want to put you out,' I replied.

'It's fine,' Roz said. 'Now we've got that sorted, let's have another drink.'

We talked for hours, until eventually we were both falling asleep. Roz brought a pillow and a blanket into the living room and I hugged her goodnight and thanked her for a nice evening before going to bed. The bedroom was light blue and felt cool and relaxing. The duvet and pillows felt light and fluffy and as I rested my head on the pillow I felt my eyes closing almost straight away. But I could hear Roz thrashing about in the next room and realised that she must be far too tall to lie comfortably on a two-seater sofa.

'Roz,' I called. 'I'm not as tall as you, I'll sleep on the sofa.' I started to get out of bed when Roz came in.

'Tell you what,' she said. 'I'm not going to bite you and there's room in here for both of us. Do you mind if I sleep in the bed too? If you have a problem because I'm gay then I'll understand.'

'Of course it's fine,' I said. Roz slipped into bed and turned the light off. I lay motionless, feeling the energy that had been building between us all evening. I couldn't understand what it was but I felt happy.

Roz turned over in the bed and moved closer. 'Do you mind if I hold you?' she said.

As she tenderly put her arms around me, every sense in my body was heightened. It felt safe, and warm and good.

I had never made love with a woman before but now that Roz was touching me it felt so right. For the first time I wasn't blocking out what was happening. Roz was gentle, patient and loving and I realised that I had never made love before, I had only had sex. I didn't feel I was being groped or mauled; this was soft and tender. We lay in one another's arms and I felt secure enough to fall asleep.

In the morning we showered and Roz made a pot of coffee.

'So,' I said, after a while. 'Where does this leave us? I mean, do you ever want to see me again?'

Roz laughed. 'Of course I do. What happened last night wasn't pre-planned you know, but it was lovely. Why don't you stay for the weekend and go back to Basingstoke for work on Monday morning?'

I never normally missed a shift in the pub but this felt too important. So I phoned Jim and told him I wouldn't be in.

I went back to Basingstoke on Monday morning walking on air. I wanted to shout from the rooftops that I was in love. Mike wondered what was up with me but I felt I couldn't tell him in case he didn't approve. Instead I waited for Fran to ring on Monday night and blurted out that I was in love with a woman. My life felt good, I had turned a corner and Roz would be my future.

Fran asked me how it felt to let Roz close to me, both emotionally and physically. I said it felt wonderful. Fran said she wasn't surprised that I was with a woman, given my past experiences with men. She was happy for me and that felt like the icing on the cake.

Over the weeks that followed I saw more and more of Roz and worked fewer and fewer shifts in the pub. Eventually, I had to explain to Jim that I had to leave. He was sorry to see me go but knew that I had found happiness with someone.

After that I worked all day with Mike and then took the

train to London most nights, coming back the next morning. I spent so little time at the house in Basingstoke that Roz suggested I move in with her.

Roz understood my past without me having to explain and she was loving, kind and funny. But I was scared of investing everything in her and giving up my independence. After three months of seeing her I agreed to move in, but I said I couldn't give up my job. I knew I wouldn't get something as good in London and besides, I couldn't leave Mike: the business was too important to him and he was important to me. Roz understood and said that if I didn't mind the commuting then it would be fine with her.

So I moved in, and despite the long commute, life was good. I felt safe living with Roz, and safety was what I needed at this time more than anything else. We had lots of fun but there was also a deep side to our relationship and she helped me to come to terms with the memories from my past. She knew all about self-harm, and the fact that she understood meant I could buy blades when I felt bad without causing panic. I didn't often cut myself because knowing that I could was the release that I needed.

Cutting was now a small part of my coping mechanism. On those few occasions when I resorted to it Roz would calmly ask me why I had done it, and take me to the hospital if I needed stitches. There was no fuss, and gradually the need to cut started to fade. I still got the urge, but I learnt to talk it through first and give Roz a chance to help me deal with it.

I let the few people in my life know that I had moved, including Dad. I had thought hard about letting him know where I was. I was afraid that if I didn't he would find me unexpectedly, and that felt worse than telling him where I was and knowing he would call. He approved of the fact that I lived with a woman, although I didn't tell him I was in a relationship with Roz. He had found a girlfriend, so was less interested in trying to see me, which was a relief, but his calls and letters still shook me. He still had a knack of making me feel like a little girl and Roz pointed out that my voice seemed to regress when I spoke to him.

Roz and I managed well in her tiny flat. By the time I got home from work she would often be out on a driving lesson, so I would have some precious time on my own before she came in. And she would get her time during the day between her shifts on the bus and her driving lessons. The two incomes meant we could afford to go on holiday together and live quite comfortably. Life felt good; this was the closest I had ever been to feeling truly happy.

I was still in touch with Katie, who had gone back into hospital following a nervous breakdown. I wrote to her every week. Every now and again a letter came and I would sit and cry as I read what she wrote. She was in a bad way and I wondered why she hadn't made it and wished that she lived nearer so I could help. I suggested to Roz that we go to visit her, but she felt it might have a bad effect on me if I couldn't reach her and save her from herself. So I continued writing, but within a few months Katie's sporadic letters stopped completely and eventually I gave up, though I never stopped thinking of her.

Fran rang regularly to see how I was. She reassured me that if I ever needed to ring the Samaritans again I shouldn't see it as a failing or a weakness. I knew she was right; I was so thankful to Samaritans for having helped me through my dark days, but I hoped I wouldn't need them again.

Fran encouraged me to write about my experiences, using the diaries and poetry that I had written over the years. I started to put my thoughts down on paper, and it was a less destructive release than cutting. I read the poems and letters that I had written in the past and it sometimes helped me to relive the emotion without needing to using a blade. At those times it reminded me that I might just hold on to life after all, even on my most fragile days.

During this time I paid another couple of visits to my birth mother, Juliet, and her husband and son. I found being with them quite natural, and enjoyable, but I didn't tell them very much about myself, so the connection was always fairly superficial. I occasionally spoke to David on the phone. We got on well, but he didn't ask to see me and I realised he was a teenager and busy with his own life. He didn't really need a big sister, so I kept my distance.

After about nine months living with Roz I received a letter from Jane Gray. I had given her my new address when I moved back to London. She explained that she had retired from social work and, as she had always felt a motherly affection for me, she wondered if I would like to catch up over a meal.

I was touched that she cared so much she wanted to see me after her professional role had ended. I agreed to see her and we met one Saturday at a restaurant close to where I had once lived. It felt strange going back and memories flooded back as I walked down the street.

Jane threw her arms around me and gave me a big hug. I realised when the waiter came back to take our order that I hadn't been taking in the words on the menu at all. I felt weird. I was in a room with my social worker, who was no longer my social worker and I felt like a little girl, yet I wasn't a little girl.

'It's so good to see you, Sophie,' Jane was saying.

'It's good to see you too, but a bit strange, because the last time I saw you I was cut to shreds and intent on killing myself,' I replied.

'I know,' she said. 'I was so worried for you, I wasn't sure you would survive in the hospital, but you were such a risk to yourself that we couldn't put you anywhere else.'

'I know,' I said. 'It wasn't your fault, it was mine.'

'It was your father's fault,' Jane said. 'We knew that all along. I'm only sorry we didn't manage to prosecute him. We let you down. I'm sorry.'

'I'm glad you didn't prosecute him,' I replied. 'It would have killed me.'

Jane knew what I meant and that I was loyal to him despite what he had put me through.

'So, tell me all about this girlfriend,' she said, smiling.

I told her how great the relationship was, how much Roz meant to me and how my life had changed.

Jane got a tissue out of her bag and dabbed her eyes. 'Sophie, I am so happy for you, I really am, and so proud of you. Despite everything you've been through, you're a survivor.'

29

Moving On

Although I had told Jane all was well, deep inside I was starting to feel uneasy about my relationship with Roz. I loved
her, but I felt that she was starting to drift away. She was
working more than ever, and we didn't need the money. She
encouraged me to do my own thing more, and I felt her
interest in me fading. I didn't want to face that I might lose
her, because if I did I would have lost everything and my life
wouldn't be worth living.

Over the next few weeks it became clear that the relationship was on the rocks. I knew it but couldn't face the reality
that my first love had been lost. I was so scared of being
alone again. We both tried to pretend that life was normal,
but I had started to self-harm regularly and I think Roz felt
that she was back in the same cycle she had been in with
Dina. A friend of hers started to appear often at the flat and
I sensed that Roz wanted to be around her more than me. I
couldn't face what I thought was inevitable, so one evening
when she was at work I packed my bags and walked away.

I headed back to Basingstoke and stayed in a bed and breakfast. Mike and the job were the security I needed at that time.
I felt numb with sadness and loss, but when Roz called me

at work I didn't return her calls. In some strange way I felt I had taken control of the situation.

But life in the bed and breakfast meant I had no boundaries again, no one knew me and in my brokenhearted state I was cutting myself every night after work. I felt like I was on a slippery slope once again.

Mike picked up on my distress and took me for a drink after work to find out what was wrong.

'Since you came back from London you haven't been the same Percy that we knew before,' he said. 'In fact, we've been really worried about you. Do you think you need some kind of counselling?'

'I've had all the counselling that I'll ever need,' I replied. 'It makes me sad that I am back where I was a few years ago. I hate myself, and most of the time I don't want to live.'

Mike was silent.

'I think I had better move on,' I said. The words came out of my mouth unconsciously. I had never intended resigning.

Mike looked shocked.

'Good God, why? I wouldn't want you to leave. I know you're depressed but you still do a great job. Don't say stuff like that unless you mean it.'

I realised at that moment that I did mean it. This job had meant such a lot to me, and until now I had managed to keep my emotional state separate from work. But since leaving Roz my emotions had spilled over and now I had started to get looks of concern and even pity from the others at work. That worried me; I was their boss and I didn't want to be seen as weak.

'Mike – I never meant to resign, but now I have I realise it's right. You've been brilliant. Who else would have employed me when I had hardly any qualifications or experience? You gave me a chance and one that I will be eternally grateful for, but now I need to move on – it's time for a fresh start.'

Silence.

'Say something,' I pleaded.

'I don't want you to leave, Perce,' he said. His head was down.

'Don't you see what I'm saying?' I said gently. 'I'm on a slippery slope and because you can see that and care about me it gives me permission not to be OK – and I need to be OK. I need to be in a job where no one knows me and where I *have* to be OK.'

'You mean I'm too nice?' he smiled.

'Yeah, sort of. You're alright for a man,' I said.

Mike smiled and held my hand as he spoke. 'I understand. But I don't want you to go. If I ignore what I see happening to you, will you stay?'

'No Mike, I don't think I can, 'cos you really are a nice guy and you wouldn't ignore me. I'm sorry.'

Mike leaned over and put his arms around me. I started to cry.

'It's OK, Perce,' he said. 'Whatever you want to do is fine by me.'

And so, within two months of leaving Roz I had resigned from my secure and stable job, was self-harming every day and had moved back to London. I had nowhere to go, so I spent the first couple of weeks sleeping in bed and breakfast accommodation and hostels. I became nameless and faceless and started drinking and cutting again on a regular basis. I was right back to square one.

By this time my father had moved to the Midlands and

while we had regular contact on the phone, I tried to keep my distance and saw him only rarely. I always told him where I lived because the fear of him finding me unexpectedly felt worse than a planned meeting which I might have some control over. He knew I had nowhere to live and repeatedly invited me to go and live with him. Despite all that had happened a small part of me still longed for everything to be alright, and I was tempted. But the wiser, stronger part of me managed to say no. He sent me some money which helped get me through, and contacted my mum. A letter arrived at the bed and breakfast asking me to meet her for coffee and I agreed.

It was with some trepidation that I went to see her. She was living in a top-floor flat in a old three-storey house in south London. It was small but comfortably furnished. We sat in the living room, the atmosphere between us awkward.

'Your dad says you have nowhere to live,' she said.

'Erm, well, temporarily – I'll soon sort something out.'

'How are the driving lessons going? Wasn't a friend helping you?' she asked politely.

I thought back to the driving lessons Roz had been giving me. Mum didn't know I'd been in a gay relationship – how would she know? We had never talked about it, but I felt sad that it was another chapter of my life she'd missed.

'I had some in Basingstoke,' I replied. 'I took my test and failed.'

'Oh. Sorry. What a shame.'

Silence.

She tried again. 'I'm seeing a man now, his name is Mark. I don't know if your dad had said.'

I shook my head. I found the reference to my father

surprising. It seemed that despite the bitter divorce and all the history between them, they were friends.

She asked if I had seen or heard from Dad.

'For God's sake, Mum – can we talk about something else?' I snapped.

'Sorry. I just wondered, sorry.' Her eyes filled with tears.

Though I was doing my best to be calm and civil, I was still very angry with her. I changed the subject. 'How's Nan?' I asked. My grandmother had been such an important part of my childhood, and I hadn't seen or heard from her – apart from one letter – since before I went into hospital.

'She's pretty frail now, and confused. But she talks about you a lot. She'd love to see you.'

A wave of emotion flooded through me.

'Yes, I'd like that,' I said.

I spent the rest of the day with Mum. We talked about insignificant topics and as we kept the conversation light I felt I could cope. A few times she tried to steer me on to conversations about the hospital, or the abuse, or my self-harm, but I closed down. Even worse than that was when she tried to offer an apology for what had happened.

'I'm so sorry about . . .' she said, starting to cry.

'God, just leave it,' I said angrily. I wanted her to stop. Her words would be meaningless, she could never put the past right.

'I just wish I could put the clock back,' she continued.

'Me too,' I said, as I walked out of the room.

I found it so much easier to blame her than to blame Dad, and this was something others around me had struggled to understand. It was partly because I had always seen her as weak, and Dad had taught me very early on that weak equalled bad, while strong (which I always struggled to be) equalled good.

But there was more to my inability to blame Dad. Dr Harvey had helped me to understand why it was that I clung so hard to my image of the good times with Dad and my love for him. Dr Harvey said that maybe what had happened was simply too big for me to accept. He said the human mind will protect us from what we can't deal with, meaning that if I ever fully faced what had happened and saw Dad in the way others saw him, then it would be more than I could endure, and it would kill me. Being able to balance the 'good' in Dad against the bad things he did, allowed me to forgive and still love him, which made what I had been through possible to bear.

I listened to the sound of Mum's sobs as I went into the bathroom and looked for something sharp. The pain inside my head was intense and I needed to let it out. I reached for the nail scissors and started to score at the skin under my bandage. The skin broke and I felt relief as bubbles of blood started to appear.

Mum knocked softly on the door.

'Come on,' she said. 'Let's go and see your nan.'

I re-bandaged my arm, hid the bandage under my sleeve and opened the door.

It was a short drive to my grandmother's house. I hadn't seen her for over two years and when she opened the door I rushed into her arms and held her tightly, taking in her warmth and smell and remembering all the times when she had held me close. I wished I could be a child again and the story could be replayed. Though she was older, she had changed very little and the house was exactly as it had always been.

'Where are you living now, Sophie?' she said, when we finally stepped back to look at one another.

The question threw me. I didn't want to say that I was in temporary accommodation. But before I had a chance to answer my mother spoke. 'She's staying with me, Mum,' she said.

I gave her a startled look.

'It's just temporary, until she gets herself sorted out,' she continued. 'We'd kill each other if it was full-time, but we can do it in the short term.'

'I'm so pleased that you two are trying to sort things out after all that has happened,' Nan said. 'And I hope we can see each other. I want my favourite granddaughter back.'

'That would be nice, Nan,' I said. 'I've missed you.'

I sat in a daze as Mum and Nan chatted. It all felt so familiar and safe. The house I had lived in with my parents had been sold when I was in hospital and I had never had a chance to clear my room or say my goodbyes. Mum's flat was alien to me and could just be anywhere, but in Nan's living room, I could recall the happy times. I could remember family Christmases and parties, my parents during happier days and times with Dad before the abuse.

I held my grandmother close again as we parted. I had missed her more than I could have imagined.

On the drive back I said, 'Thanks for saying all that about staying with you.'

'I wasn't just saying it; I meant it,' Mum said shakily.

I laughed nervously. 'You *are* joking, aren't you? We really would kill each other – and you only have a one-bedroom flat.'

Mum's face was flushed. 'I'll buy a fold-up bed and sleep on that in the living room.'

When we reached her flat she turned off the engine and looked at me. 'Please – give me a chance,' she said.

Everything inside me was screaming out 'no' but I saw the pain in her eyes and said, 'Yes, let's give it a try.'

Mum started the engine again. 'Let's go and get your stuff before you change your mind,' she said.

What on earth had I done? I wasn't a child anymore. I was a woman – I drank, I self-harmed, I cooked and cleaned for myself and now I had discovered I was attracted to women. How could this ever work?

'OK, let's go,' I said.

30

Back to Square One

In some ways living with Mum felt all wrong, but at the same time I felt I didn't know her and I wanted to try to. I couldn't cope with any sort of emotion from her — I was too afraid that it might lead us into conversations I didn't feel equipped to have. So we moved politely round one another. I wouldn't let her waste money on a bed and insisted on sleeping on the floor in the living room and bit by bit we got into a routine. She went to work and I cooked and cleaned while looking for a job. In the evening we had a meal together and at weekends she spent time with her boyfriend and I had the flat to myself.

We managed surprisingly well, given our painful past, and gradually we got to know one another better. Mostly this was on a fairly distant level, though we had moments when we allowed ourselves to get close and really get along. Neither of us pushed too hard for closeness, just chatting over dinner together was an achievement.

It wasn't easy, but it helped a lot that we had time apart at the weekends. That was when I could be me again, even if that did mean being able to self-harm. I would look forward to time on my own and buy blades and bandages, and when she had left the flat I would release everything that had been building up inside.

Although I was still self-harming I was determined to get my life back on track and not to spiral out of control and end up on drugs or on the street. I knew I needed a job to give me a routine and something to focus on, and within a couple of weeks I got one – as a trainee betting shop manager for Ladbrokes. I was only nineteen and was told I was the youngest trainee they had. I barely knew one end of a horse from the other, but getting the job boosted my self-confidence. The money was good, and at the end of the training I was made manager of a shop in south-west London. The hours were long and I threw myself into the work and spent less and less time at the flat. I was also working part-time at a local pub. Mum and I had managed surprisingly well sharing the flat, but I wanted to get a place of my own.

Life was getting back on track. I had money in my pocket and a good job, but I had lost something that I had in Basingstoke. No one at work really knew me and so no one cared. No one noticed when I was having a bad day, or gave me a call to see how I was feeling. I was still self-harming and drinking – though I never let either interfere with work – and Mum either didn't see or was too afraid to say. I had even stopped calling Fran. I told myself I didn't need the Samaritans, I could manage by myself. I was still struggling to understand my sexuality – and it was harder than I would ever have imagined. Was I gay, or was it simply Roz I had been attracted to? I started to go to some of London's gay clubs, where I stood at the side of the dance floor and was terrified if anyone approached me and asked me to dance. But gradually I began to relax and realised that watching women dance and kiss felt right. I began saying yes when someone asked me to dance, and even went home with some of them. I wanted a relationship, but most of the women I met were just looking for sex and didn't want to see me again.

A few weeks after I had moved in Mum announced that she was going on holiday with her boyfriend. She wondered if I would be alright alone in the flat. I told her I was used to being alone, but I knew it was going to be hard. Even in the bed and breakfasts and the house I shared in Basingstoke there were people around and I knew I couldn't totally lose control, but a flat on my own for two weeks would be new for me.

After Mum left I cried and cried. I was scared; the worst kind of scared in the world, because I was scared of myself. I was scared of my memories, scared of closing my eyes at night, scared of losing control and killing myself. So I did the only thing that felt like it might help – I called Dad. He would make it alright. He would tell me he loved me.

Dad's voice was warm. 'Hello, love,' he said.

I started to cry.

'What's wrong?' he asked.

I cried.

'You haven't been cutting have you?' he asked.

I cried.

'You stupid girl, why have you done that? Where are you?'

'I'm sorry,' I blubbered the words out.

'Is your mother there or are you alone?'

Desperate as I was for comfort, I knew I couldn't tell him the truth. My heart wanted to say that she was away – I wanted to see him and for him to hold me and love me like a father. But a voice in my head said a loud no.

'Yes, she's here, she's just popped out,' I lied.

I heard my father sigh.

'Ring me when you can talk properly,' he said coldly, and rang off.

I sank down on to the floor and cried.

Somehow I went through the motions of going to work and the routine kept me safe and sober during the day. At night I worked in the pub or went out to clubs. It was a painful, difficult time, but I got through, and I knew I had taken a big step forward. Saying no to Dad, and staying on my own for two weeks was something I had never done before. Despite all the times I felt I had slid back to zero, I had, for the first time in my life, chosen to resist my father and keep myself safe. I didn't feel jubilant: far from it, I felt numb and grief-stricken. But even in my dark and painful state I knew I had done something momentous and that I would never let my father abuse me again.

A few weeks later I made the decision to move out. A woman I had met in one of the clubs offered to rent me a room in her house, and I said yes. I told Mum, who was surprised, but pleased for me.

The day before I moved out, Mum sat me down. 'I was going to keep this until your birthday,' she said. 'But as you're going, I want you to have it now.'

She handed me a set of car keys. 'I bought you a car,' she said. 'It's only a second-hand one, but it'll get you started.'

I jumped up and hugged her, then raced down the stairs, where I found an old Mini Cooper parked at the front of the flats. I couldn't have been more pleased; I had passed my driving test second time around a few weeks earlier, and now this felt like the beginning of my independence.

I moved out the next day, and headed for my new start, in my new car.

A few weeks later a letter arrived.

Dear Sophie,

I hope this letter finds you well. Please excuse me for sharing my thoughts on paper. I'm sure you will understand, as you have so often used writing to describe your innermost thoughts and feelings, so forgive a sentimental old fool who needs to write things down.

What is a mother? A mother is entrusted with a small child – a gift – and expected to do her best to raise that child and keep her safe. A mother has little or no training or the skills to do the job.

I hope the time you spent with me in the flat has gone some way towards putting things right and will make amends for the years we spent apart. I wish I could put the clock back – there are some things I should have protected you from and for that I will always be sorry.

I know I can't make the past right now, but I want to make it up to you and hope you feel that the time at the flat has made us closer.

I love you and even though there must have been times when you have doubted it, I want you to know that I do.

All my love
Mum

I reread the letter before putting it back in my trouser pocket. I knew it must have taken a lot of courage for my mother to apologise. But I wasn't sure I was ready for it; I needed time to think. So I didn't answer, and although we stayed in touch, we were not as close as we had been.

A few months later, having worked hard and saved hard, I decide to buy a house. I took out a large mortgage, sold my car to furnish it and advertised for lodgers to help pay the mortgage.

My life now revolved around work. I did well at work, earned good money, bought a new car and even went back to college to try to catch up on my education, but I wondered if I would ever find happiness again.

My mother moved from London to the north-west of England, to manage a hotel. Things became distant between us again, and for many months I had little contact with either of my parents. Then, out of the blue, came a call from Dad. He told me he had married again – to a woman thirteen years younger, whom he had met while out walking his dog. They had actually been married for some months, he said, but he had been worried about how I'd take it. 'You're still my girl,' he added.

Actually, I was relieved that he had married. I hoped that now he had someone in his life my relationship with him could at last be just father–daughter, though in my heart of hearts I knew it was a foolish hope. The call shook me. If he had married again he must have convinced his wife that he was a nice, normal man. And perhaps he was, I thought. Perhaps it was me who wasn't normal, and who had made him do what he did.

I couldn't escape this thought and beat myself up with it mentally and physically – by self-harming – many times.

Not long afterwards I met a woman called Dee. She was thirty-five, a heavy drinker and self-harmed on a daily basis.

I was convinced this was someone who really understood me and soon became heavily involved with her.

I worked as normal during the week, but every weekend I went to see her in Southampton where she lived, and got into a spiral of self-destruction which we encouraged one another in. We would cut ourselves with the same blade and help bandage each other up. We drank until we couldn't stand up and then took antidepressants and collapsed into bed. I felt I didn't need anyone else – we were invincible.

One night, a few months into our relationship, I woke up in a pool of blood. I looked at her lying next to me and didn't know which one of us was bleeding. I woke her up and she laughed and told me to go back to sleep.

I got out of bed and paced around her flat. I wanted to die – I couldn't release the pain in my head. All the hurt of the past seemed to crowd in on me. I blamed myself for all the abuse and felt, as I had so often in the past, that all the treatment and help I'd received had been pointless, I was as much of a mess as ever.

I looked over at Dee. I needed her, but she was sleeping and I felt she didn't care. I went to the medicine chest and swallowed a handful of pills and then fell asleep.

Neither of us woke up for two days and when we did we were in hospital. The landlord had been worried about music playing continuously for two days and had come into the flat to find us both unconscious.

We were both full of drugs and drink and needed stitches in our cuts. We had both missed a week at work and no one had even known where I was. We were killing ourselves and each other. Dee was taken to a hospital to dry out and I was referred to my doctor for an urgent medical assessment. I didn't need an assessment – the wake-up call had been enough. The whole thing deeply shocked me and scared me and I realised how close I had come to being put in hospital again. I went back home and called Fran.

Although we had stayed in touch, I hadn't called her for help for over a year. I had believed I was coping with my life and I wouldn't need the Samaritans any more. Yet once again I needed the comfort and refuge they offered me in the darkest times.

Fran met me at the Samaritans' centre. I was twenty-two, but as I sat facing her in the sparsely decorated room, I felt like a fifteen-year-old again. I sat and cried as I explained what had happened with Dee and how I felt I was too messed up to ever find anyone who would want to be with me.

'It's like everyone has moved on,' I explained. 'I'm left with all this and everyone else is just getting on with their lives. Dad doesn't think about me, he's got a new marriage, yet I can't get him out of my head. Every time I close my eyes at night I feel his body crushing me and his breath against my face and I have to open my eyes again to check he isn't there.

'Then, around 3 a.m., which is the time when the abuse was at its worst, I wake with a start and, even with the bedroom light on, I see him standing by the door, sometimes alone and sometimes with other people. I even moved my bed so I wasn't facing the door, but that scared me more, as I thought I wouldn't know if he was there.

'When I wake in the morning he is the first person I see in my mind's eye, it's as if he haunts me.'

'Isn't it better for you that he has moved on?' Fran asked.

'I wanted to please him, I wanted him to love me, and now I'm in this mess and am alone with trying to sort it out and

I feel I just need his help.' The tears were racing down my face again and Fran put her arm around me. I felt secure when she held me, as if she could somehow erase what was in my head.

'Sophie, you need to let people around you that care be the ones who help you. You have some very good friends now – I wish I could help you to see that.'

I felt encouraged by Fran's words, but still so empty as I left her. The relationship with Dee had taken my recovery back by several steps. Why was I at the Samaritans at twenty-two years old? I was there as a child and in my head it felt as if nothing had changed. I still hated myself and I still needed help.

31

A Friendship Blossoms

Over the next couple of years I went through the motions. I worked long hours at the betting shop Monday to Saturday and during the summer evenings, to cover the night-racing calendar. I started to study at home in my spare time, and filled every waking hour, so that I wouldn't have to think. If I wasn't busy, I was drunk.

The betting shop I was managing did well and my bosses rewarded me with bonuses, which helped me to pay the mortgage and afford my hectic weekend social life. When I started the job I had worried about the fact that most punters were men, so the betting-shop environment was very male. But the regular customers in the betting shop became very protective of me and the other female staff. When we had the occasional aggressive customer or drunk who was shouting and threatening us, it was the regular male customers who used to lift them up and deposit them on the street outside.

I became good friends with the women that I worked with – in particular two cashiers called Denise and Anne. Denise was divorced with two children and had a great sense of fun. After the racing finished at 8.30 we would go to each other's houses for a meal and a drink. There was never any hint of anything romantic or physical between us – she knew I was gay and I knew she was straight. She didn't judge me and we had a good time. Life was starting to look up.

Around this time I employed a new cleaner at the betting shop called Kay. She was in her late-thirties and keen to earn the extra money. She seemed to be a serious person and on the occasions when I did try to make her laugh, she would smile politely and get on with her work. Denise and I used to joke that we should probably clean the betting shop ourselves before she arrived as we didn't want to upset her!

One winter morning I went into the shop to open up. By this stage I had an Old English Sheepdog called Sascha who I took to the shop with me every morning when I was working alone. I would normally take her home at lunchtime.

After I had set the shop up ready for opening, I went outside to raise the heavy steel shutters. I went back in and as I pushed the door shut I felt someone pushing at it from the outside.

'We're not open yet,' I called.

The door was pushed open and a man pushed his way into the shop. 'You are now,' he replied.

Before I had a chance to react he had pulled a gun from his jacket pocket and was holding it to my head.

'Give me the money or I'll blow your head off,' he shouted.

Sascha came running from the office at the back of the shop and started to bark playfully.

'Stop the dog or I'll shoot it,' he said.

I shut her into a small alcove area outside the toilets, then walked back into the office and opened the safe. The winter weather had meant that racing the previous day had been largely abandoned and the takings were low. I figured the man couldn't have known anything about racing to be robbing the shop after such a quiet day. He was still waving the gun around but I could see that his nerves were kicking in as the gun started to shake every time he pointed it at me. I passed him the money and he asked me for the keys so he could lock me in the shop.

I started to thread a chain of keys off the large bunch. 'You're not having my car,' I said calmly, and passed him the door key. A sense of calm washed over me – the same calm that had kicked in every time I had been faced with danger in the past, a feeling of inevitability that this might be the moment when I would die.

He pushed me into the area where Sascha was and I heard him lock the door. I still had the back-door key so I waited five minutes before getting out and running to the nearest house where I knew someone – Kay's house. She opened the door and I collapsed into her arms sobbing and shaking as shock set in.

From that day on Kay and I became friends. Over the months that followed the robbery, I went to her house on a regular basis and I started to see strength in her that I admired. She was an independent person who knew her own mind and was fiercely protective of anyone she cared about. And underneath the rather austere exterior she had a good sense of humour.

After work, Denise, Kay and I would often go back to my house and cook a meal together, drinking copious amounts of wine before the two of them fell into a taxi.

Gradually I realised that my feelings towards Kay were turning from friendship to something much stronger, but I didn't dare tell her, as I feared rejection and the loss of our friendship.

I spent more and more time with her, and confided in her about my past and my feelings of low self-worth. She was angry at my father for what he had done and angry at me for my continued self-harm. On many occasions she made me give her the blades, which I always carried with me.

'I'll take those,' she said firmly, holding her hand out. 'If you feel like cutting then ring me.'

So I would, and she would invite me round. We became closer, and one night, as we sat on the floor watching the music channel together, Kay leaned back against me and we shared a kiss. Kay had never had any feelings for a woman before, so it caused her great confusion. For weeks she wasn't sure whether she wanted to be with me or not, though when we were together we had a wonderful time. I knew I loved her. But I was sure it couldn't be mutual. I waited for the bubble to burst, convinced that in time she would finish the relationship. But to my astonishment, she didn't. Instead she told me she'd made up her mind – she wanted to be with me, and for us to make a life together.

32

Full Circle

Kay and I began to talk about making a new start, away from London, somewhere where we could share a brand-new beginning. I wanted to leave all my unhappy memories behind and Kay agreed that it felt right. My mother had written a few days earlier to say that she was getting remarried and would be moving from the north west to Wales with her new husband. I dug her letter out of my bag and picked up the phone.

'Hi, Mum,' I said. 'Congratulations. Where will the wedding be?'

'Hi Sophie,' she replied, 'it's great to hear from you.'

I listened patiently and made the appropriate noises of support as she told me about her new life.

Eventually she asked me how I was. 'Well,' I said. 'It's a long story, but I was wondering what you're going to do with your house when you move?'

'I'll sell it,' she replied. 'Why do you ask?'

'Can you sell it to me?' I said.

'Sell it to you?' Mum was saying. 'You want to move north? You haven't even seen it. Do you have a job up here?'

'The thing is,' I hesitated, 'I'm gay.'

'I know that,' she said.

'You do?' I exclaimed. 'How?'

'I just put two and two together. I guessed you would tell me some day.'

I was shocked. Her acceptance had floored me and I wanted to ask her lots of questions. But I decided to put my 'coming out' moment to one side and get back to the original point.

'Right, well, I'm in love with a woman called Kay and we want to make a new start. If you sold me your house and gave me a few weeks to find a job up there we'll sort out the mortgage as soon as we're settled.'

There was a pause.

'Well, fine, if that will help you, no problem. I'm ready to move out, so when do you want to move in?'

'How about next week?'

I looked at Kay and we both laughed. It was impulsive and crazy, but it felt right to just go, and worry about the details later. All our friends and the other staff in the shop were shocked by our news, but we felt fantastic. We threw a big party and everyone cried over their drinks, including us.

A week later we found ourselves sitting on tea chests full of our hastily packed possessions, contemplating our new surroundings.

We had to face a new town and a new home and we still had a mortgage to pay on the house we had just left. We needed money to live on – and we had no jobs. The enormity of what we had done seemed insurmountable. So we did the only thing that we could, under such extreme circumstances, and went back to bed – where we stayed for a week.

Once the honeymoon was over Kay found work in a local hotel. I could have looked for a job in a betting shop, but I wanted to make a new start where I wouldn't have to work every Saturday, Bank Holiday and in the long summer evenings. I looked around, and within two weeks I had started training to manage an off-licence. A week into the training I was sent away to complete a Wines and Spirits Certificate and as I sat in my hotel room at night reading books about fermenting processes and grapes I realised the job wasn't quite as simple as I had first thought.

Kay and I settled into a routine and I relished the fact that I had a new start in a place where I had no unhappy memories and someone who was committed to me. But my feelings of low self-worth were still there and I struggled with sleeping in a bed next to another person night after night. I still woke at 3 a.m. and Kay suggested that I got up if I couldn't sleep. It became a pattern and I would often sit up and watch television, before falling asleep on the sofa.

I was still cutting intermittently, and always carried blades with me as a form of security. Kay found this very hard to deal with and she would find blades and throw them away, or search my handbag or pockets if she suspected that I might be feeling low.

I would go straight to the chemist and buy more. Occasionally I would cut and bandage myself and then I'd use avoidance tactics, to stop Kay finding out. I'd opt to sleep on the sofa, feigning period pains or other ailments in the hope that my cuts would heal before she had the chance to see them.

Kay caught on to what I was doing and would regularly demand to 'check me over'. If I had cut myself she'd get very angry and refuse to talk to me. The emotional upsets hurt me far more than any hurt that I could inflict on myself and over time I stopped cutting. The control that I felt my dad had over me had been transferred to Kay. I loved her but I was also scared of her reaction to what I had done.

I had an almost constant battle going on in my head, but gradually staying safe started to seem like a better option than cutting. And as my urge to self-harm started to come under some sort of control, my self-esteem started to grow. Every time I managed to resist cutting I gradually started to believe in myself a tiny bit more. As always, my progress never went in a straight line, it was two steps forward one back – and sometimes two back – all the way. But over time, as Kay and I settled into our new life, the forward steps outnumbered the backward ones.

It took a long while for me to accept that what my father did to me was abuse. This understanding, I realised in hindsight, came in gradual stages. For so long I had found it easier to think of it as his extreme love for me that had gone wrong. I couldn't bring myself to face the truth. But bit by bit, as I put more emotional distance between him and me, I had come to accept that this was a distortion of the truth. Though I still slipped back, from time to time, into blaming myself, I knew that in reality the only person to blame was him.

Contact with him was limited to cards to mark special occasions. It was easier to allow this than to cut him off altogether, and face a confrontation with him. I knew that if I rejected all contact he would come looking for me, and I didn't want him near my home or the life I had made. But even a card every now and then made me very depressed and upset and so I tried to stay as distant as possible.

I called him on very rare occasions, when I felt it unavoidable, and once or twice I spoke to his wife, who sounded very pleasant. Sometimes he called me, but he would always do it when she was out, so that he could grill me about my eating, drinking and salary. I did my best to get him off the phone as quickly as possible.

Then one Saturday afternoon, with no warning, he and his wife turned up on my doorstep. Apparently they had been passing nearby and she had suggested it. I realised that she must have wondered why his daughter was so distant, and wanted to encourage contact, but for me it was a terrible invasion. The three of us sat for half an hour and had a polite conversation over tea. Dad and I were awkward with one another and the whole thing was an ordeal. After they left I felt desperately upset because he now knew what my home looked like and I couldn't bear the thought of that.

The last time I saw him was on his seventieth birthday. His wife called me to say she was organising a surprise party. She explained that it would be mostly her family and my dad's friends and that Dad's sister and I would be the only family from his side. I felt terribly awkward, as well as concerned that in her mind I was a pretty bad daughter. No doubt she knew nothing of the past and so thought of me as distant and uncaring. Perhaps I shouldn't have minded that, but I was used to doing the 'right' thing and pleasing others, and so without giving myself time to think it through, I agreed to go.

I hadn't been to their home before and my stomach was in knots as I drove there. When I arrived his wife was delighted. Once inside the door I walked through a throng of strange faces to see Dad standing at the end of the room. He saw me and cried. Then he held me and told me how much it meant to see me, before proudly introducing me to everyone. Most people didn't know he had a daughter, and comments like 'I never knew you had children' and 'you don't see her much' stung me. I felt I was being judged and that everyone would see me as a daughter who had failed her father.

The horror didn't end there. Dad tried to get me on my own and offered to give me a tour of his home, which I declined. I didn't even go to the loo, afraid that he might follow me upstairs. But that didn't stop him making innuendos and putting his arm round me whenever he could. His wife seemed lovely – which made the whole thing even more confusing. And meanwhile my aunt, who I'd never known well, was polite and made comments about having not seen me for a long time. I had no idea what to say.

My head was banging and I felt out of control, not knowing what anyone knew about me. I stayed for a couple of hours and then said I had to go as I had a long drive back.

As I drove away my legs started shaking uncontrollably – I had to stop the car and broke down in floods of tears. I wept for the past, for all the pain I'd been through, and because I saw so clearly, once and for all, that my father had not changed, and never would, and that I would probably never see him again.

Hard as it was, that party was another turning point for me. I had seen Dad with the eyes of someone standing at a distance, and I was no longer sucked into his deceit. I had been polite in front of the other guests, but I knew him for what he was; a sick old man who deserved no pity from me. As my recovery became more solid and real, I started to think about the Samaritans again – not about calling them for help, but about becoming a volunteer and paying something back to the organisation that had helped me so much in the past. But I wondered if they would accept me.

By this time Fran had left the Samaritans, but we were still in touch as good friends. I talked to her about becoming a volunteer and she told me she thought I was ready and would be good at it, which was the encouragement I needed.

I called and offered my services and over the next couple of weeks my application was processed. I attended the information evening, watched a video and was surprised at the level of commitment that was expected – one full-night duty every four weeks and one three-hour duty per week. And many volunteers undertook additional duties.

I scribbled down all the facts and figures, avoiding eye contact with any of the volunteers who were running the session. I felt it would be written all over my face that I had called the Samaritans in the past.

We were then invited back for a second time and had to participate in group exercises, while being observed, after which we were taken out one by one to be interviewed by two volunteers.

My heart stood still as the interviewer asked the million-dollar question about whether I had ever called before. I took a deep breath and told the truth. I said I had called as a child, had been befriended and that I hadn't now needed to call the Samaritans for several years. We talked about how I felt and what sort of calls I might find hard to deal with and the interviewer explained what it was like to be a Samaritan – confidentiality was a must and volunteers never discussed calls outside of the Samaritan movement. I was impressed with the support that was in place and surprised at the comprehensive training package, which would take a number of months to complete.

The interviewer explained that the sort of one-to-one

support I'd had from Fran was no longer policy, and that contact with callers now took place in the Samaritan centre rather than in callers' homes.

At the end of the interview the volunteers said that they were happy to accept me and welcomed me as a trainee Samaritan. I walked with a skip in my stride as I left the building. They had accepted me, and that meant a lot.

Over the next few months my life started to move in a new direction. While I didn't have paper qualifications, I had built up the experience to get myself better jobs and I was really proud when I landed a management job working for a blue-chip company in Manchester, with good prospects and pay. And I enrolled at the local college to take some A levels so that I could take an Open University degree.

I studied hard and worked hard and in the evenings I underwent the Samaritan training. I had started to take calls, alongside a trained mentor. It felt strange to be on the other end of the line, having so often been the caller in the past. At the same time it was a huge privilege that complete strangers were prepared to tell me their innermost thoughts. I realised how it might have been for Fran talking to me all those years before.

As a caller I hadn't wanted answers, just a feeling that someone would be there to care for me unconditionally, so I knew the power of simply listening, with empathy and compassion. As a child I had hung up when the voice on the end of the phone didn't sound caring and warm – and now that I was on the other end, that was at the forefront of my mind every time I picked up the phone.

I knew there must be many others out there, like me, and there was nothing in my area offering them support, so as

I became a fully fledged Samaritan and my confidence grew, I decided to start a self-help group for victims of sexual abuse.

It wasn't easy to find premises and to publicise what I was doing, but eventually I found a place for the group to meet and got an article in the local paper. I asked a friend from the Samaritans, Jenny, to support me in setting up the group and we planned our first meeting.

The evening came and Jenny and I sat drinking coffee together and waiting for people to arrive. No one came that week, or the next, or the one after. On week four a nervous-looking woman arrived and sat in silence. I told her a bit about myself to make her feel more at ease. She nodded and cried and the following week she came back.

By month three we had fourteen people coming on a weekly basis. Some didn't speak and some didn't stop speaking, though we encouraged the quiet ones to open up. The group was about more than just sharing what had happened – it was about how we coped with what had happened and with our feelings of self-hate.

It became a real success, and I was proud that I'd been able to do something for others who had suffered in the same way I had.

A couple of years into my work with Samaritans I was asked to look after the selection of new volunteers. This was a real privilege for me and I gratefully accepted the additional responsibility.

It was around this time that I was reading through a Samaritan publication and noticed a piece that had been written about self-harm. It was a long article by a volunteer from London who had been trained to deal with people who self-harmed. I read it with interest and then spotted the name at the end – Pam.

I flashed back to the time when I had been homeless in London and had stumbled into a branch and met a woman called Pam. Surely it couldn't be her, after all these years. I wasn't sure, but if it was I felt an overwhelming need to thank her.

I wrote a note.

Dear Pam

I'm sure you don't remember me but I was a caller back in the eighties and visited the branch where I think you were a volunteer. I was sleeping rough, having run away from home and you spoke to me on the phone and invited me in. I was in quite a mess, as I had self-harmed, so I was interested to read that you now work in this field. After I left you wrote me a letter and that's why I still remember you so well.

Please don't feel you have to reply and apologise if you don't remember me or if you are the wrong Pam. I just wanted to say thank you, as you did make a real difference to how I got through those really hard times. I am pleased to say that twelve years on I'm doing really well and I am now a volunteer in a branch in the north west. Just a small way of repaying an organisation that has meant so much to me.

Thanks Pam once again – all the best for the future
Love Sophie x

I felt nervous as I dropped the letter into the post box. I so wanted to say thank you to one of the people who had made such a positive difference to me at such a desperate time. A few weeks went by and I resigned myself to the fact that it must have been a case of mistaken identity. Then a letter arrived.

Dear Sophie

I have been on leave of absence over the Christmas period so only got your letter last week when I went in for a night shift.

What can I say? I was absolutely gobsmacked, I think the expression is, to receive your letter.

As volunteers we never hear how things have turned out. I'm so pleased to hear that you are doing well and have become a volunteer.

As you know I am still a volunteer – nearly nineteen years now. The work I did with the Samaritans at the time I met you led me to go back to college and retrain as a social worker, which led to work in a hospital with patients who had self-harmed. I've been there ever since, and now supervise the self-harm team.

I have always been particularly interested in this area because I feel people who self-injure are so misunderstood. There is awareness now but still nowhere near enough.

Thank you again for your letter – I was deeply moved by it and it gave me a real boost.

I hope we will be able to meet up some day.

Love Pam

I did see Pam again, when she attended a north-west Samaritans conference a year or so later. She was running a session on self-harm and I dragged my friend Jenny with me into the lecture theatre half an hour before Pam's talk was due to start. When the door opened I recognised Pam immediately. She came in and started setting up her projector and glanced up at the two of us sitting at the back and smiled.

I nudged Jenny in the ribs. 'I can't move. I'm too scared. Can you go and tell her it's me?' Jenny went down to the stage to speak to Pam and after a few moments they both hurried back up the stairs and Pam threw her arms around me. There were tears streaming down my face as Pam pulled away to look at me.

'It's so great to see you, Sophie,' she said. 'You don't look any different.'

'God, I hope I do,' I spluttered, remembering that the last time I had been sleeping rough and had cut myself to shreds.

Pam smiled.

We sat and talked for a few moments and then Pam went to present her session. I sat transfixed listening to her speak about why she felt self-harm was so misunderstood and what we as Samaritans could be doing to help. I felt lucky that I had stumbled across someone who had understood self-harm at a time when no one talked about it. And here I was listening to her, not as a caller but as a Samaritan myself.

By this time, when I was twenty-eight, my life had improved beyond recognition. I loved my job, my studies, my work with the Samaritans and being with Kay.

Mum was still in Wales; we talked from time to time on the phone and she came to stay a few times. We were still cautious around one another, but she got to know Kay and joked that she was her second daughter.

My grandmother had died, and her loss hit me hard. Even though we had never rekindled what we had before I went into hospital, my love for her had remained strong and I missed her.

Juliet, my birth mother, was still living in Essex. We didn't speak often and most of the contact was through birthday and Christmas cards. David was now grown up and had gone through university. Juliet sometimes passed on his news and gave him news of me, but I hadn't been in direct contact with him for some time. So I was surprised when I received an invitation to his wedding.

Although I was nervous at the prospect of so many people I didn't know, I decided to go. It was an almost surreal experience. Many of the guests didn't know I existed – but when I arrived looking like a younger version of my mother, the secret was out. Juliet led me round the room, introducing me to a long list of family and friends, and I was touched that she was so proud of me. But I was confused because I didn't know where I fitted in, and the whole thing, though lovely, was rather gruelling. I got home exhausted, but glad I had gone, and moved at having been welcomed so warmly.

33

A Diagnosis

One day in 1999 I was driving to work when my eyes started to become blurry. I tried to blink it away but it seemed to be getting worse. I felt scared that I was losing my sight and I pulled over to the side of the road and rang work from my mobile.

I was put through to the occupational health department who advised me to leave the car and get a taxi to hospital to be checked over. Half an hour later I lay on a stretcher with a group of doctors gathered around me.

'We're going to give you a scan,' one said.

I closed my eyes and nodded. As long as they made me feel better I didn't care.

Over the next few days I had every area of my body prodded and scanned and was eventually discharged back to my local hospital along with an urgent appointment to see a neurologist. My doctor signed me off work for a month and I went home to bed. I felt a tiredness that seemed to run through my bones. My vision was clear again, but my hands and feet were now numb and I had a burning sensation in my legs. I knew I wasn't well but no one could tell me what it was. The neurologist said he didn't know and wouldn't like to speculate.

He said he needed to admit me to hospital for tests – a full body MRI scan and a lumbar puncture, as well as brain, ear and eye tests.

The tests were awful I seemed to spend hours every day with electrodes attached to my head. As soon as the tests were over I discharged myself and came home. An appointment was made with the neurologist for two weeks' time.

The two weeks dragged by. My mother and her husband had moved back to the area a few weeks earlier, and she tried to occupy me by taking me to garden centres to buy plants and coloured stones for my large garden. I began by grudgingly helping her with the planting, but slowly started to enjoy the time we were spending together.

It was non-threatening; we weren't talking about the past but we were sharing something together, and while it didn't make me suddenly like gardening, it distracted me from the imminent diagnosis and Mum was good company. I wished I could have told her how I felt but hoped she would pick up on the thankyous that I offered.

I went back to see the neurologist with my Samaritan friend Jenny. Mum would have been too emotional and Kay was not as strong at dealing with potential bad news as she appeared. I asked Jenny to wait outside and went in on my own.

'How are you feeling?' the neurologist asked.

'Still tired, but at least my eyes aren't blurry now,' I replied.

'That's good.'

There was a long pause.

'Anyway,' he said, pulling out a sheet of graphs from my file. 'You will be pleased to know we have good news for you.'

I relaxed in my seat. Thank God, I thought.

'You haven't got a brain tumour,' he said.

I looked stunned. 'I never thought I had a brain tumour in the first place, so it's a bit of a shock.'

'Sorry,' he said kindly. 'I thought it had been explained to you that when any patient presents with your type of symptoms we start with the worst prognosis and work on an elimination basis until we find the correct diagnosis. Brain tumour would have been the worst-case scenario and we have eliminated that.'

'That's good news then,' I replied drily.

'Yes it is,' he replied. 'We are fairly sure you have a condition called MS – Multiple Sclerosis. It's quite a difficult neurological condition to diagnose but based on your various test results I would say the likelihood is very high.'

'Thank you,' I said, but immediately realised that didn't sound right.

'I have some information here for you to take away,' he said, passing me a pile of leaflets.

'So what now?' I said. 'Do I get treatment?'

'Yes – we can't cure it but we can treat it. We'll be able to get some of these nasty symptoms out of the way. And I suggest you register as disabled,' he said, handing me a form. 'It means you'll get the best parking spaces.' He smiled.

'I'll see you every three months and we can review the work situation. If we need to get you pensioned off from work I can sort that for you.'

I knew I was supposed to be pleased and grateful but I felt numb. I wasn't even thirty years old and he was suggesting I finish work, for good.

'Do you have any questions?' he asked.

'What's the cause? I mean, why did I get it?'

He rocked back in his chair and placed his glasses on the desk in front of us. 'Million-dollar question, Sophie. Depends which medical book you read. Some research suggests a genetic link, some relates to exposure to mercury, some relates to viral infections as a child and other schools of thought relate to shock or trauma in childhood. It's not easy to work out, but luckily the headway in treatment has moved on much quicker than the headway in finding a cause.'

The words 'shock or trauma in childhood' rang in my ears over and over again. My dad had done this.

Outside the room Jenny jumped up. I was in a daze.

'What is it, Sophie?' she asked. 'Did he say what it was?'

'Yes,' I answered. As I turned round to face her my eyes filled with tears. 'He said it's my dad.'

I coped with the news of the MS in the same way I have coped with everything that has happened in my life, which I haven't understood. I read and read: every book, every Internet article, every newsletter from the MS Society. I needed to understand in order to cope with the diagnosis.

I was signed off work for a couple more months in order to try different medications and in that time my mother and I carried on working in the garden. This was the first time we had ever worked closely together and shared a task and I caught myself starting to enjoy the time we shared.

Once I went back to work full time I found that I needed to sleep a lot in order to recharge my batteries. My life was filled with a routine of work, Samaritans and sleep. My legs had become painful, due to the MS, and I couldn't find a position in which I felt comfortable, so I found sleep even more difficult than usual.

By this time Kay and I were drifting apart. We were still very fond of one another, but our lives were going in different directions. Each of us had our own friends and interests and we had less and less in common. When the MS began to affect me I suggested to her that it might be better for us both if I moved to the spare bedroom, and she agreed that it would be a good idea.

When I look back, I realise this was the move that changed what we had from a relationship to a strong friendship. We never discussed it – we just evolved into something new and it still felt OK.

Over the next few months the physical pain in my legs got worse and I began to get depressed. Mostly I managed to present a cheerful front to the world, but one weekend my mask fell away and I couldn't seem to lift myself. The pain in my legs was immense and the pain in my head felt even worse. I wasn't a person prone to having bouts of self-pity and the on the whole would try to see the positives in most situations, but on this particular Saturday I was very low. I sat at home and cried – for the present and for all that had happened in the past, as the neurologist's words about 'trauma in childhood' being a cause of MS went round and round in my head.

The feelings of wanting to self-harm had never ever gone away but for some time I had always managed to fight them. But on this particular day it all felt too much – Kay was at work and I began to feel that if only I could cut myself one last time I would all be alright.

I undressed and sat in the empty bath so the blood would be easier to clean up. I took a clean blade and gently started to score at the skin on my legs, cutting long parallel lines from my knee downwards. I watched the blood start to trickle and felt an immediate rush in my head and a sense of relief.

I carried on until my left leg looked cut to pieces and with a sense of satisfaction I moved on to the right one. First vertical lines and then horizontal – I no longer felt the pain of my MS or the pain of my past – my head was buzzing and I started to feel like the teenage Sophie again. I started to cry.

All the years in between suddenly felt wasted. If I was cutting now then I hadn't moved on at all.

I washed my legs as best I could and bandaged them tightly to try and stop the bleeding, though I could still feel the blood seeping through. This would have felt good in the past, but today it felt different. I felt a sadness that I hadn't felt before, not sad that I had cut, that would come later, but a sadness that I didn't feel the same relief afterwards. The relief had been there while I was cutting, but now I just felt empty and lost. When Kay came home from work and remarked on how badly I was walking, I said it was the MS and then went to bed early and cried myself to sleep.

Over the next few days my walking became worse; there were hundreds of cuts on each leg and both legs had become swollen and raw as the skin became inflamed. It was impossible to redress my legs without the bleeding starting again, and I couldn't wash them or take a shower as the water re-opened the cuts.

A week later Kay was so concerned about my walking that she threatened to call the neurologist, and I had to tell her the truth. She was mad at me and distraught that I had done this again. She did all the things she had done in the past: searched me for blades, threatened to leave and smashed a few cups. But it wasn't Kay's anger that affected me, it was something deep inside me that had changed. I suddenly understood that I had to stop doing this because I wanted to and not because I was afraid of her reaction or of being left.

I had hoped I would never feel like self-harming again. But in reality, rather like an alcoholic who doesn't stop craving a drink, I finally had to accept that I would always feel like harming myself when I was at my lowest point. Accepting that, and embracing it, was the key that would allow me to channel in a different way the feelings that went with the urge to self-harm.

I needed to keep myself safe, not for someone else, but because I thought I was worth it.

I was thirty years old and the penny had finally dropped.

34

A Pilgrimage

It took me another year or two to stop self-harming, once and for all, but eventually I did. The urge didn't disappear, but I was able to manage it. My MS was also brought under control, with medication, and I did well at work.

I loved my Samaritans work as much as ever, and one day I received a phone call asking me to consider taking over as Director of my branch. It would be voluntary, for three years, and would mean having responsibility for one hundred volunteers and the day-to-day running of the branch.

I rang my old friend, Fran – she was the obvious person to talk to about this, as she knew me so well and had also been Director of her own branch at one point. We talked it through and she reinforced what I already felt – that it would be a privilege and honour. I was so proud that the volunteers at the branch had asked me.

So twenty years after making my first call, I became Director of my local branch. It kept me hugely busy, on top of my day job, but I loved it.

Meanwhile I had settled into a routine of seeing my mother. Through the gardening we had, at last, found a way to communicate and be around each other. When she was told she had to have a hip replacement, I visited her every day in hospital and spent time sitting with her and trying to support her. It wasn't forced, I wanted to be there. It was as if we could both cope with being there for each other if we had a purpose. A lifetime of hurt and guilt was far from being unravelled, but we both wanted to try.

I was still living with Kay, who had continued to build her own life. We were still close friends though and there was a security around being with her that I couldn't explain to anyone else. It certainly made any attempts at relationships difficult as most women wouldn't believe that Kay could be a good friend and an ex-lover. We had a history that felt impossible to explain. Despite all the difficulties, she had been there for me through thick and thin without asking anything in return. Unconditional love is hard to find.

While my job was fine, for some time now I had wanted to work somewhere where I would have a closer interaction with vulnerable people. So when I saw an advert for an assistant director for a charitable organisation, I decided to apply. Much to my surprise I was offered the job and I decided to leave my reliable well-paid job with good prospects and a pension scheme that would allow me to retire early, and take the plunge into something new. My friends told me to reconsider – a new employer wouldn't cover me for the MS, as it was a pre-existing condition. I knew that, but I was thirty-four, my life was far from over and I didn't want to stay in the same job just because I could be pensioned off. I couldn't allow the MS to be a barrier for the rest of my life. I had to break free and show myself that I was still employable and still worth something.

I left my old employer with a wonderful goodbye party and within a few months another opportunity came along. I was now in my final year as Director of the Samaritans and I received a call asking me if I would take on the role of Regional Representative. It was another three-year, unpaid post, supporting the nineteen branches in the north west. I said yes immediately – I was only sad that I would have to leave my role as Director a few months early in order to take on the new role.

I rang Pam to let her know and she burst into tears on the phone. Pam was now a paid member of staff for the Samaritans and we laughed at how far we had both come since the day I called in to her branch.

A few months later Juliet contacted me to suggest we spend the day together. We had made a number of arrangements that didn't come off, but this time it did, and she flew up to see me.

We went to visit some friends of mine, and in the company of others we both thawed and enjoyed the day. When she left she promised she would write, but in the following months I heard nothing.

It was fifteen months later, after I had sent her some impromptu flowers for Mother's Day, that her letter finally arrived.

Dearest Sophie,

It's taken fifteen months, two Mother's Days and goodness knows what else, but here is the promised letter!

The day with you last year was really great and I was privileged to meet your very good friends. The really super thing was that they know you so well and that moved us on too, with honesty. For instance, I hadn't realised that you might want me to sign myself 'Mum' on cards before we had the conversation with your friends, and I didn't really feel I'd earned the right to do so. Despite the well-chosen words in cards from you to me I'd not picked up on what you wanted me to do. It was really good too for your friends to note our similarities: turn of phrase, facial expression, mastery of the understatement etc!

Seeing you in your home surroundings has given me, when I think of you (which is a lot!), the context that was missing.

By 'a lot' I mean every night, before I go to sleep, which is the ritual / habit / comfort routine that I got into when we first parted.

Of course, it doesn't help you, not knowing that I think of you lots and talk of you when I don't tell you that I am.

I bought the same classical CD that you have in your car for mine, so we are probably playing it at the same time.

Your flowers today were a lovely surprise (and the only ones I got!).

Thank you for sharing that you are writing a book – whatever the content I will be really proud of you. All the elements that I wish hadn't happened to you, once out in the open, will show what a remarkable daughter you are. Your involvement and the inner strength you have found as a Samaritan emphasises again, how truly amazing you can be. I hope that life is good at the moment, particularly your health. There's another thing that shouldn't have happened to you.

We ought to meet up again soon; you never said if you want to wander in Geneva with me one day?

Keep safe

Love you lots

Mum x

I felt a glow inside as I read the letter. She had accepted me and wasn't judging me, and best of all she had acknowledged that I was now writing a book and said whatever the content she would be proud. It was unconditional acceptance, and it meant a great deal to me.

Soon after I received the letter I picked up the phone and called one of my closest friends, Katrina. I felt I wanted to go south and see Juliet again, as well as some of the places that had been important to me in the past.

We set off a couple of weeks later. I apologised for the fact that I was taking her on a pilgrimage of my past. It had seemed like a good idea at the time but now we were on our way I realised that this wasn't going to be the most entertaining of trips for someone else.

The first stop that we made was at Juliet's. She greeted us warmly and the smell of baking wafted over us as she opened the door.

'Did you bake a cake?' I asked.

'Yes,' she said. 'I thought that was something a mother should do and I've never baked for you before. Mind you, the icing is all runny as I didn't have a lot of time.'

'Oh, do you have a list of things a mother should do?' I replied.

Juliet smiled. 'Yes,' she said. 'Shall I tick it off?'

We stayed chatting over tea and cake for an hour and a

half. It wasn't a deep conversation but it felt fine and I was glad I had visited.

Our next stop was the house where I grew up. When we got close I drove slowly, taking in the houses and roads as ticks of recognition triggered my consciousness. As I edged the car round the corner I looked to the junction on the right where the old red phone box had been – the phone box I had fled to on so many nights. It had been replaced by a modern phone, with no door and a perspex hood.

I turned the corner and pulled up outside the house. I felt so confused. It looked different, it had an extension on the side and the long drive wasn't there anymore. The semi I had remembered as so large suddenly looked small. The fir tree I had planted with my father when I was small still stood, taller now, in the front garden. I looked up to my bedroom window at the front of the house. This was the room where I had lost my childhood and nearly lost my life.

My father had sold this house while I was in hospital and I had never had the chance to say goodbye. It was bricks and mortar, but it had been my home.

'I want to go in,' I said.

'Sophie, you haven't warned them,' Katrina said. 'If some-one knocked on your door and said they used to live there and can they see their old bedroom, what would you say?'

'I'll say I'm writing a book, that I was abused in that room and it would be good for me to say goodbye to it,' I explained.

'Sophie, you can't do that to them. How could they go on living there, knowing what happened to you in that room?'

I looked up at the bedroom windows again. She was right. We sat in silence in the car for a moment. I looked at the house for one last time and said goodbye in my head. It held memories that were both happy and sad, and some that were too hard to even think about, but those days were gone. I pulled away.

I took Katrina to see my old school, and then the house where my grandparents had lived. I stopped outside the house and once again scanned it for memories. I thought of happy days being around Nan, sitting on her lap, her soft touch and gentle voice and I realised how much I truly missed her.

I started the engine again and set off on the final leg of my pilgrimage, to a part of my past that had made the biggest difference of all. 'Where are we going now?' Katrina asked.

'The hospital,' I answered.

The traffic was bad and it took about an hour to reach the hill where the hospital stood. I swung in through the gate and my heart seemed to stop. It had been twenty-one years since I left, but it looked just the same.

When I got closer, however, I saw that there was a sign outside. 'This hospital is now closed. This site is currently being redeveloped and will be opened as a private hospital in 2008.'

'What are you thinking?' Katrina asked.

'I'm sad. I didn't expect to be able to go in, but I had always imagined it being open and life going on here in some way in some strange way it gave me a sense of security, knowing that it was there.'

I pushed my face against the window, trying desperately to see a glimpse of something inside.

Suddenly we heard a key turning and the door to the main entrance was pushed open and a security guard appeared.

'Can I help?' he asked. 'Are you looking for something?'

'Erm, I live up north now and came back to see the hospital, 'cos I used to be here.' I hesitated and the man smiled.

'Were you a nurse?'

'Yes,' I said, without really thinking.

'Come and have a look round if you want,' he said. He stepped back and opened the door and I beckoned for Katrina to follow as I walked along the corridor to the room that had been the chapel, and flung open the door.

It had been stripped bare and was now just a white room. I couldn't even work out where the pews had been, the pews where I had sat and cried and prayed for a release from my past.

The security guard had followed us. 'I've just realised I haven't locked the front door. Wait here and I'll be back,' he said.

As soon as he'd gone I shot up the corridor towards the stairs to the psychiatric unit.

'Sophie, hold on,' Katrina was shouting as she hurried behind me.

I made my way to the top of the stairs and pushed open the heavy door. I was now in the main corridor on the psychiatric ward. My head filled with memories as Katrina and the security guard caught up with me.

'Thought I'd lost you there!' he joked.

Katrina caught up with me. 'Are you OK?' she said.

My eyes filled with tears as I nodded.

We walked along the corridor and stepped into a small bare room. I walked to the window.

'This was the music room,' I said.

In my mind's eye I saw Katie, sitting in the window seat listening to Paul Young's 'A Broken Man'. I closed my eyes. I could feel her presence and hear her voice. 'Come on, babe,' Katie was saying to me.

I hurried from the room and along the corridor to the therapy room with the one-way mirror. I remembered the daily meetings – the phone ringing every time the experts had something to say, the way I had learned to open up about my past. It all came rushing back. I saw Gina, Mary, Dina and Theresa sitting in a circle, defiant, angry, funny and brave.

I walked out and along the corridor, opening each door and breathing in the memories one by one. The day room, the dining room, the medical room, the office, the bathrooms with the doors with no locks, the rows of toilets with stable doors and the area where the glass cubicles had once been for the anorexic patients. The corridors were bare and the floors were cold and hard, but I still felt the warmth that had been here all those years ago. My head was full of voices, laughter, tears and screams of joy and pain – the memories ran through my heart and straight into my head.

I walked back down the stairs in silence. I was aware of Katrina and the guard making small talk behind me but my head was still awash with voices and memories as we walked through the entrance and back into the outside world.

Outside, I thanked the guard.

'No problem,' he said. 'Have a safe trip back.'

Katrina and I laughed as we got back into the car. There was a certain irony in getting past a security guard and into a psychiatric hospital where I had once been incarcerated.

We sat in the car and the tears started to race down my face. I wasn't sad, I wasn't happy, I just felt a sense of belonging and warmth that had helped me so much.

'It became my home,' I explained to Katrina.

'This isn't your home,' she said gently. 'It's just a building.'

I nodded and choked back the tears.

It was true, this wasn't home, but it was here that the healing started and where I was loved and cared for. Now I was no longer a scared child, a scarred child, or a broken person. I had a life, a feeling of self-worth and I was able to give something back, through the Samaritans, in the only way I knew how, by listening.

I dried my eyes and looked at Katrina.

'Where to now?' she said kindly.

'I'm going home,' I replied as I started the engine. As I stopped at the main road and as I indicated to turn left I saw the hospital reflected in my wing mirror.

'Thank you,' I whispered.

Epilogue

Fran's Story: *The day I learned about the darker side of life*

The phone rang. I let it ring two, three times and then answered it. 'Hello, Samaritans. Can I help you?'

No one spoke and yet I knew there was someone there. I waited and then I said, 'Would you like to talk to me?' Again nothing – or was there a slight sound? Was it crying, or a whisper? I knew it was important to keep this caller – the feeling was very strong.

Again I waited, and then a small quiet voice said, 'Can I talk to you please?' and that is how it all began – my relationship and eventually a strong friendship, with Sophie.

Sophie was only fourteen then, and when she felt that she could trust me, she told me her story. When we had finished talking, I put down the phone and then I just sat there.

Thoughts went racing through my mind – can it be true what she has told me that she has had to endure from her father. I'd heard of child abuse but this . . . I felt terrible inside. I decided to talk it over with my colleague, to help me to come to terms with what I had just heard, and then – if Sophie rang again – to see how I could help her.

There were several more calls after that, with more sordid

details of what Sophie had been through. I felt something special towards her – I don't know what it was, and I desperately wanted to help her.

We talked lots on the phone. We met and a bond grew. During this time, Sophie had to go into a psychiatric hospital for help.

In spite of the way her father had treated her she still cared about him. She said to me one day that 'it was the only kind of love she had'.

That was a very sad statement. It haunted me.

As you will have read, a lot happened during her stay in (and out) of hospital, but we kept in touch. I think on looking back, she will agree that it did help her, although she was desperately unhappy.

There is so much more detail that I could give you, but what I want to say is that through all her traumas, and there have been many, I began to see that Sophie had a lot to offer. She was a strong person in so many ways. Through the years, I have come to admire and respect her. She is an achiever, whatever she sets out to do, she will do well.

I can't really say how you would describe our relationship now – we aren't mother and daughter but in some ways we could be. I feel that I've helped her through some of the crises in her life and I think that she knows, without doubt, that I will always be there for her.

She is much older now and I'm very glad that she made that call. I'm even more glad that I was there to take it. If I hadn't been, I would never have known her strength of character, her kindness (especially to me when I was ill) and her determination to hang on, even though I know there were many times when she felt that there was nothing worth hanging on to. She had the ability to take chances and go for it – and make it. She seems now to be very level-headed – no doubt you will smile at this, Sophie. I agree, I didn't think we'd ever see the day, did you?

Her fears will always be there and occasionally they will come back to the surface to haunt her. Because of her terrible experiences she is now able to give back into the community and cares so much that she wants to help others who have suffered as she has.

Don't look back too much now, Sophie. Keep going forward – I will be one step behind you all the way.

I could write so much more. If you have read her story you will realise how much she has suffered at the hands of her father and how she has come to terms with life, and how it must go on, or not, of course. She didn't take the easy way out, she struggled through and thank God she did – or I would never have come to know the person that she is now.

Author's Note

Fran is an amalgam of two Samaritan volunteers who befriended me. At that time, in the mid-eighties, Samaritans used to assign specific volunteers to callers who caused concern and who were at high risk. The idea was that a caller would feel more able to open up if there was continuity with the people that they spoke to.

At this time volunteers were allowed to meet callers outside the branch and call them on a one-to-one basis. Now this has changed and Samaritans offer assigned group support, meaning the caller would have a group of volunteers who would help them though a specific crisis. Samaritans are of course still available twenty-four hours a day by phone, email, branch visit and more recently through an initiative of text messaging.

'Fran' was in fact two volunteers named Frances and Avis, who I am in no doubt kept me alive during those years, when I was literally hanging on to life by a thread. Frances wrote the passage above when I told her I was writing a book, as she said she wanted the reader to know the other side of the story. When I read the words, I can almost feel her saying them. My one regret is that neither of them is alive to see my book in print. Both Frances and Avis died in recent years. It saddens me hugely that they are not here to see the end product but I hope they would be proud and that they would accept the thanks that are so rightly theirs. I like to believe they are both still by my side.

My life has not only been saved but also been enriched because I met them and my debt to them and to Samaritans is immeasurable. My book is dedicated to their memory – forever in my thoughts and heart.